PELICAN BOOKS

IRAN

Professor R. Ghirshman, archaeologist, explorer, and historian, was born in 1895, and educated at the Sorbonne, the École des Hautes Études, and the École du Louvre. His first experience of archaeology in the field was in 1930, when he accompanied the French Mission to Tello, in Iraq. The following year he was appointed head of an expedition to Iran, and made excavations at Giyan, Luristan, Assadabad, and Siyalk. In 1935 he began work on the site of Shapur, a Sassanid town founded in the 3rd century A.D., and in 1936 took part in the first archaeological expedition to Afghanistan. In 1941 he was appointed head of the French Délégation Archéologique in Afghanistan, and after the war he was put in charge of the two French archaeological expeditions to Iran by the French government. In 1949 he made a trip by caravan into the mountains of Bakhtiari, where he explored, for the first time in Iran, a cave which was inhabited in neolithic times.

Professor Ghirshman has published many works on the archaeology, history, inscriptions, and coins of Iran and Afghanistan. He is a member of a number of learned societies, both French and foreign; has been awarded an honorary doctorate by the University of Teheran and is an honorary Professor at the University of Aix-en-Provence; and is a Corresponding Member of the Académie des Inscriptions et Belles-Lettres. Professor Ghirshman is a Commander of the Légion d'Honneur.

D0927399

IRAN

FROM THE EARLIEST TIMES TO THE ISLAMIC CONQUEST

BY

R. GHIRSHMAN

PENGUIN BOOKS

Penguin Books Ltd, Harmondsworth, Middlesex, England
Penguin Books, 625 Madison Avenue, New York, New York 10022, U.S.A.
Penguin Books Australia Ltd, Ringwood, Victoria, Australia
Penguin Books Canada Ltd, 2801 John Street, Markham, Ontario, Canada L3R 1B4
Penguin Books (N.Z.) Ltd, 182–190 Wairau Road, Auckland 10, New Zealand
First published as *L'Iran des origines à l'Islam*
by Payot, Paris, 1951
This edition first published 1954
Reprinted 1961, 1978

—

—

Made and printed in Great Britain
by Richard Clay (The Chaucer Press) Ltd,
Bungay, Suffolk

To

MY WIFE

Contents

LIST OF PLATES   10

LIST OF TEXT FIGURES   14

EDITORIAL FOREWORD   17

INTRODUCTION. THE PHYSICAL ASPECT OF
IRAN   21

1. PREHISTORY   27
    Cave Man   27
    The First Settlers on the Plain   28
    The Prehistoric Civilization of Iran in the Fourth
       Millennium B.C.   32
    Iran at the Beginning of the Third Millennium B.C.   45
    Iran in the Third Millennium B.C.   50
    Iran in the Second Millennium B.C.   60
    Elam   63
    The Kassites   64

2. THE COMING OF THE IRANIANS   73
    The Immigration of the Medes and Persians   73
    The Formation of Median Unity   90
    Cimmerians and Scythians   96
    The Median Kingdom   98
    The Luristan Bronzes   99
    Cyaxares   106
    The Treasure of Sakiz   106
    The Median Kingdom   112
    Elam and the Persians – The Rise of the Achaemen-
       ians   118

3. EAST AGAINST WEST   127
    The Achaemenian Empire   127
    Cyrus (559–530)   128
       The Fall of Babylon   131
       Pasargadae   134
    Cambyses (530–522)   136

Darius (522–486) 139
    Administration 142
    The Campaigns of Darius 146
    The Political and Administrative Achievement of
        Darius 152
    Religion 155
    Language and Writing 163
    Art 164
    Economic and Social Life 181

4. THE LATER ACHAEMENIANS 189
    The Successors of Darius 189
    Xerxes 190
    Artaxerxes I 194
    Darius II 196
    Artaxerxes II 197
    Artaxerxes III 201

5. WEST AGAINST EAST AND THE REACTION OF
    THE ORIENT 206
    End of the Achaemenian Empire. Alexander the
        Great 206
    The Seleucids 219
        Art 232
        Economic and Social Life 237

6. THE PARTHIANS 243
    The Parthians and the East 260
    Organization and Administration 262
    Parthians and Greeks 266
    Religion 268
    Urban Development, Architecture and Art 272
    Economic and Social Life 282

7. THE EXPANSION OF IRANIAN CIVILIZATION 289
    The Sassanians 289
        Organization, Administration, Army 309

The Sassanians
  Religion   314
  Arts, Letters, Sciences   318
  Economic and Social Life   341

CONCLUSION   350
SELECTED BIBLIOGRAPHY   358
INDEX   360

List of Plates

1   (a) Stone tools from the cave of Tang-i-Pabda
     (b) Siyalk: Carved bone handle for flint implement
     (c) Siyalk: Grave of Level I

2   (a) Rayy: Bowl in red ware (*Teheran Museum*)
     (b) Tepe Hissar: Black ware (*Teheran Museum*)
     (c) Siyalk: Grave of Necropolis B

3   (a) Bronze statue of Queen Napir-asu (*Louvre. Photograph by courtesy of Archives photographiques d'Art et d'Histoire*)
     (b) Stele of Naram-Sin (*Louvre. Photograph by courtesy of Archives photographiques d'Art et d'Histoire*)

4   (a) Luristan: Bronze ibex (*Private collection*)
     (b) Luristan: Bronze axe (*Teheran Museum*)

5   (a) and (b) Luristan: Piece of harness (*Private collection*)
     (c) Luristan: Bronze axe (*Private collection*)
     (d) Luristan: Bronze terminal of a chariot pole (*The Charles W. Harkness collection. Cleveland Museum of Art*)
     (e) Luristan: Bronze bit (*Teheran Museum*)

6   (a) Luristan: Bronze rein ring (*Louvre*)
     (b) Luristan: Bronze statuette (*Teheran Museum*)

7   (a) Luristan: Bronze mirror (*Private collection*)
     (b) Luristan: Bronze votive object (*Teheran Museum*)
     (c) Luristan: Bronze pins (*Teheran Museum*)

8   (a) to (c) Luristan: Votive 'pins' (*David-Weil collection*)

9   Luristan: Bronze vase (*Louvre. Photograph by courtesy of Archives photographiques d'Art et d'Histoire*)

10   (a) and (b) Sakiz treasure: Gold terminals of furniture (*Teheran Museum*)
     (c) Sakiz treasure: Gold chape of a scabbard (*Private collection*)
     (d) Sakiz treasure: Gold plaque from a belt (*Private collection*)

11   (a) Sakiz treasure: Gold plaque (*Private collection*)
     (b) Sakiz treasure: Gold bracelet (*Private collection*)

12   Sakiz treasure: Gold pectoral (*Teheran Museum*)

13   (a) Kalar-dasht: Gold cup (*Teheran Museum*)
     (b) Azerbaijan: Terra-cotta rhyton (*Teheran Museum*)

14   (a) Terrace of Masjid-i-Sulaiman (*Photograph by Dr L. Lockhart*)
     (b) Persepolis: Aerial view (*Aerial Survey Expedition, Mary-Helen Warden Foundation, Oriental Institute of Chicago*)

(c) Persepolis: Stairway of the Apadana (*Photograph by courtesy of the Oriental Institute of Chicago*)

15 (a) Pasargadae: Winged genius

(b) Bisutun: Bas-relief of Darius (*Photograph by André Hardy*)

(c) Pasargadae: Tomb of Cyrus (*Photograph by Vahé*)

(d) Bisutun: Darius the Great (*Photograph by Dr Cameron*)

16 Susa: Aerial view (*Photograph by courtesy of Hunting Aerosurveys Ltd*)

17 (a) Susa: Lion-griffin in enamelled brick (*Louvre. Photograph by courtesy of Archives photographiques d'Art et d'Histoire*)

(b) Susa: Capital from the Achaemenian Palace (*Louvre. Photograph by courtesy of Archives photographiques d'Art et d'Histoire*)

18 Susa: Frieze of archers in enamelled brick (*Louvre*)

19 (a) Naqsh-i-Rustam: Fire temple

(b) Persepolis: Darius giving audience. Bas-relief from the Treasury (*Teheran Museum*)

20 (a) Achaemenian bronze vase (*Private collection*)

(b) Persepolis: Syrian tribute bearers (*Photograph by courtesy of Archives photographiques d'Art et d'Histoire*)

21 (a) Persepolis: Dog in black marble (*Teheran Museum*)

(b) Persepolis: Bas-relief from the Hall of a Hundred Columns (*Photograph by courtesy of the Oriental Institute of Chicago*)

22 (a) Persepolis: Greek marble statue (*Teheran Museum*)

(b) Persepolis: Head of a prince in lapis lazuli paste (*Teheran Museum*)

23 (a) Persepolis: Gold plaque (*Teheran Museum*)

(b) and (c) Hamadan (?): Gold appliqué (*Private collection*)

24 (a) Hamadan (?): Decorated gold handle of a whetstone (*Private collection*)

(b) Gold pendant (*Teheran Museum*)

(c) Gold wreath of flowers (*Private collection*)

(d) Gold bracelet (*Louvre*)

25 (a) to (d) Achaemenian imperial coinage (*Cabinet des Médailles, Paris*)

(e) to (h) Achaemenian satrapal coinage (*Cabinet des Médailles, Paris*): (e) Mazaeus at Tarsus; (f) Orontes at Lampsacus; (g) Pharnabazus at Tarsus; (h) Datames at Tarsus

(i) Persepolis: Elamite tablets (*Teheran Museum*)

26 Pompeii: Mosaic representing the battle of Darius and Alexander at Issus (*Naples Museum. Photograph Alinari*)

27 (a) and (b) Persepolis: Bas-reliefs of lintels of a temple below the terrace (*Photograph by Herzfeld*)

(c) Denaver (?): Head of a satyr on a basin (*Teheran Museum*)

(d) Denaver (?): Head of Silenus on a basin (*Teheran Museum*)

28 (a) to (d) Nihawand: Bronze statuettes from the Hellenistic temple (*Teheran Museum*)

29 (a) Shami: Bronze head of Antiochus IV (?) (*Teheran Museum. Photograph by courtesy of the British Museum*)
    (b) Susa: Greek marble torso (*Teheran Museum*)

30 (a) and (b) Susa: Parthian cemetery. Single grave
    (c) Susa: Parthian cemetery. Communal grave

31 Shami: Bronze statue (*Teheran Museum*)

32 (a) Shami: Bronze statuette (*Teheran Museum*)
    (b) Shami: Marble head of a prince (*Teheran Museum*)

33 (a) Bust of Vologases III (?) (*Private collection*)
    (b) Susa: Marble head of Queen Musa (?) (*Teheran Museum*)

34 (a) Susa: Limestone male head (*Louvre*)
    (b) Hamadan: Limestone male head (*Teheran Museum*)

35 (a) Bisutun: Parthian bas-relief
    (b) Bisutun: Bas-relief of Mithridates II (on the left) and of Gotarzes II (*Photograph by Herzfeld*)

36 (a) and (b) Tang-i-Sarwak: Parthian bas-reliefs (*Photograph by Sir Aurel Stein*)

37 Susa: Bas-relief of Artabanus V (*Teheran Museum*)

38 (a) Parthian horseman in terra-cotta (*Louvre*)
    (b) Bronze incense burner (*Private collection*)

39 (a) Susa: 'Emblema' in terra-cotta (*Louvre*)
    (b) Susa: Parthian figurines in carved bone (*Teheran Museum*)

40 (a) to (h) Parthian imperial coinage (*Cabinet des Médailles, Paris*): (a) Phraates IV; (b) Phraataces and Musa; (c) Orodes; (d) Mithridates II; (e) Mithridates II; (f) Gotarzes II; (g) (?) Gotarzes II; (h) Vardanes II

41 (a) Ctesiphon: Sassanian palace
    (b) Bishapur: Fire temple
    (c) Bishapur: Votive monument with two columns

42 (a) Bishapur: Model of the hall of the Sassanian palace (*Louvre. Reconstructed by A. Hardy*)
    (b) Bishapur: Sassanian palace. Recess decorated with sculptured and painted stucco. (*Louvre. Reconstructed by A. Hardy*)

43 (a) Naqsh-i-Rustam: Investiture of Ardeshir I
    (b) Bishapur: Triumph of Shapur I

44 (a) and (b) Bishapur: Mosaics from the Sassanian palace

45 (a) Bottle of gilded silver (*Teheran Museum*)
    (b) Dish of gilded silver representing a Sassanian prince hunting (*Cabinet des Médailles, Paris*)

46 (a) Rock crystal goblet (*Private collection*)
     (b) Rock crystal dish (*Treasure of Saint Mark*)
47 Post-Sassanian material (*Courtesy of Yale University Art Gallery*)
48 (a) to (g) Sassanian imperial coinage (*Cabinet des Médailles, Paris*): (a) Ardashir I; (b) Shapur I; (c) Shapur II; (d) Bahram V; (e) Yezdegerd II; (f) Chosroes II; (g) Chosroes I
     (h) Susa: Sassanian bulla

List of Text Figures

1	Relief map of the Iranian Plateau	20
2	Section of the Iranian Plateau between the Persian Gulf and the Caspian Sea	21
3	Section of the Iranian Plateau between Baghdad and the Caspian Sea	22
4	Siyalk: Painted pottery of Level I	30
5	Siyalk: Use of pestle and mortar for cosmetics	31
6	Siyalk: The earliest form of mud-brick	33
7	Siyalk: Stylization in animal design	34
8	Susa: Przewalski horse carved in bone	35
9	Siyalk: Jar from Level III	37
10	Susa: Goblet of Style I	38
11	Persepolis: Cup in painted ware	39
12	Tepe Hissar: Painted chalice	40
13	Painted pottery from Siyalk (a and c) and Susa	40
14	Siyalk: Seal impressions	41
15	Archaeological map of Western Asia	43
16	Proto-Elamite script	45
17	Siyalk: Graves belonging to the period of the proto-Elamite script	47
18	Siyalk: Proto-Elamite tablet	48
19	Siyalk: Cylinder seals belonging to the period of the proto-Elamite tablets	49
20	Map of prehistoric Iran	51
21	Stele of Horen-Sheikh-Khan	54
22	Bas-relief of Annubanini, king of the Lullubi	55
23	Susa: Pottery of Style II	59
24	Giyan: Pottery of Level IV	60
25	Giyan: Tripod vases from Level III	67
26	Giyan: Pottery of Level II	68
27	Giyan: Pottery of Level I	69
28	Town of Siyalk: Tentative restoration	77
29	Siyalk: Silver and bronze jewellery from Necropolis B	78
30	Siyalk: Weapons and tools in bronze and iron from Necropolis B	79
31	Siyalk: Stone cylinder seal and parts of harness in bronze and iron from Necropolis B	81

32	Siyalk: Painted pottery of Necropolis B	82
33	Siyalk: Painted pottery of Necropolis B	83
34	The town of Kishesim in north-west Iran from an Assyrian bas-relief	85
35	The town and temple of Musasir in north-west Iran from an Assyrian bas-relief	92
36	Luristan: Iron sword	100
37	Luristan: Bronze dagger hilt	101
38	Luristan: Bronze pick	101
39	Luristan: Bronze pins	102
40	Luristan: Bronze situlae	103
41	Sakiz treasure: Silver dish	108
42	Sakiz treasure: Hieroglyphic inscription on the silver dish	109
43	Sakiz treasure: Gold belt	111
44	A Mede from an Assyrian bas-relief	115
45	Hamadan: Stone lion	116
46	Dukkan-Daud: Rock tomb near Sar-i-Pul	117
47	Rock tomb of Fakhrica, south of Lake Urmia	118
48	Gold tablet of Ariaramnes: Old Persian cuneiform script	120
49	Plan of the terrace of Masjid-i-Sulaiman	122
50	Rock tomb of Da u Dukhtar in Fars	124
51	Pasargadae: Head of a stone lion	134
52	Ruins of Pasargadae	135
53	Pasargadae: Fire altars	136
54	Satrapies of the Achaemenian Empire in the time of Darius	143
55	Naqsh-i-Rustam: Rock tombs of the Achaemenian kings and fire altar	157
56	Susa: Achaemenian tomb	158
57	Susa: Gold jewellery from the Achaemenian tomb	159
58	Susa: Silver dish from the Achaemenian tomb	160
59	Image of the god Ahuramazda	161
60	Susa: Winged bulls in enamelled brick	167
61	Terrace of Persepolis	169
62	Columns of Persepolis	170
63	Persepolis: Human-headed capital	171
64	Persepolis: Winged bull from the doorway of Xerxes	173
65	Terrace of Persepolis	174
66	Persepolis: Bronze ornamental plaque	176
67	Persepolis: Bronze support	177
68	Persepolis: Sculptured stone dish	177
69	Cylinder seal of Darius	178

70	Bas-relief from Persepolis: Sword of a Median officer	179
71	Persepolis: Battle axe and bronze bit	180
72	Persepolis: Achaemenian pottery	184
73	Istakhr: Stone capital	233
74	Plan of the temple of Kangavar	234
75	Ruins of the temple of Kangavar	234
76	Columns of the temple of Khurha	235
77	Map of the Parthian Empire	247
78	Pahlavi-Arsacid script	257
79	Dura Europos: A Parthian cataphract	265
80	Assur: Parthian palace	274
81	Hatra: Parthian palace	275
82	Hatra: Plan of the temple	276
83	Taxila: Plan of the Parthian temple	277
84	Susa: Parthian pottery	281
85	Map of the Sassanian Empire	293
86	Bishapur: Triumph of Shapur I	295
87	Plan of the town of Bishapur (after A. P. Hardy)	319
88	Taq-i-Girre	320
89	Pahlavi-Sassanian script	321
90	Palace of Firuzabad	322
91	Palace of Firuzabad. Restored façade	322
92	Istakhr: Town wall of mud brick	323
93	Bishapur: Plan of the fire temple	324
94	Firuzabad: Tower with fire altar	325
95	Firuzabad: Stucco decoration from the palace	326
96	Taq-i-Bustan: Detail of a capital in bas-relief	327
97	Bisutun: Capitals from an unknown building	328
98	Taq-i-Bustan: Bas-relief depicting a royal hunt	331
99	Bishapur: Ossuary in sculptured stone	332
100	Bishapur: Ossuary in sculptured stone (detail)	333
101	Representations of princes in Sassanian goldwork	333
102	Sassanian silver cup	334
103	Medallion in rock crystal on the gold cup from the treasure of Saint Denis (Bibliothèque Nationale, Paris)	335
104	Bas-relief of Naqsh-i-Rustam: Ardashir before Ahuramazda	336
105	Church of Vic (Indre): Adoration of the Magi. French religious art of the twelfth century	337
106	Gold jug from the so-called treasure of Attila	338
107	Centre motif of a gold jug from the so-called treasure of Attila	339
108	Buddhist frescoes from Ming Oï (Chinese Turkestan)	340

Editorial Foreword

BY

M. E. L. MALLOWAN

Professor of Western Asiatic Archaeology, University of London

MUCH of R. Ghirshman's book on Iran was conceived and written in Susa, the Achaemenian royal city at which for many years the author has been directing excavations. That is why as we read on we begin to feel the breath of Iran, for to turn over the soil is to become a part of the land. The author has also enjoyed the unique experience of digging at Siyalk, one of the oldest prehistoric towns, as well as at centres of the Sassanian culture which brings his story to a close, *c.* A.D. 650. Thus on the most modest estimate this survey must embrace a period of not less than four and a half thousand years.

No one living could hope or pretend to give a final and authoritative verdict on the scores of complex problems that arise in the course of this study; but no one has a better title than the author to express his views in a direct narrative which must inevitably at times leave aside the more difficult and controversial aspects of the evidence. This television of antiquity must often hold our fascinated attention: the prehistoric potpainters of Bakun; the arrival on the Plateau of the first horsemen bedecked with trappings which inevitably give rise to the problem of Aryan origins; the windowed palaces of Persepolis; Darius III fleeing before Alexander; the Roman Emperor biting the dust in front of the Sassanian, and a hundred other scenes. We learn also about that inviting front door to Iran at the south-east end of the Caspian Sea through which time and again irresistible tribes of invaders forced their way from the steppes of Central Asia and renewed the life-blood of the country. Then there is the intriguing variety of religions, Zoroastrian, Christian, Mazdakite; it is enthralling to read of the Mazdakite creed, a kind of Platonic communism, born of despair under the Sassanian Empire, of its extinction and its consequences. It is not difficult to see that the Iranian problems of to-day are but a projection from its past, a past brightly illuminated by the work of archaeology. It is hoped that readers who wish to go into these matters more deeply will be tempted by the short bibliography annexed to find further enjoyment in the rich heritage of Iran.

The translation proved to be no easy task, and is mainly the work of Miss Margaret Munn-Rankin, Lecturer in Near Eastern Archaeology at the University of Cambridge. Miss Diana Kirkbride revised the first version and checked many passages. The Editor is much indebted to these two colleagues for the care and thought which they have devoted to this work, and must himself take responsibility for inevitable defects. We have attempted to turn the French into reasonably fluent English without losing the flavour of the original language. On the other hand there are times when the English is a paraphrase rather than an exact translation; a few sentences have been expanded, and occasionally a footnote or a slight addition has been made where the original sense seemed to be compressed; a few passages have for various reasons been omitted. For any inadequate rendering we must ask for indulgence, more especially from the author himself, whose French edition, *L'Iran des origines à l'Islam* (Payot, 1951), but with fewer illustrations, must be regarded as the authoritative version.

IRAN

FROM THE EARLIEST TIMES TO THE
ISLAMIC CONQUEST

Fig. 1 – Relief map of the Iranian Plateau

The Physical Aspect of Iran

THE Iranian Plateau is a triangle set between two depressions, the Persian Gulf to the south and the Caspian Sea to the north (Fig. 1). Further, as a bridge between Central and Western Asia, it forms a promontory which links the steppes of inner Asia to the plateau of Asia Minor and beyond to Europe. Geography can thus account for the historic part which the Plateau was called on to play in the course of thousands of years of human history.

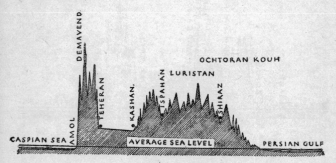

Fig. 2 – Section of the Iranian Plateau between the
Persian Gulf and the Caspian Sea

The triangle is bounded by mountains rising round a central depression, a desert region formed by the bed of a dried-up sea. The western mountains, or Zagros range, run from north-west to south-east, and are over 620 miles in length and 120 in width. The chain rises to between 3280 and 5570 feet and consists of numerous parallel folds, enclosing valleys 30 to 60 miles long and 6 to 12 miles wide (Fig. 2). Below the pastures on the higher slopes of these mountains stretch the remains of what were once dense forests of oak, walnut, evergreen oak, wild almond and pistachio. Lower down in the high valleys grow vines, figs, and pomegranates, and there is wide cultivation of wheat, barley, opium poppy, cotton, and tobacco. Owing to the summer heat in the lower valleys, goats, sheep, and horses must be taken up to the higher pastures. Thus a large proportion of the population leads a nomadic life, imposed on it by the climate and natural conditions.

From the central Zagros range a spur runs westward into the Mesopotamian plain, causing a bend in the Tigris, which at this point approaches the Euphrates. This spur has the shape of a hatchet which from aloft threatens the plain below. And, in-

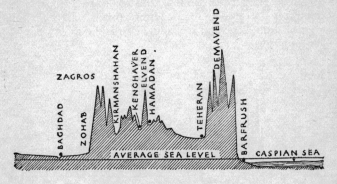

Fig. 3 – Section of the Iranian Plateau between
Baghdad and the Caspian Sea

deed, it was from here, the country now known as Luristan, that the Kassites in the second millennium B.C. invaded and then dominated Babylonia for over five centuries.

The northern part of the triangle is marked by the Elburz chain, of which the highest peak, Mt. Demavend, rises to over 19,000 feet. Skirting the southern shore of the Caspian Sea, it forms a high and narrow barrier (Fig. 3) which separates the coastal area with its luxuriant vegetation from the desert regions of the interior. At its western end, the Elburz reach Iranian Azerbaijan in the centre of which lies the salt lake of Urmia. This is the most densely populated region in Iran, and in its fertile valleys wheat, millet, cotton, rice, tobacco, castor-oil trees, and melons are cultivated. Azerbaijan, termed the

'Median isthmus', may be entered by routes leading from the north-west, north, and north-east, and is one of the easiest of countries to penetrate. This province is one of the two 'chinks' in the mountain armour of Iran, and in the course of its history has witnessed Medes and Persians, Kurds, Mongols and Turco-Tartars entering and settling in the valleys about the lake. The dynasties of the Medes and Persians arose there. There, too, at this gateway to Iran, the Persian Empire kept guard during the centuries, barring the road to the many invaders who swept across the Caucasus from the steppes of southern Russia, by erecting great fortifications which survive to this day. The mixture of races, the severe but healthy climate and the fertile soil bred an industrious and energetic racial type which greatly contributed to the development and prosperity of this ancient Iranian province.

To the east, the Elburz chain forms the mountains of Khorasan, not very high, easy to cross and with exceedingly fertile valleys in which grow wheat, barley, rice, cotton, the vine and the poppy. This granary of Iran, owing to its geographical formation, is the second gateway for penetration into the Plateau. Waves of invaders poured through it coming from the plains of central Asia which stretch thousands of miles to the north, west, and east. Like Azerbaijan, Khorasan is a 'cross-road' of peoples, and was raided by the Turcomans down to the end of the 19th century. The valley of the Atrek and the plain of Gurgan, between the Caspian Sea and the mountains, are natural oases for migration towards Iran, and to defend themselves there the Sassanian kings built a brick wall many miles in length, the remains of which can still be seen. This north-east district of Iran was the birth-place of several dynasties: the Arsacids, Safavi, and Kajars.

Finally, the mountains bordering the Iranian triangle are completed by a southern chain, the Makran, a range pierced by two passes, one to Bandar Abbas, formerly a prosperous port on the Gulf of Oman, the other leading east to Baluchistan and Quetta.

In the central part of the Plateau, which is crossed by two inner mountain chains, lies a great desert depression, the most arid in the world. This is divided into the Dasht-i-Kavir to the north and the Dasht-i-Lut to the south. The former is a series of mud and salt flats where nothing grows or lives. In some places life is possible round the hollows where the soil is less saline, and there there are true oases. The Lut, on the contrary, is a completely dry basin, and the rare explorers who have had the courage to cross this inhospitable waste say that the great deserts of Central Asia, such as the Gobi, seem fertile regions in comparison.

Thus life could develop on the Plateau only in the valleys of the great peripheral ranges or in the oases. But it also made great progress on the wide plains of inner and outer Iran. The most important of these is the plain of Khuzistan in the south-west, ancient Susiana, which geographically is only an extension of the Mesopotamian plain. Running up into the Zagros range, it forms a counterpoise to the mountainous salient of Luristan, the Pusht-i-kuh. Susiana was a country with a very old settled urban civilization, and throughout the centuries influenced the nomadic and semi-nomadic hill peoples living along its borders. When the political frontiers of the Iranian Empire extended far to the west of the Zagros, it was in this plain that the great capital city of Susa arose, an administrative centre linked by easy communications to Mesopotamia and Asia Minor.

Another outer plain backs on to the mountains bordering the Caspian Sea. This high mountain barrier catches the clouds, bringing an abundant rainfall to a narrow strip of extraordinarily fertile land. It is tropical Iran, covered with forests, swamps and jungles. Rice, cotton, tea, tobacco, sugar-cane, oranges, lemons, mulberries, figs, and pomegranates grow there and provide food for about a third of the population of the Empire.

The outer plains, however, played only a secondary part in the development of Iranian civilization. This, from earliest times, was centred in the scattered oases in the mountain ranges which encircled the Plateau and caught the rain clouds. The centre of this area is a desert except where the alluvial soil, in general very fertile, can be cultivated by means of artificial irrigation. Despite extremes of climate, intense cold in winter and heat in summer, the ground yields abundantly wherever man can bring water. At all times on the Plateau, the question of water has been vital. The country was artificially irrigated from prehistoric times, and, by the Achaemenian period, there was an extensive network of subterranean canals (*Ghanat* or *khariz*). Even to-day in certain areas, water tapped at the foot of the mountains to a depth of several scores of feet is carried to centres which may be as much as 25 miles distant. Thousands of men work all the year round, digging new canals and clearing old ones. Thanks to this water, and thanks also to the favourable rainfall in the Zagros and Elburz mountains, their inner edge is dotted with cultivated area and oasis settlements. All the capitals of Iran, ever since the rise of the first kingdom in Media, have faced towards the desert, lying along the two principal routes that skirt the inner edges of the two great ranges. From west to east on the strategic trade route along the Elburz, stand Ecbatana (Hamadan), Kazvin, Teheran-Rayy, Hecatompylos (Damghan), and Herat. On the southern route lie Isfahan, Pasargadae, Istakhr, Persepolis, and Shiraz. This fact, which is valid for the historical period of Iran and is a logical consequence of the geographical character of the country, also held good in prehistoric times, for recent archaeological investigation has shown that stone-age man, almost as soon as he came down from the mountains into the plain, settled along the same line, which describes an arc round the Salt Desert. The main sites so far identified are at Kashan (Siyalk), Qumm Rayy, and Damghan. The religious centres of the country too lay along the same natural lines of communication, and indeed even to-day two holy cities, Meshed and Qumm, are situated respectively on the east-west and north-south routes.

Primarily an agricultural and stock-breeding country, Iran possesses rich and varied mineral resources. From the third millennium B.C. its quarries provided marble and alabaster for the Sumerian princes, who also drew supplies of building woods from the forests which at that period covered the mountains, though now they are practically denuded.

Carnelian, turquoise, and lapis lazuli were all exploited from the very earliest period. Iron, copper, tin, and lead attracted the attention of the conquering Assyrians. Both slopes of the Zagros are of a gypsous rock, and contain oil-bearing deposits which were already known in the time of Herodotus, and have been worked for the last fifty years.

Thus Iran, in spite of its impoverished appearance, possesses immense reserves which are only just beginning to be exploited. Surrounded by mountains, the country is, in reality, open on all sides, to the plains of Mesopotamia and Russia as well as to India and the Persian Gulf. As it was the hub on the great lines of communication which link East and West, Iran was crossed by the oldest trade route, the Silk Road, which was also the path for invasions. For, despite the protection of its mountains and its impregnable appearance, Iran has known many conquerors. The country, physically disjointed and therefore not homogeneous, is ill shaped for defence. These features conditioned its intermittent periods of decadence and glory alike, for its peoples, although scattered in belts of cultivable soil and in oases, were endowed with the power to create a civilization. Ideas and customs, religious and artistic developments which had taken their rise in Iran left their mark on more than one foreign civilization.

CHAPTER I

Prehistory

*

CAVE MAN

RECENT geological research has shown that at the time when the greater part of Europe was covered by glaciers, the Iranian Plateau was passing through a pluvial period, during which even the high valleys were under water. The central part of the Plateau, to-day a great salt desert, was then an immense lake or inland sea into which many rivers ran from the high mountains. Fossil fish and shells, which have been found not only in the desert but also in the high valleys, illustrate the physical aspect of the country as it was many thousands of years before the Christian era.

At a period which may be put at between 10,000 and 15,000 B.C. there was a gradual change of climate, the pluvial period being followed by the so-called dry period, which is still in progress. The decreased rainfall on the one hand, and the high altitude of the lakes and inland seas on the other, slowed down the current of the rivers and streams carrying off water from the mountains. Owing to the greater regularity of their flow, alluvial deposits accumulated at the river-mouths and formed terraces which eventually rose above the water and formed a transitional zone between the future plain or valley and the mountain proper.

At this period prehistoric man was already living on the Iranian Plateau, dwelling in holes which were roofed with branches and dug into the wooded mountain-sides, or, more often, occupying one of the many caves or rock shelters, most of which are the underground channels of ancient rivers. In the spring of 1949 we identified traces of human remains of this age for the first time in Iran in our exploration of a cave at Tang-i-Pabda, in the Bakhtiari mountains, north-east of Shustar. Here man led the life of a hunter, seeking his food, and to this end employing cunning more often than force. He knew how to use a stone hammer, the hand-axe, and the axe tied to a cleft stick, all primitive tools fashioned by flaking (Pl. 1a). Bone implements, represented by awls made from tough animal bones, were far fewer than stone artifacts. But he already used a coarse, poorly baked pottery, which by the end of his occupation of the caves was deep black in colour, owing to the increased use of smoke in firing. This type of pottery has also been found with the earliest human remains on the plain, and is therefore an important pointer to the connexion between these two phases of settlement.

In this primitive society a special task fell to the lot of the woman: guardian of the fire and perhaps inventor and maker of pottery, it was she who, armed with a stick, sought edible roots or gathered wild berries in the mountains. Knowledge of plants, born of long and assiduous observation, led her to experiment in cultivation. Her first attempts at agriculture were made on the alluvial terraces. Whereas man made but little progress, woman with her primitive agriculture introduced many innovations during the neolithic period, to which the cave settlements belong. As a result, a lack of balance must have arisen between the parts played by man and woman. This may perhaps be the origin of certain primitive societies in which the woman is predominant. In such matriarchies (and also, perhaps, in societies practising polyandry) the woman directs the affairs of the tribe and is raised to the priesthood, while family succession is through the female line, the woman being considered as transmitting in its purest form the lifeblood of the tribe. We shall see that this form of matriarchy was one of the peculiar practices of the original inhabitants of the Plateau and that later it passed into the customs of the conquering Aryans.

THE FIRST SETTLERS ON THE PLAIN

The progressive drying up of the valleys, caused by the advance of drought, led to profound changes in the conditions of man's existence. The great central lake shrank, and its shores, where the rivers had left a fertile deposit of silt, became covered with rich pasture and savannah. Animals living in the mountains descended to these newly formed grasslands, and man, who lived by hunting, followed them down and settled in the plain. From this period, which may be dated approximately to the fifth millennium B.C., we can follow almost without interruption the progress made in material civilization by the inhabitants of the Iranian Plateau. This civilization was subject to diverse influences varying with the area, topography, climate, contacts with neighbouring peoples, invasion, and migration, but the resulting differences cannot be considered here. Indeed, they still often elude us, since even to-day whole areas of Iran remain untouched by archaeological research.

The oldest human settlement to be identified in the plain is at Siyalk, near Kashan, south of Teheran. Traces of man's first occupation have been found there just above virgin soil, at the bottom of an artificial mound. He still did not know how to build a house, but sheltered beneath a hut made from the branches of trees; soon afterwards, however, modest structures of *pisé* rose above these remains. Although he continued to be a hunter, man extended his agricultural activities, and to these two occupations he added a third, stock-breeding; for bones of domesticated oxen and sheep were found in the remains of Period I. To the black, smoked pottery, made by hand and without a wheel, which occurred in the caves, was added a new, red ware with black patches on the surface caused by accidents of firing in a very primitive oven. A further step was now made in the art of the potter, namely the introduction of painted pottery. The decorated pots were no more than large ill-balanced bowls; their stands, shaped like egg-cups, were covered with a white slip on which horizontal and vertical lines were painted. On closer study this decoration is seen to be an imitation of basket-work; man, who a short time before had used as receptacles baskets lined with sun-dried clay, was reproducing in paint the interlacing of twigs (Fig. 4). The large number of baked clay and stone spindle whorls is a proof that the rudiments of the textile industry were already known. The tools were all of stone: flint knife-blades, sickle-blades, polished axes, and scrapers.

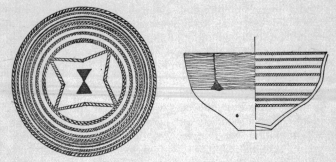

Fig. 4 – Siyalk: Painted pottery of Level I

Towards the end of this period, however, small objects began to appear for the first time. These were always hammered. Man was beginning to understand the properties of metal; he had found that copper was malleable, but was still ignorant of the art of casting. The civilization of this phase belongs to the very end of the neolithic age.

Both men and women loved personal adornment; they threaded necklaces of shells, and carved rings and bracelets out of large shells or soft stones: tattooing was probably practised or, at least, face-painting, the paint being ground with a small pestle in a miniature mortar (Fig. 5).

The artistic achievement of the age is seen at its best in carvings on bone. Before he began to paint men or animals, the neolithic artist carved bone, decorating the handles of his tools with the head of a gazelle or hare. The finest piece yet recovered is undoubtedly the knife-handle representing a man of the period, wearing a cap and a loin-cloth fastened by a belt. This is one of the oldest figurines known of Near Eastern man (Pl. 1b).

The dead were buried in a contracted position under the floors of houses; this proximity absolved the living from the necessity of making offerings, since the spirit of the deceased could share in the family repast. Man already believed that he continued to live after death as he had done on earth, for in one grave a polished stone axe had been placed by the skeleton within reach of its hand, while near the head lay two sheep jaws (Pl. 1c). Solid nourishment and, in all probability, liquid also accompanied the dead man in his grave and, since the receptacles have not been found, we may assume that they were of perishable material, such as gourds or baskets. The bones of the deceased were stained red – a practice known elsewhere. It would seem that either the body of the living man was covered with a coat of red paint or, probably, iron oxide powder was dusted over the corpse before burial.

Domestication of the first animal, which may have had its origin in man's need to have beasts available for sacrifice, was of capital importance in the advancement of civilization. Without requiring to be fed by man, the animal provided him with food and clothing, and was a source of power which could be utilized for work or transport. The care of flocks and herds required a large family of women, children, and even slaves. Thus, by this period, the basic elements of human economy were already in existence: hunting and fishing, the care of garden and field, had been followed by stock-breeding and the exploitation of mineral resources. Man had emerged from the state in which he was constrained to hunt for his daily food; he had become a producer and – the first step towards the development of commerce – was creating a surplus which he could exchange. Indeed, trade already existed. The shells worn

Fig. 5 – Siyalk: Use of pestle and mortar for cosmetics

as ornaments by the inhabitants of Siyalk I have been identified by experts as belonging to a species found only on the Persian Gulf, nearly 600 miles away. These exchanges did not, of course, take place by direct contact, and trade was probably effected mainly by itinerant pedlars. Even at this date, then, the inhabitant of a prehistoric village did not live an isolated existence; nor was the beginning of trade the prerogative of the settlers on the Plateau, for their contemporaries in Germany also received shells from the Indian Ocean and, in France and England, amber from the Baltic.

It may be that the Judeo-Christian tradition which records the expulsion of man from Paradise embodies a memory of the end of the neolithic age. The transition to the state of peasant labourer was one of the greatest revolutions in human society; indeed its consequences continue to this day.

THE PREHISTORIC CIVILIZATION OF IRAN IN THE FOURTH MILLENNIUM B.C.

The next stage in the development of the prehistoric civilization of Iran, which we shall call Period II, is only a more advanced phase of that we have just examined. Its remains accumulated above those corresponding to man's first settlement in the plain. No war or violent upheaval seems to have troubled this prehistoric village, which continued unaffected by any outside influence.

Man, though always seeking to perfect his tools, did not neglect the decoration and improvement of his dwelling. Houses became larger, and were provided with doors the sockets of which have been found. *Pisé* was replaced by the newly invented mud-brick; but at this period a brick was only a lump of earth, roughly fashioned between the palms of the hands and dried in the sun; hollows pressed into it by the thumb gave a key for the mortar-joints (Fig. 6). The new brickwork resulted in better buildings with more regular walls which were less liable to crack. Red paint, a coat of which was given to the walls of rooms, was the medium for interior decoration; this paint was a mixture of iron oxide, which was very common on the Plateau, and of fruit juice; this is a good example of man's taste for variety in his experiments and his capacity for invention. The dead lay in a crouched position under the beaten floor near the hearth; sometimes hollows a few inches deep in the floor mark the position of jars and bowls.

The refinement of taste shown in the appointments of the houses was reflected also in the new pottery. Another ware appeared side by side with the older products, smaller, but more carefully made and better fired in an improved oven. This pottery is evidence of the invention of the tournette – a simple slat of wood laid on the ground and turned by an assistant.

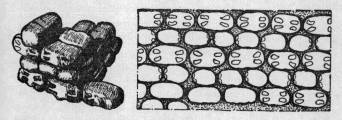

Fig. 6 – Siyalk: The earliest form of mud-brick

The great attraction and novelty of this pottery lies in its decoration, which, executed in black paint on a dark red ground, consists of rows of animals: birds, boars, and leaping ibex (Pl. 2a). With simple lines, the potter depicted creatures which were full of movement and vigorous realism; almost at the same moment he began to simplify his naturalistic motifs, moving towards a stylization in which it is often difficult to identify the original subject (Fig. 7). From this period, prehistoric Iran revealed in its pottery an art as lively and spontaneous as that of the earlier bone-carving. Nowhere else is a parallel craftsmanship known, which suggests that the Plateau was the original home of painted pottery. No other pottery has furnished at so early a date evidence of such vigorous realism passing so rapidly into an abstract style. This was achieved

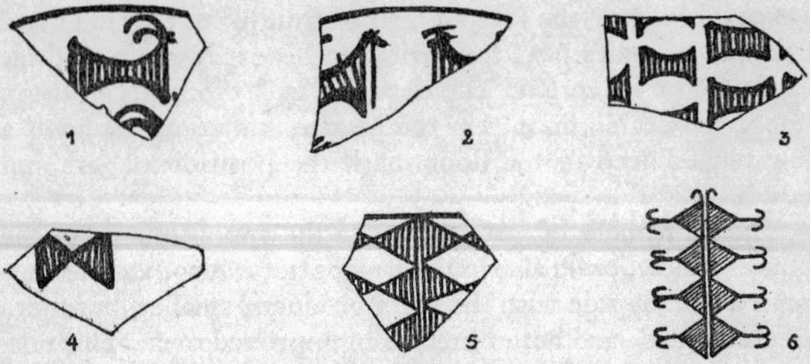

Fig. 7 – Siyalk: Stylization in animal design

for the first time, about 4000 B.C., by the prehistoric potter of
Iran alone.

Metal came only gradually into use for tools, and stone retained a predominant place; copper was still hammered, not
cast, and was worked into small awls or pins. Jewellery became more plentiful and was enriched by new materials such
as carnelian and turquoise, whose bright colours are most at-
tractive. In addition to the bones of domesticated animals
found in the previous period, there are found those of a kind
of greyhound, and of a horse of Przewalski type; this latter
was a small beast, sturdy and hardy, with a thick, erect mane,
and is thought to represent an intermediate stage between the
onager and the modern horse (Fig. 8). This solved the problem of travel and transport and at the same time made work in
the fields much easier.

The village grew quickly. As his agricultural activity extended, man, who already used the plough, was increasingly
willing to adopt a system of communal labour and to profit by
his neighbour's help, whether in building his house, clearing
the ground, or irrigation. The woman occupied herself with
the garden, prepared the food, and went on making pottery,
but this industry now passed into the hands of the craftsman
who still used the tournette. The fact that the woman continued to make pots by hand in her home is the explanation
usually given for the late invention of the wheel.

There was a great impetus to trade and an expansion of the area in which it developed. Everything man produced could serve as currency in this primitive commerce: furs, arrowheads, stone axes, and above all foodstuffs: wheat, barley, and fruit, and also cattle, which possess the great advantage of being able to increase 'capital'.

At this period, when man was only just beginning to use metal and was timidly substituting it for certain small bone tools, it is generally agreed that his commercial activity benefited humanity by a magnificent effort in the sphere of trade in plants and trees. Barley and wheat, indigenous to Iran, where they still grow wild and were probably already cultivated on the alluvial terraces, were introduced into both Egypt and Europe. Millet, a native of India, is recorded for Italy: in the opposite direction, the oats and poppy of Europe spread into Asia and reached distant China. At the beginning of the fourth millennium B.C., at the moment when he passed imperceptibly into an age characterized by a greater use of metal, man's horizons were being enlarged, to the great benefit of the expanding community.

The next phase in the evolution of the prehistoric civilization of Iran is represented by Period III at Siyalk. This comprises a large number of superimposed levels, corresponding with the greater part of the fourth millennium B.C. In architecture a new material now made its appearance: the oval-shaped brick was discarded in favour of the flat, rectangular brick, made in a mould, which is still in use to-day. The village quarters, intersected by narrow, winding alleys, marked off the

Fig. 8 – Susa: Przewalski horse carved in bone

boundaries of the estates. To obtain a play of light and shade, the external walls of houses were decorated with buttresses and recesses. Their foundations were sometimes laid on dry stones. The doors remained low and narrow, usually a little under 3 feet in height. Windows were in use, and generally looked on to the street. Large potsherds built into the walls protected the house against damp. Interior decoration continued to be in red, but white paint also made its appearance. The dead, still buried beneath the house floors, with limbs drawn up to the abdomen and bones bearing traces of ochreous paint, were accompanied by an increasing number of grave-goods.

A decisive advance, the benefits of which we still enjoy, was made in the potter's craft: this was the invention of the wheel and of the kiln with a grate. Confident in his improved tools, the potter offered his customers a great variety of pot shapes decorated with a wealth of new designs: large goblets, elegant chalices, high-footed 'champagne cups', and store jars. The colour of the biscuit, determined by the intensity of firing, which the potter could now regulate at will, varied through grey, rose, red, and green, while the painted decoration of the pottery gained in richness and variety. At first the artists showed a preference for realism: the serpent, panther, mouflon, ibex, stork, and ostrich, arranged in Indian file or in metopes, are skilfully drawn and express a naturalism which, however, differs profoundly from that known earlier. The body of an animal is no longer expressed by a simple line: volume is observed and the representation of the subject shows balanced proportions (Fig. 9). Next, stylization appears: the animal's tail becomes elongated, horns, and also the necks of waders, are disproportionately large (Fig. 10); soon only the horn is shown, describing an enormous circle attached to a minute body (Fig. 11), or a panther's body is represented simply by a triangle (Fig. 12). Though reverting to the older formulas, this art nevertheless takes a different course; it is less spontaneous, more disciplined and deliberate. Later, in response to the ever-present need for change, there is a return to realism, but it is now rather a neo-naturalism, overflowing with life and movement. Hunting scenes alternate with landscapes filled with struggling beasts; sometimes a hunter bends his bow or a peasant leads his ox by a ring passed through the nose, sometimes there is a procession of dancers performing a sacred dance (Fig. 13). For more than a millennium, the period covering the first three phases in the life of prehistoric man after he settled in the plain, the artist was never confined to the formula he had mastered, but, while

Fig. 9 – Siyalk: Jar from Level III

remaining deeply attached to this style of decoration, was constantly ringing the changes on it. Drawing on its own resources, this dynamic art renewed and transformed itself; and its power and continuity carried it far beyond the natural limits of the Plateau.

Is this painting a more or less faithful image of the life which the artist observed around him and reproduced on his pot, or does it already conceal the desire, through its many and varied signs and symbols, to express an idea? In short, was it already writing, as we are sometimes inclined to think? We shall not

Fig. 10 – Susa: Goblet of Style I

try to solve this problem. We would, nevertheless, draw attention to the fact that this flourishing period of painted pottery
on the Plateau corresponded, towards its end, with a moment
when, in the neighbouring plain of Mesopotamia, man made
one of his most marvellous discoveries: the art of writing. Are
we to believe that the inventor of writing was inspired by the

pictorial art of the craftsman on the Plateau, who placed before his eyes ready-made images and symbols? However that may be, let us recognize that this art represents a stage which showed the way to pictographic writing.

The potter was a plastic artist also. He modelled figurines of all kinds of animals, children's toys or votive offerings to a divinity responsible for the protection of flocks and herds,

Fig. 11 – Persepolis: Cup in painted ware

Fig. 12 – Tepe Hissar: Painted chalice

before whom images of the animals were placed. There are quantities of figurines of the *Dea Mater*, deity of procreation, fertility, and abundance. Very often they are found headless, a deliberate mutilation designed to prevent anyone else from making use of a figurine after the death of its owner.

The metal industry also continued to make progress: copper was smelted and cast, and the variety and number of objects were greater than before. But stone tools remained in common use and were replaced only gradually by the flat axe, copper celt, and cast socketed hoe. Daggers and knives of copper have been found in the houses of this period. The craftsman was beginning to make toilet articles such as mirrors – plain discs with slightly raised borders – and large pins with

Fig. 13 – Painted pottery from Siyalk (a and c) and Susa

hemispherical heads. Jewellery became more varied and richer in material: in addition to shell, carnelian, and turquoise, there were beads and pendants of rock crystal, lapis lazuli brought from the Pamirs, and jade from still farther afield. As commerce expanded, the need arose to guarantee the contents of a jar or bale and to ensure that merchandise was delivered intact.

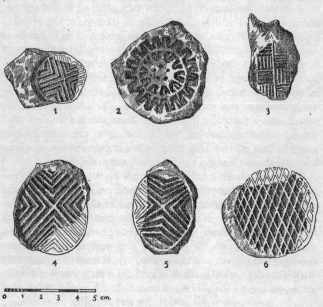

Fig. 14 – Siyalk: Seal impressions

To mark ownership, the seal was therefore brought into use, impressed on the lump of clay that stopped the mouth of a jar or was attached to a cord. The shape of the earliest seals, which remained unchanged for a long time, was that of a conical stone button provided with a loop. Geometric decoration was at first the rule (Fig. 14), but this was soon supplemented by representations of human beings, plants, and symbols, whose inspiration no doubt came from the painted decoration on pottery and, like that decoration, may possibly have had the significance of writing.

There was remarkable progress in all branches of human activity during this phase of civilization on the Plateau. The expansion of domestic economy coincided with the rise of larger communities and the emergence of urban life elsewhere. But though this was happening in the rich plain of Mesopotamia, there was still nothing comparable in Iran. Here the physical aspect of the Plateau was harsh and austere. The oases were dispersed over difficult country, the population was sparse and scattered. As a result the urban revolution was retarded, and society continued in its prehistoric stage for centuries longer, in spite of its more developed domestic economy. The only exception was the south-west region, the plain of Susiana, which was a natural extension of Mesopotamia and enjoyed similar advantages. From the beginning of the third millennium in that part of Iran there was a concentration of urban life, and there emerged the first civilized state, Elam.

The three phases of the prehistoric civilization of Iran described above have not been identified on all the sites so far examined on the Plateau. The presence of the earliest two has been recorded only on the edges of the great central desert, at Siyalk, Qumm, Savah, Rayy, and Damghan, sites forming a chain which follows the curve of the western and northern shores of the ancient inland sea (Fig. 15). It seems probable that during the dry period this belt of ground, which was particularly fertile owing to the alluvium accumulated by the rivers and streams flowing into the sea, lost water supplies more rapidly than the valleys situated in the folds of the Zagros. Sites such as Giyan near Nihawand, south of Hamadan, and Tall Bakun near Persepolis, as well as Susa, were not established before the end of Period II. But after this the painted pottery civilization flourished throughout the Plateau, and on the whole ceramic art and metallurgy then underwent a homogeneous development.

Admittedly there is little unity as far as painted pottery is concerned, but that only enhances the attractiveness of this rich and primitive art. Every district and every workshop has

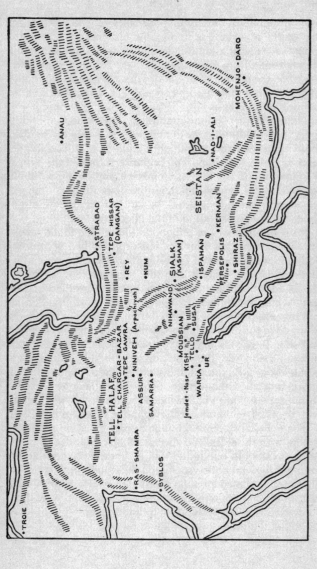

Fig. 15 – Archaeological map of Western Asia

its own individual variety of pot-shapes and decoration, and the variety of styles has its own peculiar charm. The potter from Susa fancied a tall slender goblet with thin sides, while the craftsman from Persepolis liked the shape of a truncated cone, and the potters of Siyalk or Hissar favoured the chalice. The variety of pictorial invention is but a measure of a developed artistic sense.

The potter's art became established, and owing to its vigour spread into more and more distant regions. Along the southern route it extended into Seistan, thence passed to Baluchistan and reached the Indus valley. To the north, it formed the basis of the culture found at the oasis of Merv, and in all probability reached Bactria, where the prehistoric sites still await the pick and shovel of the excavator. As we shall see, the West also benefited from the creation of the Plateau.

Many figurines of a naked goddess have been found on prehistoric Iranian sites. This goddess probably had as consort a god who was at one and the same time both her son and her husband. Undoubtedly it is in this primitive religion that we should seek the origin of marriage between brothers and sisters – a custom common in Western Asia, which the Persians and later the Nabateans inherited from the indigenous population – or of the marriage, less often recorded, between mother and son. Here also may have arisen the custom of descent through the female line which was practised by Elamites and Etruscans and Egyptians and was particularly widespread in Lycia. It is not without interest to note that among certain of these peoples women commanded the army; this was the case with the Guti, mountaineers living in the valleys of Kurdistan.

The political system was undoubtedly based on the family group, with the elders and their assembly. The idea of power being invested in one individual, in a chief who was later to become king, did not crystallize on the Plateau until later. The character of the country favoured the development of small centres which were remote from one another, and were therefore saved from disputes likely to lead to war.

IRAN AT THE BEGINNING OF THE THIRD
MILLENNIUM B.C.

The first signs of a rupture in the unity of the painted pottery civilization of Iran appeared during the second half of the fourth millennium B.C. At Susa, painted pottery suddenly stops and is replaced by a monochrome red ware with handle and tubular spout. This also occurs on the Mesopotamian plain, where it is characteristic of the period known as Uruk

Fig. 16 – Proto-Elamite script

IV: a period of capital importance in the development of Mesopotamian civilization, since towards its end came the invention of writing. Shortly afterwards, during the last centuries before 3000 B.C., a civilization arose at Susa which, though remaining under strong Mesopotamian influence, created its own writing, known as 'proto-Elamite' (Fig. 16), and was contemporary with the Jamdat Nasr period of the neighbouring plain. Susa was not the only district of southern Iran to experience western penetration: recent excavation to the north-east of the Persian Gulf has shown that all the northern shore received the new influence. During the millennia which followed, southern Iran waged a continual struggle against the strong and persistent penetration of Mesopotamian culture.

The centres situated in the western part of the Plateau do not seem to have suffered from foreign pressure. The painted pottery tradition persisted, and the Giyan potter, remaining faithful to the old fashions, continued to seek new formulas for both the shapes and decoration of his vases. There is nothing parallel in the north-east, where at Hissar, near Damghan, there was a slow, inexorable transformation lasting for several centuries. At one settlement after another the number of painted pots declined, to the advantage of the black or grey-black pottery, which both in colour and shape was completely alien to the Plateau (Pl. 2b). Transposing this substitution on to the human plane, it would seem that there was a slow infiltration of foreigners who established themselves in the midst of the indigenous population. We know nothing of the origins of this new culture, nor can we as yet say with certainty who were the people who brought it. It seems to have come from districts near the Oxus and the Jaxartes, in the plains of Russian Turkestan, or perhaps from even farther afield, towards the heart of Central Asia. It spread slowly in the north-east of the Plateau, but later became increasingly important in the north; passing, perhaps, along the Caspian shore, it penetrated as far as Cappadocia, where grey pottery with a concave body – apparently a Nordic characteristic – has been found at Kul Tepe. Resembling the culture of ancient Mesopotamia, it shows a predilection for spouted vases.

The central part of the Plateau did not escape foreign influence. At Siyalk, houses belonging to the end of Period III were abandoned and a thick layer of ash shows that they were destroyed by fire. Their ruins served as foundations for a new settlement in which painted pottery disappeared and was replaced by a monochrome red or grey ware, its shapes identical with those known at Susa at the end of the fourth millennium. The stamp seal was succeeded by the cylinder seal, a certain sign of the introduction of writing on clay tablets; indeed, tablets with proto-Elamite script were found in association with this material in the excavations. The slow and peaceful infiltration in the north-east of the Plateau by men using black pottery seems to have been very different from the arrival of the civilization bringing the proto-Elamite script, which bears all the marks of brutal conquest. At Siyalk the latter introduced a civilization which was unquestionably superior, richer, and more advanced, the result of a fusion between the native and Mesopotamian cultures which had taken place at Susa during the preceding centuries. The presence at Siyalk of Susian fea-

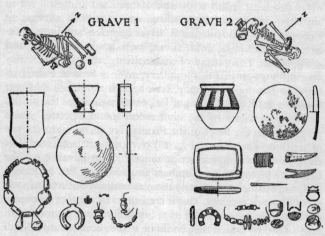

Fig. 17 – Siyalk: Graves belonging to the period of the proto-Elamite script

tures and almost complete identity between the civilizations known at Susa and Siyalk show that at the latter site it was imposed by force.

The houses were more carefully constructed, although the doorway was still curiously low. At the entrance stood an oven divided into two compartments, one used for cooking food and the other, presumably, for baking bread. At one side a small water-jar stood in the ground. There were modest furnishings of stamped earth; although rudimentary, they indicate a need for niches or little enclosures of stones to protect various objects or provisions. The dead were buried in a crouched position about a foot beneath the floor of the room, and were accompanied by varied funerary furnishings, much richer than in the modest tombs belonging to the preceding period at Siyalk (Fig. 17). Small, carefully worked alabaster bottles appear with the new ceramic. These were toilet articles, as were the copper mirrors in the shape of slightly convex disks. The dead were adorned with much jewellery: silver pendants inlaid with lapis lazuli, shell and gold set in bitumen; others of beaten silver; ear-rings with alternating pieces of gold and lapis lazuli; silver bracelets and long necklaces with beads of gold, silver, lapis lazuli, carnelian, and white stone. The variety of material used and the fine workmanship suggest that this jewellery, made at Susa or even, perhaps, in Mesopotamia, may have been the precursor of that found in the Royal Tombs at Ur, which so amazed the world.

The importance of the civilization found at Susa, which penetrated to the heart of the Plateau, lay above all in the use of writing. The tablets (Fig. 18) have not yet been read, but their semi-pictographic script represents an advance on the first pure pictography. Numbers and additions can be identified, and enable us to classify them as business documents such as accounts or receipts. This is confirmed by the fact that some of the tablets recovered by us at Siyalk had been perforated to take a cord by which they could be tied to merchandise. With writing came the use of the cylinder seal, the impression of which on the soft clay of the tablet constituted the signature of

 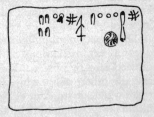

Fig. 18 – Siyalk: Proto-Elamite tablet

Fig. 19 – Siyalk: Cylinder seals belonging to the period of the
proto-Elamite tablets

the owner. The designs of this glyptic seem to connect it with
the art of the painted pottery which had flourished in the preceding period on the Iranian Plateau. Siyalk is the only site on
the Plateau which has yielded written records earlier than the
Achaemenian age (Fig. 19). The use of writing is thus attested
in Iran, though it was invented in the southern plains, which
were closely linked with Mesopotamian civilization. It was
introduced on to the Plateau by the expansion of Elamite culture following on political conquest, and certainly served an
economic purpose. It lasted as long as Elamite civilization persisted in the centre of Iran, but the abandonment of this
trading-station seems to have led to its disappearance in Iran
for several centuries.

We have noticed the different centres of Iran which at the
beginning of the third millennium B.C. were subject to

influences coming from various regions outside the Plateau.
They penetrated it unequally, coming now from the south-
west, now from the north-east, and introduced changes in the
older culture of Iran, which to a certain extent disturbed and
modified its 1,000-year-old structure. Iran, however, absorbed
them and at the same time continued to carry abroad its own
culture. To mention only one example, during the second half
of the fourth millennium B.C. the civilization which flourished
in north Mesopotamia, the future Assyria, adopted and developed a rich ceramic characterized by a chalice shape and
painted decoration which are recognized as coming, apparently, from Iranian centres, the best known of which are Siyalk
and Hissar.

Iran, as we have seen, was a highway for the movement of
peoples and for the transmission of ideas. From the prehistoric
period onwards, and for 1,000 years more, it held this important position as an intermediary between East and West. In return for what it received it never ceased to give; its role was to
receive, to recreate, and then to transmit.

IRAN IN THE THIRD MILLENNIUM B.C.

At the beginning of the third millennium B.C. the rich Mesopotamian plain entered the historic period and, thanks to the
records which its inhabitants handed down on the history of
their country, the first rays of light pierce the darkness which
was to enshroud the history of Iran for yet another 2,000 years.
This does not, however, apply to Elam, which soon made its
own contribution to a knowledge of its history. But as far as
the country to the north of the plain of Susa is concerned, such
little information as we have comes almost exclusively from
Babylonian sources. Moreover, the area with which the texts
are concerned does not extend far into Iran, for they deal only
with the frontier districts inhabited by the hill-peoples with
whom the Sumero-Semitic population of the plain was continually in contact. From south to north, these were the Elamites, the Kassites, the Lullubi, and the Guti (Fig. 20). All belonged to the same racial group; all spoke related languages;

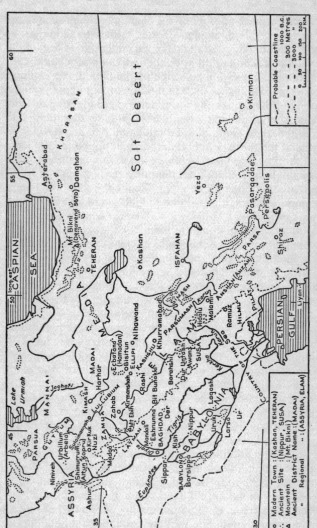

Fig. 20 – Map of prehistoric Iran

and the constant pressure of the plain, which was already organized in civilized kingdoms, forced them all to unite at about the same time, though only temporarily. The great duel of the nomad and semi-nomad with the sedentary population continued. For a Babylonian scribe of the period, the civilized world ended at the foothills of the Zagros. It was not until the arrival of the Iranians, two and a half millennia later, and the foundation of the first Achaemenian Empire, that this world pushed back its frontiers as far as Central Asia and established them to the north of the Jaxartes. Each time that Babylonia was ruled by a new and vigorous dynasty, the pressure of the plain on the mountains was intensified; the decadence of Babylonia, on the other hand, acted like a clarion call to the hill peoples, bringing them down to pillage the rich plain and sometimes, even, to occupy it for varying lengths of time.

From this general picture Elam must always be excluded. Coming from the mountains which screen the plain of Susiana on the north and east, the Elamites by the first quarter of the third millennium B.C. had already formed a dynasty which ruled over a wide area of plains and mountains, including an important part of the shore of the Gulf and Bushire district. An inscription, probably of one of the kings, has been found in this area.* It is written in Sumerian – proof that by this time the Elamites, though possessing their own script, had also adopted that of their neighbours and even used their language. With the foundation of the Semitic dynasty of Sargon of Agade, Elam entered on a fierce struggle in defence of its liberty and independence. The forces were unequally matched, and on two occasions the great conqueror was victorious; he may even have annexed Susa. One of his sons, Manishtusu, seems to have been still more fortunate in his expeditions against Iran; his armies actually crossed the Persian Gulf to secure the routes along which were brought building materials and metals from the Iranian highlands. Under Naram-Sin a general revolt broke out from Elam to the Zab, but was severely repressed (Pl. 3*b*). Susa was governed by a high official appointed by Naram-Sin, who erected important buildings in

* Cameron, *History of Early Iran*, p. 26.

the city. The Akkadian language largely supplanted the Elamite, and even proper names were more often Semitic than
Elamite. This policy of assimilation threatened the local culture, which only survived owing to the asylum afforded it in
the inaccessible mountains.

A skilful policy of submission on the part of the subject
people, however, enabled them eventually to restore the situation. One of their number, Puzur-Inshushinak, who had been
appointed governor by Naram-Sin in succession to a Semite,
was able to foster a national movement and Elam soon took
the offensive. Inscriptions in Elamite written in the proto-
Elamite script reappeared side by side with Akkadian texts.
Furthermore, the governor, on the pretext of defending his
Semitic overlord, embarked on a new policy of expansion and
extended his conquests far to the north, even coming into contact with the Guti. A great builder, Puzur-Inshushinak enriched Susa with booty carried off from the vanquished districts and erected temples and monuments; the petty kings of
neighbouring countries came to do him homage. On the death
of Naram-Sin, Puzur-Inshushinak proclaimed his independence and invaded Babylonia at the head of his army, even
reaching Akkad. He was driven back only with difficulty and
maintained his independence of Akkad, which became progressively weaker. Its decadence did not escape the notice of
the neighbouring hill peoples and, encouraged by the success
of Puzur-Inshushinak, the Lullubi and the Guti one after the
other came down from the high valleys and invaded Babylonia.

The Lullubi occupied the district lying across the ancient
road which still leads from Baghdad through Kermanshah to
Hamadan and Teheran. It is a route which makes use of one of
the few natural entries into the Plateau and has been in existence for many thousand years. Sargon of Agade had already
conquered these hill peoples, but Naram-Sin struck the heavi-
est blow; after the revolt already mentioned, the Semitic ruler
smashed the Lullubi–Guti coalition in the course of a great
battle, which he commemorated in a stele sculptured on the
rocks in the district of Shehrizor. However, here as elsewhere,
contact between the hill peoples and the inhabitants of the

Fig. 21 – Stele of Horen-Sheikh-Khan

plain was not effected only in time of war. Owing to the geographical position of their country, the mountaineers held the
road into western Iran; they therefore controlled the movement of caravans and trade. Though they were enemies, yet at
the same time they supplied Babylonia with goods, and in the
course of more peaceful transactions inevitably fell under the
influence of their more civilized neighbours. This is proved by
two bas-reliefs carved by two of their kings on the rocks of the
Sar-i-Pul-i-Zohab region, at least one of which was probably

inspired by that of Naram-Sin (Fig. 21). This local chieftain is depicted holding a bow and trampling underfoot defeated enemies who implored his mercy. A much-damaged inscription seems to give his name: Tar Lunni.

Another more important bas-relief, in two registers, is sculptured high up on the rock at the entrance to the modern village of Sar-i-Pul. It shows the King Annubanini, prince of the Lullubi, standing with his foot on a fallen enemy. He wears a long square-cut beard, a round cap, and a short garment, and is armed with a bow and a sort of harp or scimitar. Facing him is the goddess Ninni, dressed in a high mitre and fringed *kaunakes* reaching to her feet. She stretches out one hand to the

Fig. 22 – Bas-relief of Annubanini, king of the Lullubi

King, and in the other holds the end of a cord which binds two captives in the upper and six others in the lower register; all of them are naked and have their hands tied behind their backs. An inscription in Akkadian invokes several deities, most of them Akkadian, against the enemy (Fig. 22).

In view of the great rarity of monuments of this period in Iran itself, and the complete absence, so far, of texts in this part of the country, these two monuments are of very great importance for our knowledge of the level of the local culture. Everything leads to the conclusion that the inhabitants of the district did not possess a writing of their own in which to express their language. It would seem, however, that at the time they were more or less permeated by Babylonian civilization, and consequently they used the Akkadian writing and language when in contact with their western neighbours. We can also say that their few artists were strongly influenced by the art of Mesopotamia, at any rate in their more important works. Here, as in Elam, the civilization of the plain infiltrated either peacefully or by force of arms. Nevertheless the 'Iranian' role of these two bas-reliefs was great and lasting. The idea had been launched, and in the course of the long history of Iran, generations of princes left many other reliefs in all corners of the Plateau. The later reliefs drew their inspiration from these early carvings: here, high up on the mountain-sides, the pictorial record of ancient feats of arms could be seen by the caravans that passed below.

Towards the middle of the same millennium, Babylonia was overwhelmed by the invasion of the Guti, who came down from their mountains, east of the Lower Zab, into the valley of the upper Diyala. For centuries they had been a constant menace to the settlements on the plain. Investigations at Brak, a site in the Khabur valley, east of the Euphrates, have revealed the existence of a fortified palace built by Naram-Sin of Agade. This building, which was on the line of communication between Anatolia and Akkad, was no doubt designed to protect this important trade route against the depredations of these and other mountaineers. Eventually their inroads became an invasion and they put an end to the dynasty of Agade.

It would seem that Elam also did not escape them. For more than a century they remained as barbarous masters, devastating towns and cities, dismembering kingdoms, and leaving only small principalities. The very long list of their kings may indicate a troubled period. Towards the end of their domination Babylonian culture seems to have gained the ascendancy, and the destruction of the Guti was not long delayed. Resistance slowly formed against them, and a movement to drive them out was led by the new dynasty of Ur. Warrior kings of Babylonia took the offensive and smashed their power; Susa and the whole of its plain once again became a Babylonian province. But this dynasty did not last for long; little more than a century after its rise, the last king was defeated and carried off to captivity in the mountains. This time, the conqueror came from a different direction, the kingdom of Simash, probably situated in the mountains to the west of Isfahan. The hinterland of the Zagros now entered the struggle against the Babylonian kingdoms. Simash also ruled over Susa and Elam. There was eventually a reaction in the plain where the dynasty of Isin arose and expelled Simash, seizing Elam, which once more passed into foreign hands.

The role of Iran in the life of the peoples of Western Asia grew in importance during the third millennium B.C. The great kingdoms of Mesopotamia, based on an urban economy, made enormous progress in the development of their political, social, and economic life. Their need for raw materials for building, public works, arms, and objects of art increased. With the growth of royal power, great quantities of manufactured goods accumulated in the various centres of Mesopotamia. The economic policy of the princes led them to seek out more and more distant markets, and thus we learn that as early as the time of Sargon of Agade there were colonies of merchants in Asia Minor – real business centres where Semitic merchants traded and supplied their country with necessary goods. The new kingdoms also turned their attention to Iran. Owing to its proximity and its mineral wealth, it was a centre of attraction for all who were strong enough to attempt the annexation of its western districts. While Iran was a transit country for lead coming from Armenia and lapis lazuli from Badakshan, its own mineral wealth included gold, extracted in Media, copper, and tin. Various kinds of stone, suitable for building palaces and temples, were transported to Babylonia, as well as different kinds of wood, which were required for the same purpose.

In their military expeditions against Iran during the third millennium B.C., the Babylonian kings pursued two definite aims: the first, which was political, required military action against the formation of any organized state and the annexation of districts bordering on their frontiers. These were formed into provinces administered by governors who introduced the benefits of their civilization among the conquered people. In realizing this first purpose, they attained the second, the economic aim of diverting the riches of Iran to Babylonian centres. Yet, despite its political instability, Iran emerged triumphant from the struggle: twice in the course of the millennium the mountaineers brought two great Babylonian dynasties to an end. The dynasty founded by Sargon of Agade was destroyed by the Guti, while that known as the Third Dynasty of Ur received the *coup de grâce* from the kings of Simash.

We know nothing of political conditions on the Plateau, not even to the east of the region we have just studied; nor is it known how extensive was the power of an Elamite prince or of a king of the Lullubi or the Guti. At Siyalk a gap of nearly 2,000 years deprives us of any source of information. But at Giyan the life of the community went on without profound change. The art of the potter continued to be represented by a painted pottery which was very close to ware found at Susa and known as Style II (Fig. 23). Vases in the shape of small jars with button bases are decorated in black paint on the shoulder only, the most characteristic subject being the crest of a bird, which is the stylization of a motif well known in Mesopotamian art: the eagle seizing his prey (Fig. 24). Tombs found here have yielded much bronze and silver jewellery, including torques or necklaces of beads with pendants. Bronze pins for fastening garments are very numerous: some are headless, others have the upper part flattened and twisted – a type found among the jewellery of the Royal Tombs at Ur. At Tepe

Fig. 23 – Susa: Pottery of Style II

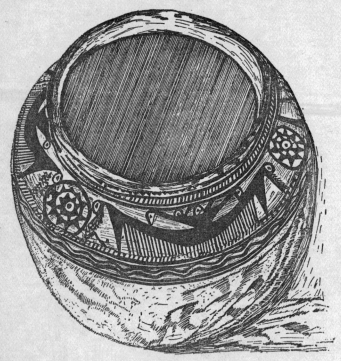

Fig. 24 – Giyan: Pottery of Level IV

Hissar grey-black monochrome pottery displaced the painted;
as in the western part of the Plateau, there is evidence of increased activity in metallurgy, particularly in the manufacture
of small objects which were usually in bronze, a metal so rare
at that time that it may possibly have been more prized than
gold or silver. Iran was passing into the age of bronze.

IRAN IN THE SECOND MILLENNIUM B.C.

The event which dominated the history of Western Asia during the second millennium B.C. was the appearance of elements

of Indo-European origin in this part of the ancient world. At first, it is true, the new-comers played a relatively small part on the scene. The Indo-Europeans seem to have left their homeland, which in all probability lay in the Eurasian plains of southern Russia, as the result of pressure from other peoples in their rear. In the course of their migration they apparently split into two groups. One, which we shall call the western branch, rounded the Black Sea, and, after crossing the Balkans and the Bosphorus, penetrated into Asia Minor. Settling among Asianic peoples who appear to have been the original inhabitants of the country, they rapidly became the dominant element in the population, and formed a Hittite confederation.* Their empire was subsequently one of the most active members of the concert of Western Powers at the time. The Hittites extended their conquests in Asia Minor and even made a successful raid as far as Babylon, which they took and sacked – a barren victory, however, for they failed to follow it up and almost immediately retired. After a temporary eclipse, there was a great revival in the second half of the millennium, during which the Hittites absorbed a number of neighbouring kingdoms, notably those of the Hurrians and the rulers of Mitanni; this brought them face to face with Egypt, then at the height of its expansion in Syria and Palestine.

The eastern branch, known as the Indo-Iranians, moved eastward round the Caspian Sea. One group, which apparently consisted mainly of the warrior element, crossed the Caucasus and pushed as far as the great bend of the Euphrates. There they settled among the indigenous Hurrians, a people of Asianic origin, and after some time formed the kingdom of Mitanni. They established their suzerainty over northern Mesopotamia and the valleys of the northern Zagros, and kept Assyria confined within narrow limits. The greatest period of this kingdom was about 1450 B.C.: Egypt became an ally, the most powerful pharaohs marrying the daughters of the kings of

---

* The problem of the origin of the Hittites is, however, a controversial subject. A different view has been expressed by Sir Leonard Woolley, *A Forgotten Kingdom*, p. 35, where it is admitted that the evidence is still defective.—EDITOR.

Mitanni. But revolts and rivalries between members of the royal family weakened the country, so that it was unable to maintain independence in face of the rising power of the Hittite kingdom. At the end of the fourteenth century the political dynasty of Mitanni disappeared; yet something remained of its civilization, and especially of its vigorous art, which, though rooted in Sumerian origins and influenced by Egypt and the Aegean, yet possessed an individuality of its own. There are perhaps some grounds for thinking that by the time the kingdom of Mitanni was formed, the Indo-European element had already been absorbed by the Hurrians, leaving behind it vestiges only of its religion and the names of the gods of its pantheon. Thus, a treaty concluded between a king of the Hittites and a ruler of Mitanni mentions Mithra, Varuna, Indra, and the Nasatya, all divinities known among the close relatives of the rulers of Mitanni, the Indo-Europeans who about the same time settled in India; certain of their gods are also known among the Hittites and Kassites. These Indo-Iranians also left treatises on the training of horses which they seem to have introduced into Western Asia. The survivals of their Indo-European religion reveal the existence of a divine couple consisting of the great god, divinity of the natural elements, of mountain tops, of the storm and of rain, and of the great goddess who is sometimes the sun, sometimes the earth.

A branch of these warrior horsemen moved along the folds of the central Zagros and penetrated into the region south of the great caravan route – a district later famous as a centre of horse-breeding. They settled there as an active minority and seem to have been quickly assimilated by the mass of the Kassite people of Asianic origin. The penetration by this reduced branch of Indo-Europeans resembles to a certain extent a later episode, the invasion of the Cimmerians and Scythians in the eighth century B.C. One fact seems to emerge from this rapid survey which has traced the appearance on the soil of Western Asia of a new ethnic element. Whenever there is an amalgamation of two blocks of races as different as the Asianic and the Indo-European, even though the former is the stronger element, the issue of this hybrid emerges with an astonishing vitality: a vigorous diplomacy, military and economic expansion follow in its wake, even in countries which hitherto had no history. Regions that before were only a scattering of little principalities, city states, and temple states, were transformed into powerful confederations, and even into empires, infused with a dynamic force that carried them into the first rank among the powers of their age. Such was the case with the Hittites and the rulers of Mitanni; and, as we shall see, the same thing happened with the Kassites.

Finally, the bulk of the tribes, forming the eastern branch of the Indo-European movement, slowly passed eastwards, crossed Transoxiana and the Oxus, the modern Amu-Daria, and then, after a short halt in the Bactrian plain, scaled the passes of the Hindu Kush and, following the classic route of the invaders of India, descended along the Pandishir and Kabul rivers.

It may be that during their passage through Bactria certain tribes thrust towards the west. Were they already capable of bringing to an end the occupation of the site of Hissar? The difference of opinion concerning the date of the end of the latest settlement at this site – which, as excavations have shown, fell to a violent assault – leaves the question open. If it is dated to the middle of the second millennium, the cause of this destruction could be attributed to the movement of Indo-Europeans described above. If it is brought down to the last centuries of the same millennium, it may be that the cause was a new wave of Indo-Europeans, this time bringing the Iranians on to the Plateau.

ELAM

The second millennium found a new national dynasty in Elam, whose kings styled themselves: 'divine messenger, father and king' (of Anzan and Susa). The business documents of the period were written in Akkadian, but the presence of many indigenous words testifies to the development of the local civilization. This is evident also in religion. The goddess Shala and her consort, Inshushinak, were frequently invoked and were more popular than the gods of the Babylonian pantheon. At the beginning of the second millennium the Elamites invaded Babylonia, one of their princes founding a dynasty at Larsa. Shortly afterwards the Elamites overthrew the dynasty of Isin and also became masters of Uruk and Babylon. The accession to the throne of Babylon of Hammurabi, a powerful and outstanding ruler, checked Elamite expansion; but it took that king thirty-one years to defeat Rim-Sin his Elamite opponent. After several unavailing attempts to maintain their dynasty at Larsa, the Elamites were defeated and Elam disappeared from the annals, to reappear a century later under a national king, Kutir-Nahunte, who re-established a stable kingdom. The documents of his reign were written in Akkadian, showing how strong had been the renewed pressure of the Semitic world during the preceding century. After a few more decades our knowledge of Elam fails. It was the period of the great conquests of the Kassites.

THE KASSITES

Early in the reign of Hammurabi's son, the records speak of the repulse of attacks by the Kassite army. Thereafter, for 150 years, Babylonia was exposed to the peaceful penetration of these mountaineers who came down into the plain to seek employment as agricultural labourers. Towards the middle of the eighteenth century they arrived in force and seized the country. Their domination, the longest foreign conquest known in Mesopotamia, lasted 576 years, not ending until 1171 B.C. The area of the Zagros inhabited by the Kassites corresponds to the central part of the range, modern Luristan, but their rule also extended north and east of that province and, according to certain scholars, included the district round Hamadan. The bulk of the population, which was Asianic in origin, had at the beginning of the second millennium been permeated by Indo-Europeans, who, forming a small military aristocracy, established themselves as a ruling caste, though they soon lost their own language. Babylonian texts referring to the Kassites show that there was a hybrid pantheon in which gods of Asianic origin existed side by side with those of Babylonia and with Indo-

European deities such as Shuriash, the Hindu Surya, Maruttash, the Indian Marut, and Buriash, the Greek Boreas. The horse seems to have been a divine symbol to the Kassites and was probably introduced by the ruling caste, as was the case in the kingdom of Mitanni. The native god, Kashshu, doubtless bore the name of the people, as is known to have occurred among other Asianic tribes.

The earliest reference to the Kassites is found in texts of the twenty-fourth century B.C. belonging to the time of Puzur-Inshushinak; they appear to have been relatively unimportant during the third millennium. The Assyrians knew them under the name of *Kassi*, which in the form of *Kossaioi* is mentioned by Strabo, who places the Kassites fairly far to the east at the Caspian Gates above Teheran. It is thought that the name of the town of Kazvin, as also that of the Caspian Sea, may preserve the memory of this people. The Greek word for tin, κασσίτερος, means metal 'coming from the country of the Kassites', while the name of Hamadan before the Medes was *Akessaia*, the Assyrian *kar-kassi*, meaning 'town of the Kassites'. It may be, however, that the term *kas-si* or *kas-pi* had a wider ethnic sense than the designation of a single people among the many peoples of the Zagros and that it included all the Asianics occupying Iran. The name of the Kassites as applied by Strabo to the Caspian gates is but a legacy from an ancient occupation of a country whose new rulers were unrelated to the old.

The memory of the Kassite invasion made a deep and lasting impression on the minds of the Babylonians, who associated it with a strength and power unusual among foreign invaders. There must have been good grounds for this, when we consider the length of the Kassite domination. The rather meagre information which is all that can be obtained from Kassite documents is, however, surprising: it seems that no vital innovations were introduced under their rule. But although the records are relatively inarticulate about Babylonian and Elamite affairs, we know from other sources that the Kassites were in touch with Egypt during the Amarna age. During this period there occurred a revival of Assyria, which by treaty secured a frontier in the Holwan district, after a campaign conducted by Adad Nirari I.

The overthrow of the Kassites was the work of Babylonian forces. Elam was the first to revive while the Kassites were still firmly in occupation of Babylonia, and once again it delivered the final blow. About the beginning of the thirteenth century B.C. a new dynasty established itself in Elam which, with rulers of the calibre of Shutruk-Nahhunte, Kutir-Nahhunte, and Shilhak-Inshushinak, marks the 'golden age' of Elam. A predecessor of these kings, Untash-Huban (or Untash-Gal), the great builder of this regenerated empire, studded the country with new towns or renovated old ones. The arts, above all that of the metal worker, reached a very high degree of perfection, to judge by the statue of the wife of Untash-Huban, Queen Napirasu (Pl. 3a). Babylonia, with its decadent Kassite dynasty, was no longer a dangerous adversary; the menace came rather from Assyria, which extended the hand of friendship to Babylonia. A war broke out, in which Elam registered its first successes.

Elam attained its apogee in the reign of Shutruk-Nahhunte I (c. 1207–1171), who built temples in all the important towns of his kingdom. Moving ahead of the Assyrians, Shutruk-Nahhunte invaded Babylonia and overthrew the last representative of the Kassite dynasty, replacing him by his own son, Kutur-Nahhunte, who carried off to Susa the statue of Marduk, the national god of Babylon. Babylonia had escaped from the domination of the Iranian mountaineers only to fall under the yoke of the Iranian plainsmen. Under King Shilhak-Inshushinak (1165–1151), Elam extended its conquests still farther afield: its armies were victorious in the north, where they penetrated the Diyala district; they reached the Kirkuk area, pushed as far as Assur, and besieged Babylon. The whole of the Tigris valley, most of the shore of the Persian Gulf, and the Zagros range fell under Elamite domination. All western Iran, enlarged by territories west and south of the mountains, was united, and formed the first empire under the Elamite sceptre. Hand in hand with these conquests went a national Elamite revival: inscriptions were written almost exclusively in Elamite in the proto-Elamite script. The reaction against foreign culture grew stronger; Inshushinak became a national god and the king and royal family were deified during their lifetimes. The renaissance found expression in the arts and architecture, and one of the chief cities to benefit was Susa.

But, as so often happened in the history of the peoples of the ancient world, the period which brought them to the summit of their power was followed by one of rapid decline. This was the fate of Elam at the end of the second millennium B.C. Its disintegration coincided with the advent of a new Babylonian dynasty, whose King, Nebuchadrezzar I, after several abortive attempts, smashed Elam and seized Susa, bringing back the statue of Marduk in triumph to his temple at Babylon. Once again Elam disappeared from history, this time for three centuries. The two regenerated kingdoms of Babylon and Assyria engaged in a long rivalry for domination of the plain. The Plateau declined in importance, and, although still to be reckoned with, was obliged to await events which, several centuries later, entirely changed the face of the ancient world.

The hiatus at Siyalk during the third millennium lasted through most of the second, and life was resumed at this site on the central Plateau only towards the end of the second millennium B.C. We have already seen the fate of Hissar in the north-east, which finally disappeared during the second half of the second millennium. But Giyan in the west has yielded valuable information and throws light on the varying currents influencing Iran at this time. Level III, which seems to represent a continuation of the native painted pottery tradition (Fig. 25),

Fig. 25 – Giyan: Tripod vases from Level III

is marked by the appearance of a new ware with strange shapes such as the *kernoi* and tripod. Their introduction in the area inhabited by the Kassites coincided with the penetration among these people of the Indo-European warriors to whom reference has already been made. With their near relations, the rulers of Mitanni, they formed a chain which followed the contour of the 'Fertile Crescent', running from the Zagros to Asia Minor across north Syria. The origin of these peculiar vases is rather to be sought in the west, in Syria or Asia Minor, where, in fact, both types are known to have occurred. The

Fig. 26 – Giyan: Pottery of Level II

tripod seems to have been much in vogue in certain parts of the Zagros, and remained in use there, particularly in Luristan, where tombs with bronzes, dated to the first millennium, have yielded a number of vases of this type.

In Level II at Giyan proto-Iranian pottery continued, but there was a return to animal decoration, abandoned in Period III. This decoration, however, assumed a new form characterized by metopes, the fashion for which in the middle of the second millennium spread far beyond Iran, and even reached Palestine (Fig. 26). Parallel with this native pottery was another ware with fine, light clay, decorated with strictly geometric designs in dull and sometimes poor-quality black paint. This so-called 'khabur' ware spread to the West as far as the Mediterranean region. This level corresponds in date to the invasion of the Hyksos and the conquest of Babylon by the Kassites – two connected movements which once more threw a bridge between the Mediterranean and the Zagros.

The settlement of Giyan I, which existed during the second half of the second millennium, was subject to extremely complex and confusing influences. It is difficult to examine all the

Fig. 27 – Giyan: Pottery of Level I

changes that affected the pottery of this period without taking into account political conditions among the neighbouring peoples of the Zagros, both to the west and east. Thus the oldest part of the settlement is characterized by vases in the shape of a chalice or slightly curved goblet, decorated with animal or geometric designs and with the guilloche (Fig. 27). We know where this pottery originated: it was derived from the so-called 'Hurrian' ware, found in particular among the rulers of Mitanni, who at this moment, the fifteenth and fourteenth centuries B.C., were expanding their kingdom towards the east and annexed the area of the Zagros inhabited by the

Guti. Later tombs were found at Giyan containing related pottery which, however, for the first time since the foundation of
the site, was without decoration. We have long emphasized the
identity of this pottery and its associated jewellery with everything that we know at Babylon towards the end of the Kassite
domination, in the thirteenth and twelfth centuries B.C.

The western currents which influenced the west of the
Plateau for several centuries seem to have ceased at this point.
Babylon and Assyria entered on a long rivalry, and their
struggle may have interrupted contact between the Zagros
and the western world, for at this moment eastern influences
appeared. The first sign of change was the arrival at Siyalk and
Giyan of a grey-black or black pottery, not previously recorded there. It had, however, already appeared in the third millennium at Hissar, where the people associated with it gradually
established themselves, in time eliminating the painted pottery
and spreading in the north of Iran. This civilization arrived in
force at Siyalk, and in Cemetery A practically nothing but the
grey-black pottery was in use; at Giyan it was more or less sub-
merged by the survivals of the preceding period, but retained
its peculiar ware and shape. The theory that it was introduced
by tribes coming from the north and north-east driven by some
external pressure is a plausible hypothesis which would allow
for the destruction of Hissar. This 'mountain crescent' had
hitherto formed a shield between the plateau-dwellers and the
world to the north and north-east, but it was here that the pressure started, before the invader himself actually appeared, an
invader whom we think we can recognize in the civilization of
Cemetery B at Siyalk. Indeed, shortly afterwards a new wave,
with an original and highly individual culture, replaced the
grey-black pottery civilization: it was the culture of Cemetery
B at Siyalk to which we shall return, and was identical with
that of tombs of 'Luristan type' at Giyan. A link between
these two cultures has been found by peasants of the village of
Khurvin, about 50 miles west of Teheran, in the southern foothills of the Elburz chain. Elements characteristic of both
Cemetery A and B at Siyalk were found together there, but the
pottery was almost exclusively grey-black (except for certain

pots in a common coarse ware). There was a more extensive use of iron than in Cemetery A, although it was mainly confined to jewellery; thumb-guards in the form of a ram's head were common, and there were already many vases with long spouts, probably funerary ware.

The evidence suggests that the successive phases were interdependent, and that there were three stages in this settlement, the logical effects of an identical cause: (1) About the twelfth century B.C. the peripheral tribes started to move towards the west and south-west as the result of external pressure. These were the people of Cemetery A at Siyalk. (2) At Khurvin there was a mixture of civilization A of Siyalk and the culture whose pressure had given rise to the movement. (3) Finally, Cemetery B at Siyalk was the material expression of this new force which had initiated all the large-scale movements that took place on the Plateau at the very end of the second millennium. We have already had occasion, when referring to the discovery of Cemetery B, to state our theory that this culture belonged to the first Iranian tribes who about 1000 B.C. reached the western districts of Iran.

The advent of the Bronze Age, which took place in Iran about 2000 B.C., does not seem to have caused important changes in the economy of the country. The rural centres, which we can observe from the end of the neolithic period, grew larger, but they never attained the importance of the cities of the West, and their economy remained backward in relation to that of the great urban centres of Babylonia, Asia Minor, and Egypt. Elam, of course, formed an exception, and seems to have kept pace fairly closely with neighbouring Mesopotamia. This state of affairs was certainly due not so much to the topography of the Plateau and the difficulty of interior communications, as to shortage of water, which prevented the expansion of agriculture, and to the climate and natural conditions which too often imposed a nomadic or semi-nomadic existence. But in the second millennium Iran stood less apart from the world than ever before; owing to its mineral wealth, it had much to contribute to the progress of urban economy in the western countries. Commerce, however, was carried on under difficult conditions. The wealthy merchant, in order to conduct his trade, would often have been obliged to travel in disturbed and insecure country. Consequently he elected to invest his capital in the hands of royalty, nobles, and religious bodies, who extracted considerable profits therefrom and made the merchant himself dependent on them. At this period, too, there were many small traders who bought up scrap metal and acted as smelters and smiths: these men travelled far and wide and spread their merchandise over different countries which would otherwise have been out of touch with one another.

The invention of bronze brought improvements in the methods of production of metal objects, and created an expanding demand for raw materials. This source of wealth enabled Iran to enter the concert of nations as one of the most important suppliers of copper, tin, lead, wood, and stone. Her western neighbours had formerly been her only customers, but now India entered the sphere; thus her commercial transactions grew, but without supplanting those of Babylonia. As commercial relations expanded, caravans became more frequent and men travelled greater distances than ever before. Political expansion, such as that of the kingdom of Mitanni, brought greater knowledge of the country to the east behind the Zagros barrier and of its potentialities. An illustration of the connexions between Iran and the West is provided by the many changes in the pottery of the second millennium, which often supply evidence of the close relationship between the Plateau and the country to the west of it. The moment had been reached when Iran could claim to have acquired a place in the economy of Western Asia. The political supremacy which it exercised for more than five centuries in the second millennium over a country with a civilization as advanced as that of Babylonia must have considerably strengthened the development of economic relations with the West.

CHAPTER 2

The Coming of the Iranians

*

At the beginning of the first millennium B.C. two unrelated events of capital importance affected the history of the peoples of Western Asia: the invasion of the Indo-Europeans and the increased use of iron. Despite this coincidence, however, there is no reason to suppose that the new-comers introduced the use of this metal.

The arrival of the Indo-Europeans seems to have been very similar in character to their earlier invasion, and they probably came from the same regions. Just as towards the end of the third millennium B.C. the future founders of the Hittite Empire thrust across the Balkans and the Bosphorus,* so from about 1200 B.C. Thraco-Phrygian tribes, pushed by Illyrians, penetrated Asia Minor. Balkan peoples, Phrygians, Armenians, Thracians, and Mycenaeans fell upon the Hittite Empire and destroyed it, bringing disaster upon vassals and enemies alike. The wave included the Philistines, who settled in Palestine, a country that still bears their name. With strong forces of cavalry and chariotry and accompanied down the coast by ships, the invading armies of these 'peoples of the sea' passed through Syria and Palestine and reached the gates of Egypt, where only the energetic action of Ramses III saved his country from disaster. Driven back from Egypt, these young and vigorous peoples swarmed over Syria and Asia Minor, in the former country establishing a number of 'neo-Hittite' states, at Aleppo, Hama, Carchemish, and Malatia, and in the latter forming two kingdoms: that of the Phrygians in the west and that of the Mushki in the east.

The penetration of Iran by the Iranians at the beginning of

* This interesting view would not command universal assent, but is one of several theories on a controversial subject. – Ed.

the first millennium B.C. affected the country in a different
manner from the previous invasion, 1,000 years earlier. The
invaders arrived in force and in successive waves, apparently
following the same two routes as on their first appearance: the
Caucasus and Transoxiana. This time, however, they were not
absorbed by the native Asianic population, as the Hurrians,
the rulers of Mitanni, and the Kassites had been. After a slow
penetration lasting several centuries, they finally established
themselves as masters in the country from which, later on, they
were to set out to conquer the world.

The eastern branch of these Iranians, coming from Transoxiana, was unable to spread to the south of the Hindu Kush,
since all the district of Arachosia as well as the Punjab was already in the hands of the sister branch of the Aryans, the future
Indians, who had settled there at the time of the earlier Indo-
Iranian invasion. The new arrivals were therefore forced to
turn west towards the Plateau, along the natural route leading
from Bactria into the heart of Iran. This land of Iran was less
favoured than India, being 'rich only in square miles', and the
Iranians never abandoned the idea of re-taking Arachosia.
They bitterly contested the province with the Vedic tribes in
the course of a long struggle that finally ended in the Iranization of the disputed territory.

This great migration of Indo-Europeans in Asia, with
Thraco-Phrygian elements in Asia Minor and Iranians on the
Plateau, must have been in some way connected with the very
extensive movements of invading peoples in central and western Europe, which occurred about the same time. The nomads
who invaded Europe, like the Iranians, were primarily a pastoral people, and, to a less extent, agriculturalists. Above all,
they were breeders and trainers of horses, and their cavalry and
chariotry contributed greatly to the success of their venture.
Their tombs, like those of the ancient Iranians, had a gabled
roof, imitating a Nordic house,* and doubtless reflected the
same conception as the funerary urn in the shape of a house
known in Etruria at the beginning of the first millennium B.C.
Like the Iranians, these Nordic peoples advanced slowly, and

* Herzfeld, *Iran in the Ancient East*, pp. 199–200, 209.

under their 'prolific impetus' Europe underwent profound changes.

It was not the parallel ranges of the Zagros, though difficult to cross and forming a protective curtain, that checked the Iranian advance. To the west lay a barrier of states with a long history and cultures developed by hundreds, if not thousands, of years of sedentary and civilized life. The Iranian tribes moving south-east along the folds of the Zagros were faced from south to north by Elam, which included Susiana and extended to the mountains of its hinterland; by Mesopotamia, which to the north of Babylon had a common frontier with Assyria; and finally, farther to the north and north-east around Lake Van, where the Zagros merges into the Caucasian massif, by the young kingdom of Urartu (Ararat), which four centuries later was to become the kingdom of Armenia.

For the time being, the Iranians were unable to break through this barrier. In the course of the next four centuries they absorbed the aboriginal population, and established their own civilization, which inevitably had roots in the cultures of the neighbouring states, which, although barring their advance westwards, were not continuously hostile. Settled in the valleys of the Zagros, the invaders cast their political, cultural, and even to a certain extent their religious life in the mould fashioned for them by the civilizations they were later to absorb.

The first half of the first millennium B.C. was a turning-point in human history. The centre of the 'world politics' of the age shifted; instead of valleys with a favourable climate conducive to the birth of magnificent civilizations, as the Nile valley was for the Egyptians, or the plain watered by the Tigris and Euphrates for the Sumero-Semites, it was more to the north, in regions less clement in physical aspect and climate, that the struggle for world power was centred. There were three principal actors in the drama: the Semitic Assyrians with their vast empire; Urartu, a powerful kingdom of Asiatic origin, tenacious opponents of the Assyrians, over whom they were sometimes victorious; and finally, the Aryans, the Iranians who, after a long and arduous struggle, triumphed over their two adversaries and, with the spoils, founded the first World Empire.

It is not easy to determine the causes of these extensive movements which had as their theatre the Eurasian world in which Indo-European tribes made their appearance. It is thought that increased numbers of flocks forced their owners to seek new pastures; the drought which periodically brings desolation to the Eurasian steppes may equally have driven them to seek relief in more favoured countries. These warrior horsemen were a menace to the sedentary peoples; but they learnt the arts of civilization as a result of war. Their migrations continued for centuries, and eventually the conquerors became so far identified with the conquered as to lose all traces of their origin.

It was not a case of obtaining 'residential permits' like those distributed by Rome at the end of the fourth century A.D. to settle the barbarians. These Iranian horsemen arrived with women, children, and flocks and, taking advantage of the division of the country into numerous petty states, most of them, together with their bodies of cavalry, entered the service of local princes. Men who lived by the sword and mercenaries, they became praetorians who were one day to supplant the very princes they had served. In this way, these small states, often no more than towns surrounded by a belt of gardens and fields, passed into the hands of the new-comers. In the course of centuries a slow substitution took place, affecting different parts of the Plateau unequally, and the indigenous inhabitants were progressively forced to surrender possession to the invading army.

It is still impossible to write the history of these developments, for the sources are too few and fragmentary. The royal annals of Assyria are practically the only records, and the identification of the names of princes, towns, and countries mentioned in them is still far from certain. What occurred must have been somewhat analogous to the struggle of the Roman Empire against the barbarians, with this difference, that instead of the Rhine and the Danube, it was a mountain barrier that separated the civilized world from the irresistible onrush of the tribes. There it was united Rome, here a diversity of civilizations. The composite character of the material culture found among the Persians may thus easily be understood.

We are beginning to know something of the civilization of these warriors, and in particular that of the tribe which gained control of the oasis of Kashan. At Siyalk, already mentioned in connexion with its prehistoric settlements, one of these princes

Fig. 28 – Town of Siyalk: Tentative restoration

built an imposing residence on top of the artificial mound, and the town, including the houses at the foot of the mound, was surrounded by an enclosure wall, flanked with towers (Fig. 28). There was an important change in the method of burial – generally considered to be a sign of the radical replacement of an old by a new people. Graves were no longer dug beneath the house floors. Several hundred yards from the town was a vast cemetery, a 'city of the dead'. The dead were still laid in the ground with numerous and varied grave goods, sometimes several hundred objects in one tomb (Pl. 2c). On their heads

were helmets of leather; these have now disappeared, but
worked silver plaques had been sewn on as decoration. There
was much jewellery, particularly of silver, though also of

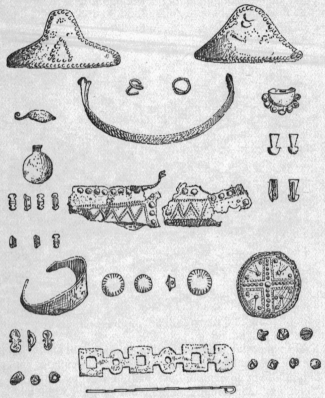

Fig. 29 – Siyalk: Silver and bronze jewellery from Necropolis B

bronze: pins with animal heads – a Nordic ornament *par excellence* – bracelets, ear-rings, hair ornaments, rings, and belt
plaques, all worn by men as well as women. Anklets were
usually of bronze, but might also be of iron (Fig. 29). Weapons

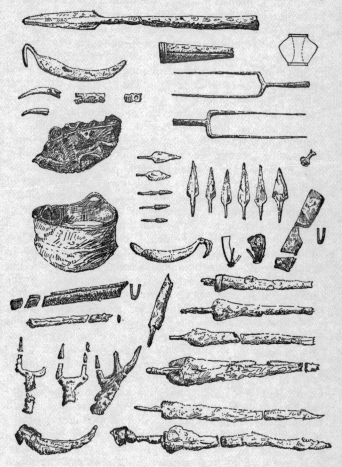

Fig. 30 – Siyalk: Weapons and tools in bronze and iron
from Necropolis B

– swords, daggers, shields, arrow-heads – were as common in
bronze as in iron (Fig. 30). Tombs of warriors contained
bronze or iron harness, including broken bits and multiple
elements for adorning the head and breast of a horse (Fig. 31).

The most common class of object, however, was the pottery: painted or monochrome, grey-black, red, or drab, vases
for ritual or for domestic use, it provides evidence of great
activity in the potters' workshops. The most striking shape is
that of a vase with elongated spout, too fragile to have been
in daily use and probably intended for libations at the time of
burial (Fig. 32). This very characteristic pottery sprang up
everywhere in Iran: it is found at Siyalk and Giyan, in Luristan, west of Teheran, near Karaj, south of Lake Urmia, and at
Solduz. We were even able to identify it at Nad-i-Ali on the
banks of the river Helmand on the fringes of the desert of
Afghan Seistan. At Siyalk its painted decoration is particularly
rich and instructive: its origins certainly go back to the art of
painted pottery on the Plateau, the production of which, in
practice, never ceased. But on the Siyalk vases the abundant
and elaborate painting reflects a new taste: the *horror vacui*. In
addition to the geometric motifs, among which the sun-disk
holds a place of honour, is the ibex, soon to be replaced by the
horse, as in Hallstatt art. The horse and the sun, two symbols
associated by practically all Indo-European peoples, gradually
assumed a preponderant place in the art. The winged horse is
found painted on Siyalk pots and in *repoussé* work on a bronze
disk, possibly the trappings of a charger, from Solduz.

On the Siyalk pottery there are pictures of men fighting on
foot and wearing a helmet with crest and plumes and a short
fitted jacket (Fig. 33); on one cylinder seal there is an engraving of a warrior on horseback fighting a monster; he is dressed
in similar fashion, and wears turned-up shoes (Fig. 31); finally,
on another seal, very clumsily engraved, a man stands in a
chariot drawn by two horses and shoots an arrow at the animal
he is hunting. Thus he is portrayed both as warrior and huntsman by the potter and stone-engraver who created subjects
which were to become classical at all periods of Iranian art.

The low mound formed by the earth-filled grave was pro-

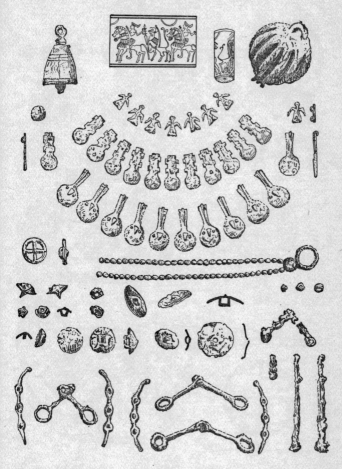

Fig. 31 – Siyalk: Stone cylinder seal and parts of harness in bronze and iron from Necropolis B

Fig. 32 – Siyalk: Painted pottery of Necropolis B

tected by heavy slabs of stone or burnt brick, placed in such a way that the tomb resembled a gabled house. We may recognize here the same idea of giving the grave the shape of a Nordic house* as has been already noticed among the Indo-European invaders of Italy. Among the Iranians this formal link with earlier European burial practices did not disappear for some time despite the changes which soon took place, as is proved by a tomb such as that of Cyrus the Great.

Fig. 33 – Siyalk: Painted pottery of Necropolis B

The majority of the human skulls found in the cemetery are brachycephalic, a shape previously unknown on the Plateau. In this connexion it should be remembered that about the same time brachycephalic peoples belonging to the great Indo-European family penetrated not only into Italy, but also into western Europe.

The top of the mound at Siyalk which overlay a long succession of prehistoric villages was re-levelled, and on it the new chief built his residence. This no longer exists, but a solid mass of masonry, over 40 yards square, formed its foundation.

---

* Herzfeld, *Archaeological History of Iran*, pp. 15, 16, 33 ff.

The alternating courses of crude brick and dry stones of which the walls were composed illustrate building techniques hitherto unknown on the Plateau. The conquerors must have learnt them elsewhere, probably farther to the north, from neighbouring peoples during their slow migration. This method of constructing a terrace on which to build the palace and residences of the nobility required an army of workers, masons, bricklayers, and quarrymen. The prince therefore employed serfs to work for him and for certain nobles of his retinue and bodyguard. Thus society was already divided into sharply differentiated social classes; even the contemporary cemetery provides proof of this. Some tombs contained bodies bedecked with silver jewellery and furnished with a variety of weapons and tools, while others had only a few modest ornaments of iron and a small number of pots. Some of the poorer graves were without the roofing-slabs which simulated the appearance of a Nordic house. Perhaps these were the original inhabitants subjugated by the invader. This is not an impossible hypothesis, for the few objects found with them were tools of farmers or artisans.

The prehistoric village of Siyalk, which had been overrun by a powerful clan of horsemen, changed into a fortified town: its palace, with subsidiary buildings and perhaps a temple and living quarters, was surrounded by an enclosure wall with redans and towers to withstand a siege. The new chiefs not only fought the local princes and one another; they also fought the great Powers of the West, especially the Assyrians. The aspect of the Plateau changed, and the royal monuments of Assyria reproduce, more or less exactly, the fortified towns of Iran with their double or triple enclosure wall surrounded by moats or diverted rivers, projecting towers manned by defenders, stone foundations, and crenellated terraces. It was an age notable for the growth of urban life, a new development in Iran, probably to be ascribed to the enterprising spirit of the new ethnic element. It formed a prelude to future developments when, in place of a plurality of princes and nobles, the unity of the Iranians was to be realized (Fig. 34).

The prince lived with the vassal lords of his retinue and

ruled over the peasantry. He drew his revenues from his estates and levied dues on hunting, fishing, and stock-breeding. He owned private lands worked by slave labour, and his peasants owed him service in all kinds of *corvées* and also for public works such as roads, canals, bridges, and fortifications.

A Court, a retinue, vassals who formed the core of his army, friendly relations with other princes involving the exchange of

Fig. 34 – The town of Kishesim in north-west Iran from an Assyrian bas-relief

presents, gifts to his subjects, perhaps also to the priests – all this required expenditure which taxes and dues were often inadequate to meet. Recourse was then had to war, and, if the outcome was successful, loot restored the royal finances.

Society was divided into several groups: the prince, the nobles, free men owning land, those who had nothing, and, finally, slaves. Already there were signs of the future struggle of the non-propertied classes and peasantry against the nobility. The situation in Iran during the early years of the first millennium B.C. must have closely resembled that of Greece as described by Homer. In Iran the households of the great lords of the ninth and eighth centuries seem to have consisted of male and female servants, slaves, and all kinds of artisans who produced everything needed by their masters. The free artisan certainly existed, but was more rarely employed. The surplus of these closed economies was sold; it no doubt consisted primarily of the products of agriculture and extensive stock-breeding.

It was also the age in which the small estate began to develop, and it is generally agreed that the peasantry of the time enjoyed much greater liberty in Iran than in Mesopotamia or Egypt. Agriculture showed a tendency to split up into smaller units and towards individualism, a very notable advance on the situation existing in the Ancient East during the Bronze Age, a system which was to become one of the bases of agricultural economy throughout the world.

Exploitation of the mines owned by the princes developed alongside agriculture. Iran continued to be a producer country, as we may see from the annals of the Assyrian kings who, in the course of war, obtained very considerable quantities of copper, iron, and lapis lazuli.

The prince could not live solely on agricultural produce, or by the exploitation of mines and booty; he also became protector of the merchant, who was still in most cases non-Iranian and could not carry on his business without the patronage of the prince who, for his part, was interested in increasing his revenues. Large-scale commerce dealt mainly in luxury articles of gold, silver, and precious stones or richly embroidered cloths. Without being neglectful of his domains and his peasants, the prince interested himself in the development of trading centres and entrepots and in the business carried on by the merchants in towns and cities. Thus a peculiar hybrid economy grew up in Iran; yet, despite the development of the towns, the country lived essentially by agriculture and stock-breeding; and this rural economy remained Iranian throughout the centuries, under both the Achaemenians and their successors.

The increased use of iron during the first millennium had a far-reaching effect on the economic structure of society. Although known to the Hittites and rulers of Mitanni in the fifteenth century B.C. and in Egypt in the fourteenth century B.C., this metal did not become widespread until the ninth to seventh centuries B.C. The use of new tools led to increased production, and this inevitably caused a considerable drop in the price of goods. Improved methods of agriculture opened up new tracts of hitherto uncultivated land. Rich sources of iron ore enriched countries that had previously played only an unimportant part in international trade, and this particularly affected northern Iran and the neighbouring countries. From Spain to China, the great changes taking place in the world led to an outburst of commercial activity in which Iran must have participated.

When speaking of the use of iron at this period, however, a reservation must be made. Although this metal came into general use, this does not mean that it finally replaced copper and bronze, for these continued to be widely employed for a very long time. This transitional period during the early centuries of the first millennium is well illustrated by the cemetery at Siyalk. The tombs of the ruling class of horsemen show that weapons as well as harness, and even utensils, were made of iron, although there was still a number of bronze objects. Nevertheless the quantity of iron used was not yet as great as that of copper. If we consult the lists of booty amassed by the Assyrian armies, it appears that the weight of iron carried off from Iranian towns never equalled that of copper, and indeed scarcely amounted to half the latter. This explains the fact that about 500 B.C. certain peoples of eastern Iran, such as the Massagetae, were, according to Herodotus, still unacquainted with the use of iron. The presence of iron jewellery in the modest tombs of Siyalk is hardly a criterion of the amount of iron which was available elsewhere, for we know that Sargon II's troops (end of the eighth century B.C.) were still armed with bronze picks and axes; that the treasury of Alyattes, king of the wealthy state of Lydia, at the beginning of the seventh century B.C. possessed iron vases as well as gold and silver vessels; and that Croesus, his successor, presented worked vases of iron to the oracle at Delphi. Many iron arrow-heads and javelins were also found in the tombs at Siyalk. It should, however, be recalled that the excavators of the wealthy towns of the kingdom of

Urartu found that iron objects were much less common than bronze.

Cemetery B at Siyalk marks the end of that city's existence. At Giyan, above the level containing analogous tombs, there was an imposing structure with door-hinges in the pure Assyrian style of the eighth century. This suggests that the partial destruction of these fortified towns was the work of the Assyrian army, and that it took place not later than the ninth to eighth centuries B.C., a period when the Assyrian Empire was engaged with all its forces against the rising strength of Iran.

We have already said that the introduction of iron into general use as a metal both of war and agriculture changed the character of commerce at the beginning of the first millennium B.C., a commerce that had previously been based on trade in copper and its alloys. There was a shift in the centre of gravity of exporting countries. Assyria, which was a great consumer, had no iron mines; for a time, especially during the earlier half of the eighth century B.C., it was denied access to the mining centres of the southern coast of the Black Sea and Transcaucasia by the neighbouring kingdom of Urartu. Inevitably it turned its attention to Iran, not so much because this country was a source of iron, but because it obtained this metal from regions inaccessible to Assyria; in addition, copper and lapis lazuli were much in demand in Assyria. Finally, the plains and valleys of Iran constituted a reserve of horses of the finest breed and indispensable to armies of the importance of those of Assyria. There were, of course, other factors shaping the aggressive policy followed by Assyria towards Iran: it was necessary at all costs to pacify the Zagros district on the eastern frontier of the Empire and to subdue its mountain people, among whom the warrior Iranian element was always on the increase. This territory was particularly susceptible to the intrigues of the kings of Urartu, and constituted a real and continual menace to the very existence of the Assyrian state. The Assyrian kings were not always successful in their attempts to reduce these districts to the status of provinces, and when they did succeed, their administration remained precarious. Usually their campaigns developed into *razzias* on towns, which they captured, pillaged, and burnt, looting their stores of metal or semi-precious stones and carrying off horses and cattle. The population saved itself by taking to the mountains, coming back after the army had left, and the Assyrian victories rarely produced the decisive results claimed by the scribes: nearly always the defeated people were left in enough strength to resume the struggle after a short respite.

These hostilities went on for centuries and left their mark on the military organization of the Assyrians. Just as the China of the Han dynasty was forced to adapt its army to the conditions of warfare imposed on it by the horsemen of the nomadic Huns, and to change both its armament and costume, so in like manner the Assyrians were forced to adopt new formations for their expeditionary forces. Thus, before the reign of Assurnasirpal (884–860) cavalry was not yet used in the Assyrian army; the shock troops were the chariotry, which, owing to rudimentary harnessing, was a somewhat inefficient arm, its effect being mainly a matter of morale. It was inferior to the cavalry of its opponents, especially for operations in the rough country of the Zagros mountains. To ride along the mountain tracks in a chariot or to cross passes suitable only for caravans was no mean exploit, and explains why Assyrian artists depicted the king crossing mountains and torrents in his chariot. To fight against cavalry, cavalry had to be created, and this the Assyrian army hastened to do. Many centuries before they measured themselves against the Romans and imposed on them a cavalry arm, the Iranians in their struggle with Assyria obliged the latter people to adopt this reform.

Cavalry rapidly altered the character of warfare: the light Assyrian formations, whose aim seems often to have been to bring back remounts rather than to conquer the country, thrust deeper and deeper into the hinterland of the Zagros, and in their annals the kings triumphantly boasted that they had penetrated districts reached by none of their predecessors. Frequent mention is made of Mount Bikni, identified as Mount Demavend near Teheran, and of the Salt Desert, the region stretching to the south of that city.

THE FORMATION OF MEDIAN UNITY

The annals of Shalmaneser III make the first mention of the Iranians who lay in the path of the Assyrian army in its campaigns in the Zagros: in 844 B.C. the Assyrians knew of the Persians (Parsua) and in 836 B.C. of the Medes (Madai), but there are no grounds for believing that the former people arrived before the second. If we may accept the account given by the Assyrian scribes, the Persians at this period lay to the west and south-west of Lake Urmia, and the Medes to the southeast, in the neighbourhood of Hamadan. It is not thought, however, that these names, Parsua and Madai, express ethnic concepts, but rather that they refer to the areas where the tribes were settled from the middle of the ninth century B.C. The general movement of Iranian tribes was far from over: a third and fairly important group of Iranians, the Zikirtu, or Sagartians of the Greeks, settled farther to the east, perhaps thrusting as far as the Tabriz district and the frontier of the kingdom of Urartu. A branch of the Medes spread to Isfahan, where they were checked by the Elamites. Farther to the east, the Parthava, the future Parthians, settled round the Caspian Gates, while the Haraiva occupied the oasis of Herat in the southern district of Khorasan.

The King of Assyria, Shamshi-Adad V (823–810 B.C.), mentions the defeat of an Iranian chief from the country north of Lake Urmia, with 1,200 of his cities. This figure is very significant: the fortified towns under feudal chiefs, spread over western Iran, normally had only small forces of cavalry, numbering some 2,000 or 3,000 men. Their rivalries and lack of unity were a trump card for the Assyrians, and contributed greatly to the success of their operations. It is true that at this period Iranian-named 'kings', as the scribes call them, were in a minority. This is proof that their migration was still in progress or, where they are found already stabilized, that power passed only slowly into their hands. Iranian names also occur at this period in the army of the kings of Urartu. In the interior of the country, south of Lake Urmia, lay the kingdom of

Mannai, comprising a large part of modern Kurdistan; it was a country with an Asiatic population strong enough to check the expansion of the Medes.

The Persians do not seem to have stayed long in the northwest of Iran: either it may be, as a result of Assyrian operations, or of pressure exercised against them by the Urartu (their northern neighbour) or by other tribes. The fact remains that already in the eighth century B.C. they were on the move and proceeding slowly south-east, along the folds of the Zagros. Probably about 700 B.C. they settled in the western area of the Bakhtiari mountains to the east of the modern town of Shustar, in the country they called Parsuash or Parsumash, a name found in Assyrian annals. As so often happened in this period, the tribes gave their name both to the country where they settled and also to their principal city.

The end of the ninth century B.C. and the first half of the eighth century marked a decline in Assyrian power, of which the neighbouring kingdom of Urartu took full advantage. The formation of this kingdom was of recent date, and could not have taken place before the beginning of the ninth century B.C., when one of the many princes of the Nairi lands, with whom Assyrian kings had first been in conflict in the twelfth century B.C., succeeded in unifying the country. It stretched to the east of the junction of the two branches of the Euphrates, included Lake Van, and reached as far as the valley of the Araxes. From an ethnic point of view it was an extension of the Hurrian population of north Mesopotamia. The language spoken there, known to us in the so-called Vannic inscriptions left by the kings of Urartu, was closely related to that of the Iberian or Georgian branch of the Caucasian family. Although there are high mountains, the greater part of the country consists of very fertile plateaus, well watered by springs and rivers. It was an agricultural district and well stocked with flocks, while horse-breeding provided a large part of its revenues. In addition, it had extensive forests, an abundant supply of all kinds of minerals, and a very healthy climate. It is not surprising, therefore, that it evolved an individual and relatively powerful

civilization, much of it outwardly shaped on an ancient Babylonian pattern.

Assyrian monuments and annals, as well as inscriptions of
the kings of Urartu, supplemented by finds obtained in
archaeological excavation, enable us to reconstruct with the
help of documents a picture of the civilization of this state,
which, under a strong dynasty, united a number of tribes dispersed in the valleys and on the plateaus. Excavation has revealed the existence in Urartu of fortified towns with a Cyclo-

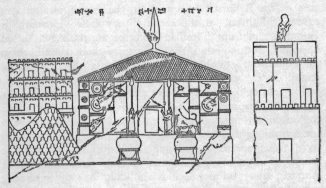

Fig. 35 – The town and temple of Musasir in north-west Iran
from an Assyrian bas-relief

pean construction unknown to the inhabitants of the Mesopotamian plain. A particular feature of the architecture was the
impost, which was never developed into a column with capitals (this being decorated with a pair of volutes as if forming a
stage in the evolution of the proto-Ionian column). Buildings
had gabled roofs. In short, there were certain architectural
peculiarities which we shall encounter among the Persians at
Pasargadae and Persepolis, and also in the districts they occupied after leaving the frontier of Urartu before the final conquest of Fars.

When they entered Iran, the Persians settled on the frontier
of this young and dynamic kingdom with its feudal organiza-

tion and borrowed largely from its civilization. During the remarkable period of Urartian expansion consequent on the decline of Assyria, the Persians, along with other peoples in the north-west of Iran, passed under the suzerainty of these new masters. King Ishpuinis, who associated his son Menuas with him on the throne, seized from Assyria all the districts along the upper Tigris and the upper Zab, and even annexed those of Mannai, south of Lake Urmia. He followed up this conquest by building a series of fortification works and new towns, round which future resistance to the eventual Assyrian reaction was to centre. A country such as Musasir, an important political and religious centre in the north-west angle of Lake Urmia, remained a vassal of Urartu down to the Sargonid period (Fig. 35). It is not known how long the Persians remained under Urartian domination, but when they left the district, they had, as assets, sufficient knowledge of this civilization to take a number of its features away with them. This is particularly noticeable in architecture, an art of which they knew nothing in their nomadic existence and which they developed in the country where they finally settled.

Extending their conquests to the south as well as to the north, Ishpuinis and Menuas built up a kingdom which in area equalled, and even surpassed, that of Assyria, while remaining more compact. The inscriptions show that their civilizing mission equalled their military success. They undertook gigantic irrigation works, digging imposing canals, partly constructed of stone, which transformed formerly unworked country into agricultural land. The Persian tribes must have watched the work, and so learnt the technique of irrigation.

The struggle between the two kingdoms continued during the reign of Argistis, a contemporary of Shalmaneser IV (782–772 B.C.). Urartu maintained the upper hand, although the Assyrians undertook a number of campaigns, expeditions in which the name of Parsua, among others, again occurs. In widespread conquests, Argistis annexed all the districts round Lake Urmia, and then, turning towards the west, asserted his supremacy over most of the small states of eastern Asia Minor, hitherto vassals of Assyria. It may well have seemed that Assyria was

stricken with such weakness that it could never again become
a great Power or prevent its role from finally passing to Urartu.
Yet with the accession of Tiglath-pileser III the situation was
once again reversed.

In rapid campaigns the new King of Assyria recovered all
the territory lying between the Euphrates and the Mediterranean, and defeated Sarduris II, King of Urartu. He next carried the war into the very heart of the enemy country, conduct-
ing an unsuccessful siege of the Urartian capital, a proud and
impregnable city on the shores of Lake Van. He undertook a
number of campaigns in the Zagros district, and once again
his annals mention the names of Iranian princes, as well as
Asianic or Caucasian rulers. His troops carried off enormous
booty: one captured town alone furnished ten tons of lapis
lazuli(?). He next carried the war among the Medes, to the
north-west of Hamadan; Parsua was among the countries list-
ed. The conquering Assyrian pushed his arms as far as Mount
Bikni, or Demavend, and the borders of the Salt Desert.
Among the names of captured towns and fortresses is Shirkari
or Shilka(ki), which might be Siyalk. The annals also speak of
the land Nishai, the Nisaean plain, south of the great Hamadan
road, and famous for its horses; this is the Giyan district. The
conquered lands were organized in provinces under governors, and towns destroyed in sieges were rebuilt. This may
have occurred at Giyan, where on top of the mound are the remains of a fortified Assyrian palace. Tiglath-pileser III was an
outstanding administrator as well as a great conqueror. Without depopulating his country he established Assyrian colonies
in the annexed districts with the object of holding them more
securely, and transplanted the vanquished populations. It was
a veritable shuffling of peoples: from his Median campaign he
brought back 65,000 prisoners, whom he settled on the Diyala,
along the frontier of Assyria proper, replacing them on the
Plateau by Arameans. Even Babylonia did not escape, and he
attached it to the Assyrian crown.

The new King of Urartu, Rusas I, tried to retaliate by gain-
ing the support of the small tribal chiefs along his frontier and
seeking to band them together in a federation. His new policy

made much headway, and won over a certain number of Median chiefs, among whom the name of Daiukku appears for the first time. This was none other than the Deioces whom the Greek historian Herodotus credits with the creation of the Median kingdom. The truth as revealed by the Assyrian annals is less pretentious. Daiukku is to be regarded as a Median chief who, conscious of the serious threat hanging over his people, split up as they were among dozens of tribal chiefs, was apparently one of the first to devise a plan for their union.

The accession of Sargon II (722–705) was marked by the capture of Samaria and the dispersion through his Empire of nearly 30,000 Israelites, one group of whom was carried off and settled in Median towns. To the mixture of peoples in the Zagros at the end of the eighth century B.C. was thus added a further element which founded a community that has persisted to this day. The absorption of Babylonia gave the Assyrian Empire a common frontier with Elam, and Sargon was soon involved in war with this country, without, however, achieving any success. There were mutterings of revolt from Elam to Asia Minor, but although Sargon was fighting on many fronts, Media remained his principal theatre of operations. A revolt of the Mannai under an Iranian chief, fomented by the intrigues of Rusas, was severely put down, but not for long, for the prestige of Urartu remained high. Parsua suffered a fresh Assyrian invasion and twenty-eight Median chiefs were compelled to recognize Sargon as suzerain.

Confident in the support of the Mannai, the King of Urartu in 715 B.C. invaded this kingdom. Daiukku, one of the Median chiefs and an ally of Urartu, to prove his loyalty sent a son as hostage to the capital of Rusas and worked for his interests. The reaction of Sargon was swift. Once more the coalition was smashed, and Daiukku was taken prisoner and deported with his family to Hama in Syria. Did he owe his life to his prestige among the Median tribes, or to the calculations of Sargon, anxious to have at his disposal a warrior chief whom he could use, if occasion arose, as the King of Urartu had used him? However that may be, the policy of Rusas, which certainly aimed at the creation of a buffer state with Iranian elements, had failed. It seems certain that the deeds of the first Deiocides were attributed to the earliest of the line, known to history owing to Herodotus, although in reality his descendants were the true founders of Median unity and inspired the struggle for Median independence.

Sargon was again in Media in the following year, and the Iranian names of princes become more numerous. He continued the struggle in 713 B.C., subduing forty-two Median chiefs, some of whom lived beyond the district of Hamadan. In his annals the Assyrian King boasted of conquests over powerful Median kings, but in reality these were no more than chieftains who, surrounded by retainers, ruled over the numerous towns of Media. One of them was Daiukku, who was deported and whose tribe, Bit Daiukku, was called on to take the lead among the others. Under his son – whom Herodotus calls Phraortes, but whose name was Khshathrita, as is confirmed by the inscription of Darius at Bisutun – the ideal for which Deioces seems to have fought was finally realized in the union of the Medes.

The severe pressure exercised against Media by Sargon II seems to have been relaxed in the reign of his successor, Sennacherib (705–681), who was busy elsewhere warring with a Babylonian pretender with Elam, Egypt, and Judaea. Perhaps this was one of the reasons that led Iranian forces to rally round the 'house of Deioces' in the person of his son Khshathrita. At first governor of a town, he soon became head of a powerful coalition, and was certainly a person of importance, for Esarhaddon, who succeeded Sennacherib, sent him an embassy. Indeed, he united under his authority not only the Medes but also the Mannai and the Cimmerians. The last were tribes of Iranian origin who with the Scythians crossed the Caucasus in a new wave and appeared on the horizon of the two rival kingdoms of Assyria and Urartu.

CIMMERIANS AND SCYTHIANS

From the end of the eighth century B.C. these Iranian tribes caused serious disturbances in the north-west of Iran, which had already been shaken by the military activities of Assyria, Urartu, and the Medes. The Cimmerians and Scythians likewise brought trouble to Asia Minor, Syria, and Palestine. Their invasion differed from the slow penetration of the Persians and Medes some three or four centuries earlier. It was no longer a case of tribes seeking safe pastures or a safe refuge. Aggressive horsemen and plundering hordes of warriors poured like a stream of lava down the southern slopes of the Caucasus. Herodotus has preserved the memory of this episode, and the Assyrian annals also give details of great historical value. The Cimmerians and Scythians are known in the annals as the Gimirrai and Ishkuzai, names which also occur in the Bible. The former people appears to have come from the Crimea, which preserves their name. The account of Herodotus, which represents the Cimmerians as being driven forward by the Scythians, need not be accepted in its entirety. These two peoples were closely related; they spoke almost identical languages and lived by plunder. Already during the reign of Sargon II, Urartu had been the first country to suffer the impact of the Cimmerians. Although they were driven back, they so laid waste the country that its king, Rusas I, committed suicide. Splitting into two, one group of the Cimmerians moved along Lake Urmia and shortly afterwards appeared among the allies of Khshathrita, while the bulk of their cavalry continued its devastating progress westwards in the direction of Asia Minor. Other Indo-Europeans, such as the Treres, a Thracian tribe, were driving into Asia Minor at this period. The Cimmerians established themselves on the southern shore of the Black Sea in the neighbourhood of Sinope and the mouth of the Halys, whence they periodically set out to plunder the rich districts of Asia Minor. They were the people who brought the Phrygian kingdom to an end, its king, Midas, committing suicide. Lydia was not spared, and, although supported by the Greek cities of Ionia, its king, Gyges, was killed. Shortly afterwards Assurbanipal defeated them in the gorges of Cilicia and their scattered remnants fled and joined up with the Scythian bands.

The latter had thrust in another direction at the beginning

of the reign of Esarhaddon. Having driven out the Cimmerian horsemen to the south of the Hamadan road, they firmly established themselves to the south and south-east of Lake Urmia, in the country of the Mannai, which passed out of Assyrian control. These dangerous enemies are mentioned together with the Medes and Mannai in contemporary Assyrian omen texts foretelling the issue of operations which Assyrian troops undertook towards the centre of Iran, in order to procure horses for the army. Under King Partatua of the Assyrian records, the Protothyes of Herodotus, the Scythian kingdom included the greater part of the province later called Atropatene, modern Azerbaijan, the centre of which lay south of the Lake. The King of the Mannai acknowledged his suzerainty, and relations with the Medes seem to have been good. As Urartu was still a danger, the King of Assyria sought to win over the Scythians. Emboldened by these advances, Partatua demanded the hand of an Assyrian princess, and this was probably granted him, although history does not actually tell us so.

THE MEDIAN KINGDOM

The settlement of the Scythians round Lake Urmia did not impede the rise of Median power. The chief Khshathrita-Phraortes seems to have succeeded in uniting the Medes, who occupied a broad tract of territory which extended from Hamadan to the east of Demavend and southwards to the borders of the central desert of Iran. With the Cimmerians and Mannai as allies, and confident, perhaps, in Scythian promises, Khshathrita, after he had made vassals of the Persians – who from the end of the eighth century lay more to the south-east in the country round Parsumash – decided to strike against Nineveh. This was a daring operation which proved disastrous for the Medes: taken in the rear by the Scythians under Madyes, son of Partatua, an ally of the Assyrians, Khshathrita was defeated and lost his life (653). The Scythians, profiting from this reverse, invaded Media, which, according to Herodotus, remained under their yoke for twenty-eight years (653–625). Emboldened by this victory over the Medes, the Scythians launched an attack westwards. They laid waste Assyria, their erstwhile ally, and, joined by the Cimmerian horsemen who had escaped after the victory of Assurbanipal, they sacked and pillaged Asia Minor, North Syria, Phoenicia, Damascus, and Palestine. The memory of this raid is preserved in Jeremiah iv. 13, who foretold it in dread words: 'A destroyer of nations ... is on his way .... Behold he shall come up as clouds and his chariots shall be as the whirlwind: his horses are swifter than eagles. Woe unto us: for we are spoiled'. Pharaoh bought their withdrawal from the Egyptian frontier, and, falling back towards the Zagros, the Scythians continued their pillaging.

THE LURISTAN BRONZES

For more than twenty years, finds made by peasants in the Kermanshah district, particularly at Harsin, Alishtar, and Khorramabad – that is, in the north of Luristan – have enriched private collections and the museums of Europe and America with thousands of bronze and iron objects. All or practically all these objects came from tombs none of which has yet been scientifically excavated. These are reported to be pits, sometimes paved with stones and always closed by great stone slabs laid flat. Very often the tumulus is marked by a stone circle.

Civilizations such as that of the people who made the Luristan bronzes and created something which was entirely new to the country are of rare occurrence. If we consider this rich and varied collection of bronzes and the variety of symbols which they portray, we may conclude that they must have belonged to an *élite* clan of warrior horsemen and charioteers, who were reluctant to settle on the land and for this reason valued portable goods. Objects from Luristan which are not portable are rare. This observation seems to be confirmed by the absence of any traces of settlement in the neighbourhood of the tombs. These have yielded a great number of weapons: long iron swords with iron hilts decorated with heads of men or animals (Fig. 36); short bronze swords with hollow handles; daggers of bronze or iron, the hilts representing a human being or the stylized head of an animal (Fig. 37); many picks and axes of iron or bronze, often decorated with animals or parts of animals (Pl. 4*b*); most characteristic are axes with the blade or handle emerging from the open jaws of a wild beast (Pl. 5*c* and Fig. 38). Mention must also be made of spear-heads, jav-

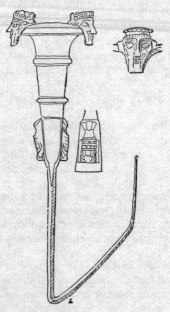

Fig. 36 – Luristan: Iron sword

elins and large numbers of bronze or iron arrow heads, laurel-shaped, conical, or trilobal; pieces of harness or the trappings of chariots, in particular, straight or broken bits and headstalls, which gave the bronzesmith almost unlimited scope in the choice of motifs: horses (Pl. 5*d*), ibex, bulls, mythological and composite beings, or chariots. Among the rarer items should be noted a bronze object provided with a bobbin and ring for attachment and decorated in openwork with two figures strug-

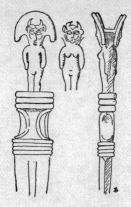

Fig. 37 – Luristan: Bronze dagger hilt

gling with lions, surmounted by two bulls and above them again two monkeys – a piece which may have secured the embroidered cloth to the end of the chariot pole and the body of the chariot, as seen on chariots in Assyrian bas-reliefs (Pl. 5a). To the same class belong the end of a chariot pole in bronze, decorated with two stylized lions above an eagle with out-stretched wings (Pl. 5b), and rein rings surmounted by two figures apparently taking part in a scene of investiture (Pl. 6a).

There are many toilet articles: pin-heads show great variety,

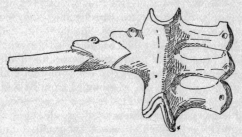

Fig. 38 – Luristan: Bronze pick

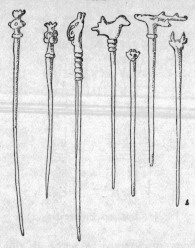

Fig. 39 – Luristan: Bronze pins

representing heads of animals and birds or complete animals
(Pl. 7*c* and Fig. 39); on richly worked belt plaques there are
very elaborate hunting scenes or mythological subjects; the
bronze mirrors now have handles in the shape of a naked
woman in the pose of a caryatid, with the sabre-blade profile so
characteristic of Luristan (Pl. 7*a*). Among votive objects of
uncertain purpose are opposed ibex or felines in heraldic grouping (Pl. 7*b*); or openwork motifs representing the 'hero' struggling with two wild beasts. To the ritual objects belong a number of bronze situlae decorated with banquet scenes or genii
standing by a sacred tree (Fig. 40). Special mention must be
made of 'pins' with a large disk bearing a head in relief in the
centre. Our plate (Pl. 8*a–c*) explains the origin of this head,
shown full face, which must be that of the mother goddess of
the Asianic peoples who was worshipped from Asia Minor to
Susa. One piece from the series represents her squatting in
childbirth. She holds her breasts, a gesture also shown on the
next object (Pl. 8*c*), which is that of thousands of figurines
found on Near Eastern sites, particularly at Susa, where, under

the Elamite name of Kiririsha, this fertility goddess was worshipped through the centuries. Under the name of Nanaia her
cult continued down to the Parthian period, and we found
many terracotta figurines representing her in the Parthian
cemetery at this important site. The question arises whether
this ancient mother-goddess, symbol of fertility and procreation, had not already by syncretism become the goddess Anahita, and whether it is not she who is to be recognized in certain of these representations. Support is lent to this hypothesis
by the borders of some of the votive disks which are decorated
with fish and pomegranates, two symbols of this divinity of
water and fertility, and also by the *appliqué* figure on a fine

Fig. 40 – Luristan: Bronze situlae

bronze vase in the Louvre, which may perhaps be the prototype of the representation of Ahuramazda (Pl. 9). These 'pins'
with disks were apparently found inserted in the interstices of
the stone walls of a building (temple?), a practice that recalls
the ancient Roman custom of hammering nails into the temple
wall in order to ward off the plague. In Luristan, the little
figures of goddesses seem to have been made with the idea of
promoting fertility. These images were represented full-face,
so that the sense of personal contact with the divine power was
enhanced. The Luristan plaques are among the oldest illustrations of the 'law of frontality', which may also be observed
in designs on the painted vases of the Siyalk cemetery, and in
the much later productions of the Parthian period.

It is said that not far from the places where these pins were
found there are communal graves containing the bones of
several individuals, lying in disorder. It may be asked whether
we are here already confronted with the custom of secondary
burial, in accordance with the funerary rites of the Magi, the
fraternity which, among the Medes, formed the priesthood
and, like other 'Nordic' and nomadic peoples, practised exposure of the dead.

We have also to remark the ibex with large horns (Pl. 4a), a
masterpiece of the animal artists of Luristan, who inherited in
a very high degree the power of expression of Assyrian art and
who, in their manner of attenuating the object, were already
precursors of Achaemenian animal portraiture. They were far
less successful with the human form, which is too flat, lacks
volume, has too prominent a nose and round, wide-open eyes
(Pl. 6b).

There are few civilizations whose art and whole material
culture are as composite as that of the Luristan bronzes. Traditions of older local cultures are represented only by a few tripod vases, which we have already encountered in these regions
from the beginning of the second millennium B.C., and which
seem to have remained popular over a long period. However,
the painted pottery of Luristan seems to be 'autochthonous'.
These survivals, to which may perhaps be added a few weapons
belonging to a type known from the end of the second millen-

nium B.C., comprise only a relatively limited part of this vast assemblage of objects. More numerous are connexions with the civilization of Cemetery B at Siyalk, in which we recognized the remains of the Iranian tribes who shortly before had arrived on the Plateau. Luristan furnishes us with many typical examples of the culture of these horsemen with their weapons, decorated harness, and the peculiar spouted bronze and clay vessels which we have already described; in addition there are little bronze figurines and toilet articles such as pins with animal heads. Nevertheless the collection as a whole bears a preponderant impress of foreign influence, both in form and in subject. The ancient art of Mesopotamia is represented by many examples of 'Gilgamesh' struggling with various kinds of animals; the Kirkuk glyptic, which enriched Assyrian iconography, appears in heraldic subjects, and left its imprint in the ritual *situlae* for libations, or in the terminals of chariot-poles shaped like a ram's head. Axes with the head of an animal 'spitting out' the blade appear to be an element characteristic of Hurrian art; certain belt plaques betray, if we are not mistaken, the classic art of the Scythians as known from excavations in South Russia. Subjects current in Syro-Hittite art of the eighth to seventh centuries occur, as for example the hunter whose arrow pierces an ibex which, with an astonished expression, turns its head towards its attacker. This subject is typical of the art of these small 'neo-Hittite' states which studded Asia Minor and north Syria. A fine example of this scene, on a bas-relief, has recently been brought to light in the course of excavations at Kara Tepe. Comparisons can be made with even more distant regions, and links may be recognized with the civilizations of Cis- and Trans-Caucasia, or even perhaps with China, as in the mask of Tao-t'ie.

The ethnic implications of this complex evidence are by no means easy to interpret, but some scholars may assent to our view that a clan of warrior-horsemen was grafted on to an Asiatic stock which had already been more or less permeated by Iranian tribes: this new warrior element in the course of its migration, plundered, devastated, and overran many a region of Western Asia. One cannot avoid the conclusion that the

majority of the Luristan objects belong to the eighth and
seventh centuries, or even later. The attentive student of history will seek to distinguish in the medley of Asiatic peoples
those Scythians and Cimmerians who after their terrible razzias from the Caucasus up to the frontiers of Egypt and the
coasts of Asia Minor, were thrown back from the Zagros
which was dominated by the power of Media. These wanderers
established themselves in the district where their cavalry encountered the finest breed of horses, and there they became a
valuable warrior nucleus for the young Median state, then at
the height of its expansion.

CYAXARES

Herodotus maintains that the years during which Cyaxares,
son and successor of Phraortes-Khshathrita, had to recognize
Scythian suzerainty were not unprofitable for the military
future of Media. Cyaxares reorganized his army; introduced
formations of archers and infantry, separate from the army,
and also probably adopted the tactics of the Scythian horsemen, who were skilled in mobile warfare. It may well be that
certain traditions of Scythian art were borrowed from them
during this period. This prince consolidated his political position by annexing certain regions situated around Lake Urmia,
and finally, according to Herodotus, won a brilliant and decisive victory over the Scythians of Madyes, who, with his followers, probably abandoned the territory of Mannai.

THE TREASURE OF SAKIZ

This Scythian episode of Iranian history is illustrated, we believe, by an accidental discovery recently made by peasants
near the town of Sakiz, to the south of Lake Urmia. This is
probably a royal treasure which, we conjecture, may once have
belonged to Partatua or his son Madyes, but it is not known
whether it came from a tomb or a cache. The collection falls
into four very distinct groups: the first is undoubtedly As-

syrian in inspiration and execution; the second is typically Scythian; the third is Assyro-Scythian in inspiration, but was probably executed by Assyrian artists; and finally the fourth group consists of products of local workshops, probably Mannian.

To the first group belongs a splendid open bracelet in gold, the two ends of which are in the shape of lion heads, one with open, the other with closed jaws; the latter is detachable to permit the ornament to slip over the wrist and is fastened with a pin; the circle of the bracelet is formed of four flat surfaces widening towards the centre, and at its widest point it has a pair of crouching lion cubs in high relief. This is a masterpiece of the art of the Assyrian engraver and jeweller. A golden plaque has a design in relief of two processions of animals and winged figures moving towards a stylized tree of life. On the bronze plaques that originally covered the wooden coffer containing the treasure were engraved ibex, rendered very freely, and separated by the classical Assyrian rosettes of daisies. To this group also belong much oxidized fragments of the rim of a bronze bowl on which there is a delicate engraving of a procession wherein the lower part of thirteen figures can be distinguished. The first five, dressed in long fringed garments, are perhaps officials in the suite of the Assyrian king, while those behind, with bare legs, may be the soldiers of the guard. These subjects are familiar from monuments such as bas-reliefs, frescoes, enamelled plaques, and glyptic. Certain peculiarities, however, seem to indicate that the group belongs to the reign of Esarhaddon (681–668 B.C.) or shortly after; and this dating does not exclude the possibility that part at least of the treasure may have been the gifts made by the king on the occasion of the marriage of the Assyrian princess to the Scythian king, Partatua. The place where the discovery was made is one of the few villages of Kurdistan that have preserved their name from this period. Indeed, everything leads one to believe that Sakiz, in which we may recognize the name of the Scythians, or Sakka as they called themselves, or Ishkuzai as they are called in the Bible and by Assyrian scribes, was the capital of the Scythians when they settled south of Lake Urmia, in the country of Mannai which they had conquered. We know that the name of a people was often given to its capital.

In the second group, Scythian pieces are represented by a fine gold scabbard, decorated in relief with a cluster of ibex heads,

Fig. 41 – Sakiz treasure: Silver dish

shown full face, the curve of the horns forming a lyre. This scabbard ends in a massive gold chape, barbarian in workmanship, depicting on each side a head, front face; this is strongly stylized and is almost a mask of Tao-t'ie (Pl. 10a). One hesitates to ascribe a purpose to the splendid gold plaques which perhaps decorated coffers (Pl. 11a). Their decoration in relief consists of heads of lynxes full face, joined to each other by ribbons. In the field are alternate crouching ibex and stags, the horns lying along the back in classical Scythian style. An object of particular interest is a silver dish, some 14 inches in diameter, the rim slightly curved towards the inside and decorated with a row of gold studs with convex heads (Fig. 41). The finely engraved decoration consists of rows of different subjects disposed in concentric circles. In the centre, which is an omphalos, is a rosette of sixteen petals in the shape of elongated lozenges. This is surrounded by seven circles, followed by rows of lance-head motifs, separated by seven other circles. Next come crouching animals facing to the left and resembling lynxes; these are followed by hares running towards the right, from which they are separated by a row of heads of wild ani-

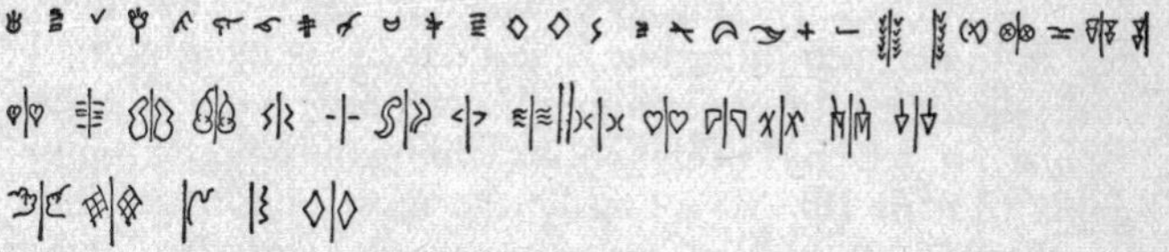

Fig. 42 – Sakiz treasure: Hieroglyphic inscription on the silver dish

mals facing right. These heads, of which one only is in gold, occur in two further rows, turned in one case to the left, in the other to the right, above the hares and the same lynxes, which this time are squatting on their haunches in a begging attitude and arranged in opposed pairs, exactly as on the chapes of Scythian swords from Kelermes and the excavations at Melgunovo. The decoration is completed by a band of lanceolate motifs whose base touches the row of golden studs; each is divided by a vertical medial line on either side of which are engraved hieroglyphic signs; these must certainly together form an inscription, the only one known on a Scythian object (Fig. 42). The art and writing of this dish constitute evidence of the highest order on what we may consider to be the oldest known Scythian monument. Is this writing in some way related to the 'Hittite hieroglyphs' which appeared in Asia Minor and north Syria shortly before the date of this object?

A certain number of small and very simple gold fibulae indicate that the treasure is to be assigned to a date after the eighth
century, and we are inclined to place it between 680 and 625
B.C.

To the third group may be attributed the gold terminals of
furniture, one of which represents the *protome* of a bird of prey
with a curved beak and round eye; this is a motif of Scythian
art *par excellence* as known to us from the many examples coming from Scythian tombs in southern Russia, and is also a subject of the Eurasian art of the steppes (Pl. 10*d*). Another terminal is a lion (Pl. 10*a*), but this is a placid beast which does not
belong to the family of Assyrian lions with their fierce beauty;
this also finds parallels in the Scythian art of southern Russia.
Another object that we are tempted to include in this group is
a gold bracelet the terminals of which are fashioned as ducks,
which touch each other but have their heads bent back; the
bracelet-circle is turned in a spiral, a favourite motif in Achaemenian art, which is richly represented by the objects from the
Sakiz treasure (Pl. 11*b*). Finally, the most important object,
of which by a miracle all the pieces are preserved (the objects
of the treasure were ruthlessly cut up by the peasants who
divided it between them), is a very large gold pectoral (Pl. 12).
This is decorated in two broad registers in crescent shape on
which we may see in relief a number of animals and composite
beings converging on two stylized trees in the centre. The
trees, the ibex standing on each side, the winged genii, the
winged human-headed bulls (*lamassu*), the sphinxes, the border
of pine-cones, are so characteristic that this piece could be
classed as gold work of pure Assyrian workmanship were it
not that in the corners are a running hare and a crouching animal, clearly Scythian in style and both identical with the animals engraved on the dish described above. This object, better
than any other in the treasure, gives an idea of the new art
which developed in the north-west of the Plateau and drew,
on the one hand on Assyrian sources, on the other on those of
the Scyths, two cultures which bordered this region on the
west and north.

Finally in the fourth group we have a thin gold plaque

which was probably sewn on a leather belt and is decorated in
repoussé in two registers with processions of tribute-bearers
leading a row of animals by a rope (Pl. 10*d* and Fig. 43). Apart
from a few small differences, we have here a replica of the art
of Luristan, showing the same figures, their noses protruding
level with the forehead, chinless, with a straight goatee beard
and wearing a little skull cap perched on the back of the head
and a long belted garment. The animals are also treated according to the conventions of the Luristan bronzes: the eye is a
lozenge, fur is indicated by a parallel series of strokes; the
muscles are accentuated by outlines, and the hooves, strictly in

Fig. 43 – Sakiz treasure: Gold belt

profile, show the dividing cleft, which normally would not be
visible. This object is of great interest for our understanding of
the local art: the obvious connexions with that of Luristan are
a logical consequence of the fact that both were contemporary
and executed in neighbouring districts; here already we find
the procession of tribute-bearers, a subject later developed by
Achaemenian art on the staircase of Persepolis.

The importance of this collection, the richest and most representative of the art of the Assyrian and Scythian jewellers,
may easily be appreciated. The treasure of Sakiz is an unexpect-
edly complete illustration of the arts with which the Medes
must have been in constant touch while their civilization was
in its formative stages; clearly, Assyrian as well as Scythian
artistry was leaving its impress. It will suffice to draw attention

as an instance of this to the scabbard of one of the Median nobles belonging to the retinue of Darius in the decoration of which Scythian survivals may be recognized (Fig. 70).

The local art of north-west Iran should not be neglected; it may perhaps be attributed to the Mannai who formed the largest political unit in this part of Iran, but our knowledge of it is very limited, for it is represented only by a few rare objects, none of which has come from a scientifically conducted excavation (Pl. 13a and b).

THE MEDIAN KINGDOM

Having defeated the Scythians and imposed his overlordship on the Mannai and the Persians, Cyaxares was master of the western part of the Plateau, and undoubtedly had his capital at Ecbatana, the modern Hamadan, whose name means 'place of assembly'. He turned against Assyria, which had withstood an attack by his father, whose temerity had cost him his life. Cyaxares seems to have begun by taking Harhar on the Diyala, an Assyrian administrative centre in the Zagros district which opened the way for him to Nineveh. He was not left to attack the Assyrian capital single-handed; Nabopolassar, the governor of Babylon, had through his own astute policy and the weakness of Assyria become absolute master of Babylon and in his turn attacked his former suzerain, who, however, was on this occasion saved by Egyptian intervention. Not for long, however, for in 615 B.C. Cyaxares marched against Nineveh, which resisted his onslaught. He then pushed farther to the north and took Assur, the ancient capital of Assyria. Nabopolassar hastened to meet him, and the Mede and the Babylonian concluded an alliance, sealed by the marriage of the Babylonian heir, Nebuchadrezzar, with Amytis, granddaughter of Cyaxares. The records explain the reason for the reverse suffered by Cyaxares outside the walls of Nineveh – once again bands of Scythians were helping Assyria. Cyaxares resumed operations against them and defeated them. In the following year, 612 B.C. the two allies, Cyaxares and Nabopolassar, captured Nineveh. The last King of Assyria fled to Harran, but two years later, in spite of Egyptian help, a new blow by the allies finally caused Assyria to disappear as a world power. It must be assumed that the kingdom of Urartu also fell about the same time and Cyaxares pushed farther to the west, towards Lydia which had now become a flourishing centre of world commerce. For five years the armies of the Medes and Lydians fought without decisive result, until, according to Herodotus, an eclipse of the sun, and also, probably, the mediation of Nebuchadrezzar – who had succeeded his father at Babylon – brought this war to an end. Peace was once again strengthened by a marriage between the daughter of the Lydian king and Astyages, son of Cyaxares, who in 584 succeeded his father. The frontier between the two States was fixed on the Halys.

Apart from Lydia, all Western Asia was divided between Media to the north and Babylonia, with Syria, Palestine, and Elam, to the south. The power of Media was a reality with which a kingdom such as Babylonia had to reckon, and King Nebuchadrezzar, foreseeing the impending threat, built strong fortifications on his northern frontier, to guard against an attack. Babylonia awaited this event; the prophecies of Ezekiel are significant, as are those of Jeremiah, who foretold the arrival of the Median armies, augmented by fighting men of Urartu, Mannai, and Scythians. The struggle was resumed under Nabonidus, the last Babylonian prince, and centred round Harran, which Astyages sought to seize from Babylonia. It was there that Nabonidus was patron of the great temple of Sin which was in fact a great commercial and banking centre. It commanded the road towards the maritime outlets, the Mediterranean ports, and was the switch-point for commerce from the north and east with the west. Nabonidus prepared himself for defence against Astyages, and astutely entered into alliance with Cyrus II, King of the Persians, who was trying to seize control of the great trade route through Hamadan. A fresh adversary, the kingdom of Persia, had appeared; it had come of age, and guided by its king, one of the most brilliant leaders of antiquity, this young and vigorous people embarked in its turn on the conquest of the world.

Practically nothing is known about the organization of the Median State: it has been seen how by patient effort the members of the house of Daiakku had succeeded in creating a kingdom out of scattered principalities, some rallying to them of their own free will, others being coerced. The unification of the Iranians was indeed a tardy process, when we reflect that peoples such as the Egyptians or Sumerians had been organized as monarchies, almost from the moment when they passed from the condition of hunters to that of an organized society of farmers and stock-breeders. The reason is to be sought as much in the composite character of the population as in the physical, geographical, and climatic conditions in which the society formed by the people of the first millennium B.C. developed. The Iranian conquerors needed time to seize, reduce to submission and absorb the Asianics, who were presumably the indigenous inhabitants. At the end of the eighth century B.C. this process was still not complete. The settling of the Iranians was a long and arduous process.

Iran is not watered by rivers like the Nile, Tigris, and Euphrates which by their yearly floods bring fertility to the country. Nor does it enjoy a regular season of beneficial rains stimulating the earth to production. From earliest antiquity, the question of water has been vital, for man could settle only where irrigation was possible. Thus the inhabitants were perforce scattered, and the population was far less dense than in Egypt or Mesopotamia. This is well illustrated by the dispersion of *tells* or artificial mounds, remains of ancient settlements, which the modern traveller finds lying scores of miles apart. Physical conditions thus led to the development in each district, and even in each valley, of a kind of particularism, traces of which have not even yet disappeared. This is the reason why Iran contained, and still contains, so many nomadic, semi-nomadic, and sedentary tribes who have preserved their dialects, manners, and customs. This is why, politically, the unity of Iran depended, and still depends, on the character of the reigning dynasty. External factors, however, contributed to the formation of Median unity: threatened by the kingdom of Urartu, and still more by the imperialist policy of Assyria, the

Medes were forced to choose between existence under the banner of unity and possible disappearance under a foreign yoke. They chose the first solution, which finds eloquent expression in the name of their capital, Ecbatana, 'place of assembly'. This city was founded on the route along which Assyrian armies penetrated the country, and was destined to

Fig. 44 – A Mede from an Assyrian bas-relief

block the invaders' path. The unstable conquests of the Assyrians led them to introduce a policy of colonization, as is shown by the settlement of Jewish colonists at Rhages, near Teheran; this, however, was only a palliative, which could not prevent the empire of Nineveh from passing to Ecbatana. If the royal annals of Assyria are to be believed, no people subject to their power rebelled as often as the Medes; they defended their independence with their arms and united the better to resist. The beginnings of the kingdom were far from being as peaceful as the idealized tradition of Herodotus would have us believe.

But if the political organization of the Median kingdom to a certain extent resembled that of Assyria – and this is a matter of conjecture – its spiritual and material culture remains practically unknown to us. And no more can be said of a people who knew only the rude life of the peasant and fought to conquer land on which to live, than of the literary culture of the Vandals, Visigoths, or Franks. As to their artistic achievement, the Medes, like the Scythians or Cimmerians, must have had a

Fig. 45 – Hamadan: Stone lion (Scale 1 : 50)

taste for richly ornamented weapons, decorated harness, vessels of precious metal, and garments with coloured embroidery. The appearance of the common people may be judged from representations on the Assyrian bas-reliefs: the men have moustaches and beards; animal skins are thrown over their garments; they wear high, laced boots with turned-up toes, and lead in their horses to the victorious Assyrians (Fig. 44). In the light of the Sakiz treasure, we may form an idea of their art, which in time to come will be supplemented by other evidence of what they borrowed from the more civilized peoples whom they conquered. Only a few rare vestiges of their monumental art have survived, such as the gigantic but much-damaged lion from Hamadan (Fig. 45) and some rock-tombs,

Fig. 46 – Dukkan-Daud: Rock tomb near Sar-i-Pul

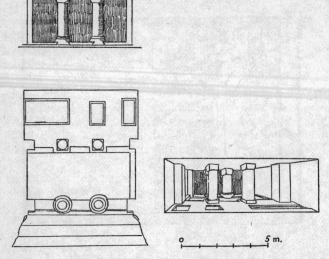

Fig. 47 – Rock tomb of Fakhrica, south of Lake Urmia

one near Sar-i-Pul, in the western foothills of the Zagros (Fig. 46) and others in Kurdistan (Fig. 47): these are princely sculptures dug into the mountain-side: the first is decorated in relief with a religious scene, and depicts a figure holding the *barsom*, the bundle of branches used in cult ceremonies.

ELAM AND THE PERSIANS

The Rise of the Achaemenians

Practically nothing is known of Elam between the twelfth and the middle of the eighth century B.C., beyond the fact that the struggle with Assyria flared up sporadically. The lack of records coincides with the eclipse of the Elamite kingdom; developments at home and abroad seem seriously to have disturbed the country. The establishment of new ethnic elements, Persian or perhaps Aramean tribesmen, who had long been settled on the left bank of the Tigris, almost certainly contributed to the weakness and decline of Elam.

By about 700 B.C. the Persians are found at Parsumash in the foothills of the Bakhtiari mountains to the east of Shushtar, a district straddling the Karun, near the great bend of the river before it turns south. Elam was no longer strong enough to oppose the occupation of a territory which hitherto had formed part of its domains. Although they probably recognized Elamite overlordship, the Persians under Achaemenes founded in Parsumash the small kingdom which was destined to have so brilliant a future.

The struggle between Assyria and Elam was periodically renewed owing to the attitude adopted by Elamite kings towards Babylonian affairs. Thus the Persians of Parsumash are mentioned for the first time in the reign of Huban-immena (692–688), who mustered a mighty army against the Assyrians in support of the legitimate aspirations of the Babylonian prince. A bloody but indecisive battle was fought at Halule; shortly afterwards Sennacherib succeeded in recapturing Babylon, and Elam was once again repulsed.

Following up its action against the enemy, Assyria brought its full military and diplomatic weight to bear against the declining power of Elam. On the one hand it pursued a policy of dismemberment, on the other, it lent support to such princes as would pledge themselves to remain loyal to the Assyrian crown. The Assyrian sovereign made and unmade the kings of Elam at will. In this troubled atmosphere, further aggravated by internecine struggles among the Elamites themselves, who were divided into pro- and anti-Assyrian factions, the small Persian kingdom continued its slow expansion. Teispes (675–640), the son and successor of Achaemenes, already bore the title of 'king of the city of Anshan' and held the district to the north-west of Parsumash. Although he may have thrown off Elamite sovereignty, he was forced (about 670), if we may credit Herodotus, to recognize that of the Medes under Phraortes-Khshathrita, who, as we know, gathered together a great coalition for the purpose of attacking Assyria. The defeat of this attempt and the death of Khshathrita (653), followed by

the Scythian invasion and vassalage of the Medes for twenty-
eight years, freed Teispes from Median control. In face of the
declining power of Elam, he grew more powerful and added
to his kingdom the province of Parsa, modern Fars. His patient
efforts seem to have been of the very greatest importance for
the future of this young and rising kingdom; by a policy of
boldness tempered with prudence he acquired a good deal of
territory. As far as possible he avoided being drawn into the
struggle between the great Powers; thus Teispes wisely rejected the appeals of Elam, which supported Shamash-shum-
ukin, the Babylonian king who had been dethroned by his
brother Ashurbanipal.

On his death, the Persian kingdom thus consisted of the

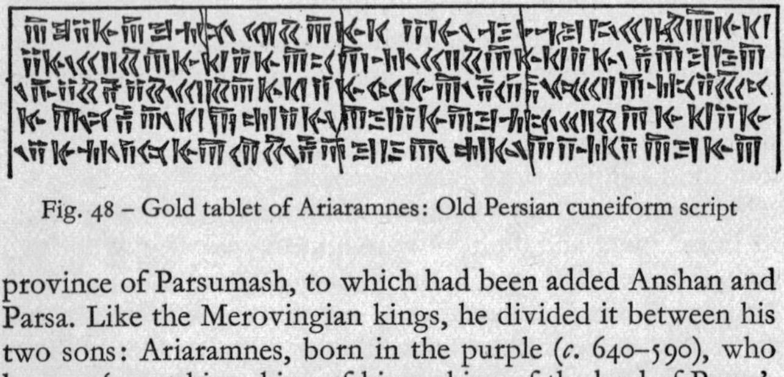

Fig. 48 – Gold tablet of Ariaramnes: Old Persian cuneiform script

province of Parsumash, to which had been added Anshan and
Parsa. Like the Merovingian kings, he divided it between his
two sons: Ariaramnes, born in the purple (c. 640–590), who
became 'great king, king of kings, king of the land of Parsa',
and Cyrus I (c. 640–600), who was 'great king' of Parsumash.
A chance find made at Hamadan has brought to our knowledge a gold tablet on which is engraved in cuneiform signs
and in the Old Persian language, the titles of Ariaramnes (Fig.
48). 'This land of the Persians', says the King, 'which I possess, provided with fine horses and good men, it is the great
god Ahuramazda who has given it to me. I am the king of this
land.' This tablet is the oldest Achaemenian object known and
bears the earliest Old Persian text. It shows the great progress
that had been made by the beginning of the seventh century
B.C. by Persian tribes who had but recently passed from the
semi-nomadic state into that of a semi-sedentary people. Their

alphabet, expressed in cuneiform signs, is a very real advance on the ideographic and syllabic writing of Assyria or Elam which were still in use and inspired its creation. At the dawn of their history, while their small kingdom was still in the formative stage, the Persians achieved something that the original inhabitants of the Plateau never seem to have attempted during the centuries, and indeed millennia, of their settlement there, namely to express their language in their own writing. The discovery of the tablet of Ariaramnes, which, as we shall see, is not the only one of its kind, seemed so extraordinary that certain scholars have refused to accept it as a genuine document. From the beginning of their civilization, the Persians showed the originality of their creative spirit, which could adopt a foreign idea and yet reshape it along the lines of their own genius.

Events in Elam provoked Assyria into taking military reprisals against this kingdom. Tammaritu, a king who ventured to make a parade of his loyalty to Assurbanipal, was deposed by a native general. He fled and, falling into the hands of Assyrian troops, was taken to Nineveh. The attitude of the new Elamite King towards Assyria soon appeared so equivocal that Assurbanipal decided to strike before worse should befall. The Assyrian commander had two objectives: Susa to the south, and Madaktu, in the valley of the middle Karkhah, to the north. Madaktu was captured, and the same fate befell a number of Elamite towns along this river. Finally Assurbanipal had Tammaritu crowned again at Susa, and the Elamite King recovered his authority from the hands of the Assyrian sovereign. This restoration did not, however, last long and, the Assyrian *protégé*, after being deposed a second time, again sought refuge with his protector.

The anti-Assyrian forces were becoming active, and Assurbanipal decided to finish with Elam once and for all. Assyria, itself only a quarter of a century away from its own fall, was responsible for the disappearance of Elam, the oldest enemy of Babylonia.

Madaktu was retaken, the Karkhah crossed, and Susa pillaged. Pursuing the Elamite King, the Assyrians captured

many Elamite towns, among them Dur Untash, modern
Tchoga-Zembil, a royal Elamite city founded by Untash-Gal.
Continuing their victorious march, the Assyrians crossed the
river Idide, the modern Ab-i-Diz, and reached Hidalu, which
must be located in the district of Shushtar. Pushing still farther

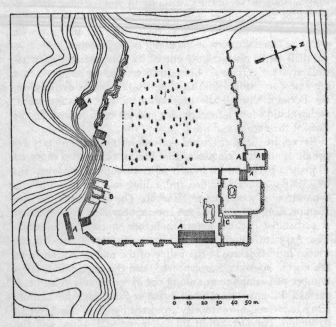

Fig. 49 – Plan of the terrace of Masjid-i-Sulaiman

east, the Assyrian general reached the first foothills of the
Bakhtiari mountains, the western frontier of the kingdom of
Parsumash. The king of this country, whose name is rendered
as Kurash by the Assyrian scribe, was Cyrus I, son of Teispes.
As pledge of his loyalty to the victorious Power, he agreed to
give his eldest son, Arukku, to the Assyrians as hostage.

This episode, the first direct contact between the Persians

and Assyrians, has provided us with some very interesting clues to the extent of the territory of Parsumash.

This included the district in which lies the modern town of Masjid-i-Sulaiman, a centre of oil production. In this very place are the remains of an imposing artificial terrace built up against the mountain-side (Fig. 49). Certain scholars, recalling the presence of oil in the valley, believe this to have been a fire temple in which the eternal flames were fed by escaping gas. Excavations have disclosed that princely dwellings once stood on this terrace, where a triple *iwan* is still visible to-day. The construction of the walls, which are built of enormous stones laid without mortar, resembles that generally called cyclopean (Pl. 14*a*). The whole enclosure wall was built with buttresses and recesses, clearly designed for defence; five staircases, one over 25 yards wide, led up to the terrace. This very distinctive complex was an innovation on the Plateau: neither the Elamites, Babylonians, Assyrians, nor the original inhabitants were ever associated with constructions of this type. The only other country on the borders of Iran which employed precisely this method of wall construction, and that very extensively, was the kingdom of Urartu. The peoples of Urartu were the immediate neighbours of the Persians when they were dwelling west of Lake Urmia, and for a time even counted them among their vassals. We therefore attribute the terrace of Masjid-i-Sulaiman to the Persians who after the eighth century left north-west Iran and settled in the Bakhtiari mountains. This terrace is not, however, the only one known: 15 miles to the north-west, at Bard-i-Nishundah, a mile or two from the left bank of the Karun, is a similar structure. There the same method of construction and the same kind of plan can still be observed; but the site as a whole is more extensive, and by the side of a large cistern are the ruins of an ancient village. Here may still be seen the remains of the stone columns which supported the roof of a triple *iwan*, of which the stone foundations have been exposed. It is possible that the first royal cities of the Persians stood on these two sites, built perhaps by Achaemenes or Teispes. We are inclined to see in the terrace of Pasargadae, which remains an enigma, a similar construction, and would attribute it to the kings of the branch of the Achaemenian family which with Ariaramnes – whose gold tablet we know – reigned over Fars. Thus the terraces of Masjid-i-Sulaiman and Bard-i-Nishandah, as well as that of Pasargadae, would be 'ancestors' of the terrace of Persepolis. In its principles of construction this again is evidence of the old methods

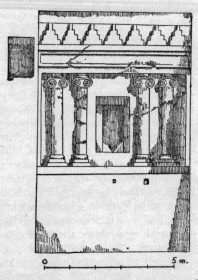

Fig. 50 – Rock tomb of Da u Dukhtar in Fars

employed by the Persians from the time of their arrival in south-west Iran, a technique which, derived from northern neighbours, was previously unknown in the country. In our opinion, the rock tomb of Da u Dukhtar, near Fahlian in Fars (Fig. 50) should be similarly considered. It must have belonged to one of the princes of the line of the first Achaemenians, and have served as a prototype for the rock tombs which, from the time of Darius, were sculptured on the cliff of Naqsh-i-Rustam.

As the power of the Medes increased under Cyaxares, the two small Persian kingdoms could not escape the suzerainty of the conqueror of Nineveh, although, according to the treaty dividing the lands between Media and Babylonia, Susa and Susiana were included in the latter kingdom. Ariaramnes was succeeded by his son Arsames; a golden tablet of this king is also known, apparently found at Hamadan at the same time as that of his father. He also styled himself 'Great king, king of kings, King of Parsa, son of Ariaramnes', and the text does not differ from that of his father. These two small objects must have formed part of the royal archives which Cyrus the Great moved to Ecbatana. We learn this from the evidence of the Bible, and excavations at Susa and Persepolis seem to confirm it. In fact, none of the documents found at the sites of these two ancient capitals – and they number many thousands of tablets – can be classified as royal archives dealing with imperial affairs.

The tablet of Arsames seems to prove that before losing his sovereignty, he reigned over Persis on the death of Ariaramnes. It was probably Cambyses I who forced him to abdicate; Herodotus tells us that his son, Hystaspes, was the governor of Persis at the beginning of the reign of Cyrus the Great. But although Ariaramnes' branch of the family lost their title to the crown they continued to govern the country under the orders of the family to which Cyrus belonged. A text of Darius, brought to light at Susa, explicitly states that at the time of its redaction, in the first years of his reign, his father Hystaspes and his grandfather Ariaramnes were still alive.

Cambyses I, King of Parsumash, Anshan, and perhaps also Parsa, married the daughter of Astyages, King of Media, his overlord. This marriage must have enhanced the importance of this branch of the Achaemenian family, and the prestige of the two kingdoms was united under one crown. From this union was born Cyrus the Great, who established his capital at Pasargadae, where he undertook the building of a great complex of palaces and temples. The inscriptions carved on the columns of his palace name him 'Great king, the Achaemenian', a formula in which he still recognized the suzerainty of his grandfather Astyages. He soon began to reduce to obedience the tribes both of Iranian and Asianic origin living to the east, south-east, and north-east of the kingdom inherited from his father. Nabonidus, King of Babylon, recognizing the ambitious nature of Cyrus, astutely enlisted his aid in order to create a diversion that would enable him to retake Harran from the Medes who had cut his road to Syria. Astyages got wind of this hostile alliance; Cyrus, summoned to Ecbatana, refused to obey. The Median King had no option but to suppress the revolt by force. The struggle was hard and was decided in the course of two battles, in the second of which Astyages commanded in person. This did not save him: he was defeated and fell into the hands of Cyrus, who treated him with great generosity. Ecbatana was chosen by Cyrus as the capital of united Iran. With the victory of Cyrus over Astyages, a new era opened for the Persian people whom fate had united to the Medes.

CHAPTER 3

East Against West

*

THE most important developments in the history of the Empire created by the military prowess of the Achaemenians occurred between the seventh and fourth centuries B.C. During that period the Achaemenian Empire was at its prime, and the historian must generally consider events in the terms of its history. The Achaemenians conceived of Iran as a state, and turned that concept into a reality. Its survival no less than its independence was the legacy they bequeathed to posterity.

The administrative achievement of the Achaemenians bears no resemblance to that of the Romans, in whose Empire conquered peoples were forced to adapt themselves to the common culture and to participate in the collective economy. This usually entailed a levelling upward, and was required from men whose origins were as diverse as their traditions and abilities. The position under Cyrus and Darius was different. Apart from certain outlying regions with a low level of culture, these monarchs incorporated in their Empire, the most extensive in the history of the world, a synthesis of ancient civilizations, for they included under their rule Mesopotamia, Syria, Egypt, Asia Minor, the Greek cities and islands, and part of India. To make these countries conform to the level of their own civilization would have been a retrograde step, and, as newcomers in the concert of peoples, the Achaemenians were aware of the superiority of these ancient civilizations. Hence the large amount of autonomy granted by Cyrus; hence also the astute policy of Darius, as a result of which these ancient cultures were preserved and favoured at the expense, perhaps, of the stability of the State. Throughout the history of the Empire this lack of balance was to be a latent and sometimes dangerous weakness, and, in face of the expansionist tendency of the young and vigorous Persian people, was one of the causes of its greatest defeats and final fall.

The Roman Empire was the result of a slow development extending over centuries, and its late formation ensured it both strength and stability. Out of a small kingdom obscurely situated in the foothills of south-west Iran, the Achaemenians created a vast empire in the span of a single generation; but what had grown so fast could hardly have been established on a firm foundation. The first convulsions within the kingdom occurred on the death of Cyrus' son, and were so violent that only a man of the calibre of Darius was capable of restoring the situation. A comparison may be made between this almost fatal episode in Achaemenian history and the civil wars of Rome. Under Darius, as under Augustus, violent upheaval was followed by a period of reconstruction and administrative reform which affected both society and politics. Nevertheless, despite wise and far-sighted measures, the centrifugal forces constantly pulling at the heart of the Achaemenian Empire in the end brought about its overthrow.

CYRUS (559–530)

When once he had decided on open conflict with the Median power, Cyrus could not count on the aid of his distant Babylonian ally: he was then dependent on his own forces alone. These had already been consolidated as the result of a great movement for union between tribes of both Iranian and non-Aryan origin. Herodotus gives a list of these peoples who, from the south-east corner of the Caspian Sea as far as the Indian Ocean, formed the core of the kingdom of Cyrus. Their unification seems to have been achieved on the whole peacefully, and it is thought that the college of seven princes may date from this period. This body formed the royal council of the Persians, in which the king was the first among the seven. Thus, within the borders of Iran proper, there came a union in which the tribal chiefs took an active share in the formation of the State, while preserving their character, whether nomad or sedentary.

The victory over Media was not the kind of bloody and destructive triumph which the Assyrians or Babylonians, the Elamites or Carthaginians inflicted on a vanquished people. Not only was Ecbatana spared, but it remained the capital; and there Cyrus installed his archives, including perhaps the tablets of Ariaramnes and Arsames among them. The Median officials, in association with a number of Persians, were kept at their posts, and the change in the seat of power took place so discreetly that for the western peoples, the Persian was still the Median kingdom. With two realms united under his sway, Cyrus found himself at the head of an empire whose geographical situation and natural wealth enabled him to play the part of intermediary between the civilization of the West and that of the Far East.

This outstanding leader and able strategist had two political objectives. In the west, his aim was to gain possession of the Mediterranean coast with its seaports which were the terminals of the great routes crossing Iran, and to secure Asia Minor, where, in addition to the wealthy state of Lydia, the Greeks had their maritime bases. In the east, his aim was security. The creation of a vast civilized state, absorbing part of the older cultures, had pushed the frontiers of the civilized world far to the east, to the confines of the Oxus and Jaxartes, where peoples and tribes of 'Outer Iran' were still on the move. Cyrus devoted his life to the pursuit of these two ends and sacrificed it to the second.

As heir of the Median kingdom and master of Assyria, Urartu, and eastern Asia Minor, Cyrus found himself face to face with Lydia, where Croesus had been reigning since 561 B.C. By peacefully establishing his overlordship in Cilicia, he cut the route along which any future help from the Egyptian and Babylonian allies of Lydia would have to pass. Thereafter, assured of support at the Court of the Lydian King, Cyrus, who was a good gambler, proposed to Croesus that he should recognize Persian sovereignty, promising in return to leave him his throne and kingdom. When Croesus refused this offer, Cyrus assembled his troops in Assyria, crossed the Tigris, and, following the later Royal Road, marched towards Cappadocia.

On the way he seized Harran, the important commercial centre
held by Nabonidus, thus driving his old ally into the camp of
Lydia, which was already allied to Egypt and Sparta.

The first battle, near the Halys, was indecisive. As winter
was approaching, Croesus assumed that Cyrus would cease
hostilities, and he therefore withdrew, but the Persian pressed
after him. He was forced to send his famous cavalry into battle,
and against it Cyrus drew up his camels. The Lydian horses,
terrified of an animal they had never seen, refused to advance.
After this disaster, Croesus sought refuge in his capital city of
Sardis: this was believed to be impregnable, but Cyrus besieged
and captured it. According to Herodotus,* Croesus was con-
signed to a funeral pyre, and when the flames had already been
kindled was miraculously rescued by the intervention of Apollo
after Cyrus had given him a last-moment reprieve. Lydia became a satrapy under a Persian governor. Cyrus then turned to
the wealthy Greek cities on the coast, and demanded their
complete surrender. The Greeks refused. It seems certain that
they had been subjects of the Lydian King, but, enriched by
commerce, the Lydian yoke sat lightly on them. Their reply,
however, was tantamount to rebellion, and Cyrus dealt with
them accordingly. Except for Miletus, the only town to sub-
mit at once, the Greek cities were conquered one by one, some
by force, others by treachery, for Persian gold proved as
powerful as Persian arms. The littoral was divided into two
satrapies; the Ionian satrapy being joined to Sardis, while the
Black Sea satrapy was named 'those of the sea'.

We shall see that the problem of the Greek cities of Asia
Minor was the touchstone of Persian policy throughout
Achaemenian history; these same cities led to the crusade of
Alexander the Great. There were many reasons why the Persians, from Cyrus onwards, held on to these possessions. Ob-
viously the political and international prestige of a great empire could not brook the independence of a few cities which
had been enriched by commerce. In addition to their strategic
value, these cities constituted an important reserve of man-
power; they possessed skilled technicians as well as excellent

* *Herodotus*, I. 87.

soldiers. Their ports, which looked out towards European Greece, ensured a connexion with the Greek world. These wealthy and prosperous settlements formed an influential element in the commercial life of the Empire which, by absorbing them, freed itself from what would otherwise have been a barrier to trade. The weakness of the Greek cities, arising out of their failure to agree among themselves, invited attack, just as it attracted Persian gold, which proved irresistible even to the Oracle of Delphi. Indeed, in all these centres there was one class of society, and that not the least important, which found it advantageous to favour Persian enterprise; this was the merchants who foresaw in the Empire a profitable source for their commercial activities.

Having completed the conquest of Asia Minor, Cyrus and his armies turned to the eastern frontiers. Hyrcania and Parthia, united before the Median period, received Hystaspes, the father of Darius, as satrap. Cyrus then pushed farther east, Drangiana, Arachosia, Margiana, and Bactria, one after another, became new provinces of the Empire. He crossed the Oxus and reached the Jaxartes, which formed the northeastern limit of his state; there he built fortified towns with the object of defending this line against the attacks of the nomadic tribes of Central Asia.

The Fall of Babylon

Returning from the eastern borders, Cyrus undertook operations along his western frontiers. The hour for the attack on Babylon had sounded. Everything appeared to favour the enterprise: the weakness of Nabonidus, who was devoting himself more and more to the cult of the god Sin; his preoccupation with ancient monuments and cities and 'archaeological' research; the discontent of the priestly class, which felt itself abandoned by the King; and the fact that defensive measures were left to the Crown Prince. The storm gathered over the great city. The Jewish exiles foresaw the Persian attack and their prophets hailed Cyrus as liberator. Babylon fell without resistance, the royal citadel alone holding out for a few days. The King was taken prisoner, but Cyrus, as was his custom,

treated him with great clemency, and when he died in the
following year 538 B.C., a state of national mourning was proclaimed in which Cyrus himself took part.

Cyrus presented himself to the Babylonian people not as a
conqueror but as a liberator and the legitimate successor to the
crown. To emphasize the importance he attached to his new
possession, he took the title of 'king of Babylon, king of the
land'. He restored to their temples all the statues of the gods
which Nabonidus had brought into the capital and, at the great
New Year Festival, following the custom of the Babylonian
kings, he took the hand of the god Bel and by this gesture
legalized the new line of Babylonian kings.

As lord of Babylonia, he also became master of its depen-
dencies, and in particular of Syria, where he pursued a benevolent policy. The Phoenician kings came to assure him of
their loyalty and put at his disposal their ships, which as a fleet
could match that of the united Greeks. In the first year of his
rule at Babylon, Cyrus issued a decree permitting the Jews to
return from captivity and to rebuild their temple at Jerusalem
as it had been before its destruction; further, he gave orders
that all the gold and silver vessels that had been carried off and
held by Babylon should be restored to them. In 537 B.C., under
the leadership of Zerubbabel, more than 40,000 Jews left
Babylonia to return to the promised land. They were accompanied by a high Persian official, specially commissioned to see
that the royal orders were executed. Once again the generous
character of Cyrus, who sought to bring peace to mankind, is
in evidence; at the same time, as a statesman he did not forget
that Palestine was a road that led to Egypt, as yet unconquered.
It should also be remembered that at this period politics and
religion were closely linked. But if Cyrus, and after him Darius,
adopted a friendly attitude towards the Jews, this was not only
because it served their own interests, but also because the religious ideal of the Jews, whose religion they certainly thought
superior to many others, was far closer to their own than were
the cults of Chaldea or Egypt. The Jews, for their part, were
conscious of this attitude, and their gratitude to the Iranian
people found expression in songs of joy after the dark days of

their captivity. For it was to the Persians that the 'chosen people' owed their rebirth.

Events on the eastern marches of the Empire next forced Cyrus to resume military operations against the nomads. After putting his son Cambyses in charge of preparations for a campaign against Egypt, Cyrus left for the east, and shortly afterwards was killed in battle. His body was brought to Pasargadae and placed in a tomb, the general appearance of which is reminiscent of the graves of the first Iranians to enter the Plateau and recalls their original Nordic home (Pl. 15c).

Few kings have left behind so noble a reputation as that which attaches to the memory of Cyrus. A great captain and leader of men, he was favoured by the fate that befell him. Generous and benevolent, he had no thought of forcing conquered countries into a single mould, but had the wisdom to leave unchanged the institutions of each kingdom he attached to his crown. Wherever he went he acknowledged and honoured the gods of the different religions. He invariably represented himself as the legitimate successor of the native rulers. Alexander was not the first to adopt this policy; he had only to imitate the example of Cyrus to be acclaimed by his new subjects. A new wind blew across the world, carrying away the cries of murdered victims, extinguishing the fires of sacked cities and liberating nations from slavery. More than anyone else Cyrus was conscious that 'the ancient world, civilized cities, and barbarian hordes, dimly obey inner forces which strive to merge in a common humanity'. We never see Cyrus, like the Romans, ally himself to a rival people, treat it as an equal, and then, turning upon it in a moment of weakness, subject and oppress it. The Persians called him 'father', the Hellenes whom he conquered regarded him as a 'master' and 'law-giver', and the Jews as 'the anointed of the Lord'. While his aggressive spirit never weakened even after years of war and conquest, he was always magnanimous towards the defeated enemy, to whom he extended the hand of friendship. In a historical text written in Babylon he himself says: 'Marduk had visited all lands in search of an upright prince, a king after his own heart, whom he took by the hand. He named his name

"Cyrus of Anshan" and to the kingdom of the whole world he called him by name.'

Pasargadae

The campaigns in the east and west occupied most of the reign of Cyrus and left him little time for other activities, such as urban development. Having chosen Susa as his capital while still ruler only of Anshan, and subsequently Ecbatana and Babylon, he lived in each of these cities at different times. Nevertheless he bequeathed to posterity the royal residence at Pasargadae, built, according to tradition, on the site of a decisive victory over Astyages. The name, thought to be a corruption of *Parsagad*, means the 'camp of the Persians', and if this amendment is correct, it gives a faithful picture of the town. It was indeed a vast camp, surrounded by a retaining wall within which, amid parks and gardens, rose palaces and temples. The entrance to the park was flanked by two winged bulls; at the door of the north room there still stands one of a pair of four-winged genii (Pl. 15a). The trilingual inscription

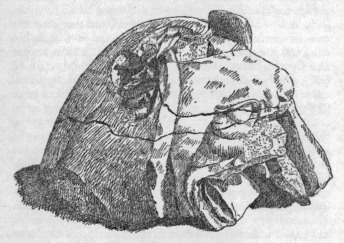

Fig. 51 – Pasargadae: Head of a stone lion

Fig. 52 – Ruins of Pasargadae

in Old Persian, Babylonian, and Elamite reads: 'I am Cyrus, the king, the Achaemenian' and must date from the time when he was still a vassal. The great audience-chamber is decorated with orthostats showing priests bringing animals for the sacrifice and genii with the heads and claws of eagles. The columns are surmounted by imposts in the form of horses, bulls, lions (Fig. 51), and horned lions. The pilasters of another palace (Fig. 52) bear a second trilingual inscription in which Cyrus calls himself 'great king', and this building must certainly have been erected after the conquest of Media. Elsewhere the columns were of wood, brightly coloured in blue, green, red and yellow. On the doorposts the king is depicted carrying a sceptre, the eyes and part of the clothing being inlaid with gold. A fire temple in the form of a square tower, well constructed of dressed stone, is identical with that standing in front of the tomb of Darius at Naqsh-i-Rustam. Some distance away are two stepped fire altars (Fig. 53) round which religious ceremonies took place, in the open air.

Pasargadae is indeed an impressive manifestation of a Persian art whose beginnings are still unknown. Although it is a composite art, with its Assyrian winged bulls, Hittite orthostats, its Babylonian polychromy and Egyptian symbols, yet fundamentally it reflects a national culture of a high order. In

Fig. 53 – Pasargadae: Fire altar

it all foreign influences had been recast and transposed in a co-
herent and balanced manner, and the result was a new art in
which architectonic features were predominant. Appreciating
the play of colours in sunlight and shadow, the artists introduced the use of alternating white and black stone, while in
the representation of the human form there was a notable advance in the treatment of the folds of draperies. Each detail,
whether original or of foreign provenance, is infused with the
Iranian spirit, and for many scholars the art of Pasargadae is an
even greater achievement than that of Persepolis.

CAMBYSES (530–522)

The eldest son of Cyrus and of an Achaemenian princess, Cambyses was associated with his father during the last eight years
of the latter's reign, and bore the title 'king of Babylon'.
Cyrus, during his lifetime, also entrusted his second son, Bardiya, with the administration of the eastern provinces of the
Empire. On the death of the great King, disorders, to which
Bardiya may have been party, broke out on all sides. Cambyses, an experienced statesman, very different in character
from his father, decided to nip in the bud any movement that
threatened to weaken his power and the stability of the throne,
and had Bardiya secretly assassinated. To enforce recognition
of a single state ruled at the sole behest of the King; to cen-
tralize authority with the object of pursuing his conquests;

to reign as a complete autocrat; these seem to have been the aims of the new sovereign, whom the Greeks called 'despot'.

The expedition against Egypt had been planned by Cyrus, who had placed Cambyses in charge of the preparations. On the death of his father, Cambyses first restored order in Iran and then, at the head of his army, marched towards the Nile valley. The Pharaoh Amasis, perhaps foreseeing after the capture of Sardis that the ambitions of the young empire would one day extend to his own country, had allied himself with Polycrates, the powerful tyrant of Samos. But while the Persian army lay at Gaza, the tyrant deserted his ally, and one of the best Greek generals in the service of the Pharaoh went over to the enemy, to whom he revealed the secrets of the Egyptian defence. With the help of Beduin, Cambyses crossed the Sinai desert and arrived before the walls of Pelusium where Psammetichus III, the son of Amasis, who in the meantime had died, had concentrated his Greek mercenaries. After a fierce battle the Egyptian army was forced to retire upon Memphis. The city fell to the Persians, who deported the new Pharaoh to Susa. Cambyses seems to have behaved in Egypt as the successor of the Pharaohs: he paid homage to the Egyptian gods, entrusted a high Egyptian official with the administration of the country, and ordered reforms in the interests of the Egyptian people.

Three new campaigns were planned with the object of extending Persian hegemony over the entire world. One of these was directed against the Carthaginian power which dominated the western Mediterranean; another against the oasis of Ammon, which controlled the route to Cyrenaica; and the third against Ethiopia. But the good fortune of his father seemed to have deserted Cambyses, and none of these grandiose schemes was realized. The operations against Carthage were never undertaken, because the Phoenicians refused to use their fleet against a sister colony. According to Greek sources, an army of 50,000 men sent against the Oasis of Ammon failed to attain its objective and was overwhelmed in a fearful sandstorm. Yet, although it failed, this attempt bore fruit, for the Greeks of

Libya, Cyrene, and Barka submitted. A part of the Greek world thus fell under Persian domination.

Finally, Greek sources, probably influenced by Egyptian tradition, relate that the Ethiopian expedition led by the King in person also ended in failure. The army ran short of provisions, and in its retreat lost the greater part of its effectives. It may be that while on the march Cambyses received bad news from Iran and that, forced to return to Memphis, he took a short cut across the desert, and so met with disaster. In any case, Cambyses was the first to occupy the entire country, a feat not accomplished by earlier conquerors, Assyrian or Babylonian. Egypt was held by three garrisons stationed at Daphnae, in the east of the Delta, at Memphis, and at Elephantine, where Cambyses maintained a garrison of Jewish mercenaries.

The short stay made by Cambyses at Memphis on his return from the Ethiopian campaign has been the subject of much controversy. If Greek sources are to be believed, Cambyses abandoned the religious policy of his father which he himself had at first followed. He mocked Egyptian religion, destroyed the temples, and stabbed to death the sacred Apis-bull at Memphis. Opinion is divided on this subject and modern research, based on a study of the Serapeum stela, tends to the opinion that Cambyses could not have wounded the Apis.* The real lords of Egypt were the gods, as was recognized by all rulers of the country, and it would be surprising indeed if a statesman like Cambyses had been so lacking in foresight and common sense, unless indeed some mental disorder, epilepsy, or even madness, was the real cause of the conduct which the Greeks sought to impute to him. It is certain that, owing to the war and the foreign occupation, gifts to the temples diminished, and this fact alone would account for the legend that represents the Persians as hard-hearted conquerors.

The news from Iran became alarming, and Cambyses decided to return. In the course of his homeward march, probably in northern Palestine, he received confirmation of the revolt of the Pretender Gaumata, the Magian, also known as the false Bardiya or Smerdes. This man, whose physical appear-

* Olmstead, *History of the Persian Empire*, p. 89.

ance closely resembled that of the brother whom Cambyses had assassinated, proclaimed himself king and the true heir to the throne (522 B.C.). Nearly all the provinces of the Empire accepted this new ruler, who ingratiated himself with the people by remitting taxes for three years, and attempted a religious reform by destroying the existing temples. His success seems to have been fairly rapid. It is not known whether Cambyses on learning of this revolt accidentally wounded himself in the course of an epileptic fit, or committed suicide. However that may be, the army remained loyal to the Achaemenian cause, and followed the seven young conspirators of the Persian nobility, led by Darius, son of Hystaspes, the Satrap of Parthia, whom from the beginning they probably regarded as their future king. According to legend, the seven conspirators agreed to choose as king him whose horse neighed first after sunrise, and the ruse of his groom won Darius the throne. The speed with which Darius took action gives the measure of the man: two months after the death of Cambyses, Gaumata was taken prisoner and executed.

DARIUS (522–486)

The disappearance of Gaumata did not, however, immediately restore peace to the country. For nearly two years the young King was compelled to deal with revolts which broke out in all quarters of the Empire. As a record of his victory, he caused a gigantic bas-relief to be cut in a high cliff on the road between Kermanshah and Hamadan. This represents him under the benevolent protection of the great god, Ahuramazda, whose head and shoulders rise out of a winged sun disk. The King, followed by two arms-bearers, tramples underfoot the prostrate body of the false Bardiya, while behind him, attached by a long rope, stand eight 'false kings' (Pl. 15*b* and *d*). Round this scene is sculptured in several columns the story of their revolts and the victories won over them. The inscription, written in Old Persian, Babylonian, and Elamite, states that Darius was the ninth Achaemenian king. In this number are included both branches of the dynasty which, with Achaemenes,

Teispes, then Cyrus I, Cambyses I, Cyrus II, and Cambyses II on the one side, and Ariaramnes and Arsames on the other, agrees with other known records. 'Ahuramazda and the other gods helped me', said Darius: the new King invoked the aid of the Great God and presented himself as the legitimate successor of Cambyses II, who had died without issue.

The text seems to belittle the extent of the sedition. The truth was far otherwise. Practically the whole of the Empire was embroiled in the revolts; even Persis was not spared, and the reintroduction of the taxes remitted by the false Bardiya seems to have aroused discontent. The over-liberal policy of Cyrus had proved ineffective; a mere eight years after his death the Empire had to be reconstructed on a different basis.

To his enemies Darius was only an impostor, and the failure of their widespread insurrection must be attributed to the absence of a unified plan. Each 'king' worked for his own ends, and each was separately defeated and executed by Darius.

In Elam the rising was soon put down, but this was not the case in Babylonia, where Nidintu-Bel claimed to be a descendant of Nabonidus and was proclaimed king as Nebuchadrezzar III. The capital was difficult to approach, being defended by a strong army and fleet on the west bank of the Tigris. After losing some time there, Darius crossed the river in a surprise attack, defeated the army and besieged the city. At this point a second revolt broke out in Susiana, but the Persian pretender, Martiya, had been executed before Darius arrived. More serious events were taking place meanwhile in the north, in Media and Armenia, where a certain Phraortes claimed to be the descendant of Cyaxares and King of Media. With only weak forces at his disposal, Darius was forced to detach part of the army besieging Babylon and to send it against Phraortes under the command of his lieutenants. The struggle remained indecisive both in Media and in Armenia until, having captured Babylon, Darius took over the command in person. Phraortes was defeated and pursued as far as Rhages near Teheran; after being taken prisoner he was mutilated and hanged at Ecbatana. This warning did not, however, prevent another Mede from raising the Sargartians, a north Median tribe. He suffered the

same fate as Phraortes. In the east, the difficulties facing Darius
were no less serious. Hystaspes, his father and the governor of
the provinces of Parthia and Hyrcania, dealt firmly with the
insurgents. The satrap of Bactria fought against the rebels in
Margiana; while in Persis a certain Vahyazdata, who claimed
to be Bardiya, was defeated and hanged with his followers. A
party of these, however, succeeded in raising Arachosia and
fought their way through to the city of Kapici, the modern
Begram, north of Kabul at the foot of the Hindu Kush. A fresh
revolt also broke out in Babylonia, where another Nebuchadrezzar appeared, only to be defeated by a lieutenant of Darius.

Darius spent most of the first two years of his reign in these
struggles: in nineteen battles he defeated nine kings. The disturbances that had shaken the Empire also spread to the west.
A satrap such as Aryandes, who had been left by Cambyses in
in charge of Egypt, did not indeed defy the King openly, but
his conduct showed that at the least sign of weakness on the
Persian throne he would have declared his independence. Because of this he was put to death by Darius, who visited Egypt
in person, and in order to pacify the people introduced a series
of reforms, and gave the high priest of Sais an important post.
The situation in Asia Minor was no better, for there the satrap
Oroetes seems to have taken advantage of the difficulties in
which the King was involved to make himself independent,
holding up the prompt dispatch of reinforcements. He also
was removed.

Even little Judaea did not remain undisturbed. The legitim-
ist party, believing the moment propitious for placing on
the throne a descendant of David, perhaps Zerubbabel himself, started to intrigue. The high Persian official in control of
the country stopped work on the rebuilding of the Temple.
An embassy was sent to Darius who established the right of
the Jewish people to rebuild its sanctuary in accordance with
the edict of Cyrus. As the text of the decree had been found in
the royal archives in Ecbatana, Darius ordered it to be put into
effect. This did not, however, prevent him from taking severe
measures against the Davidites and installing a high priest at
the head of the community, thus creating a theocratic state.

The work of restoring the Temple was resumed, and ended in 515 B.C. The road to Egypt was assured.

The Empire had been reconquered. The small army of Darius, which had remained faithful to him, had re-established its unity from Egypt to the Jaxartes. Darius as a young officer had carried his lance in the last expedition of Cyrus and had been commander of the Ten Thousand Immortals, the royal body-guard, under Cambyses, in the Egyptian campaign. When, on the death of Cambyses, he was recognized as king, he was acclaimed by these same veterans and loyally followed by his former comrades in arms. He showed his gratitude towards this *corps d'élite* – a survival of the retinue of the conquering chief which shared in his victories and which, in the form of a royal guard, still survives in certain kingdoms. In each new palace that he built, whether it was at Susa or Persepolis, he caused representations of these Immortals to be sculptured in stone (Pl. 14c) or depicted in colour on enamelled brickwork (Pl. 18), so that their memory should be perpetuated.

Administration

The troubles which for several months flared up over most of the Empire were a grave warning. The setback suffered by the over-liberal policy of Cyrus showed the necessity for its revision and impressed the young sovereign with the importance of establishing a state on more solid foundations. The tendency towards autonomy shown by the diverse peoples of the Empire during the recent events seemed to confirm that only the Persian people could be trusted to remain loyal to their king. They therefore must govern as masters and direct the affairs of all the countries included in the Empire. Except in a few rare cases, it was the representatives of the Persian people who, richly endowed with land and alone exempt from taxation, as were the Arabs in the early days of Islam, were placed at the head of the newly created organs of administration.

There was, however, no question of a policy of force: this would have been impossible, since the ruling people was in an obvious minority in relation to the conquered masses. A

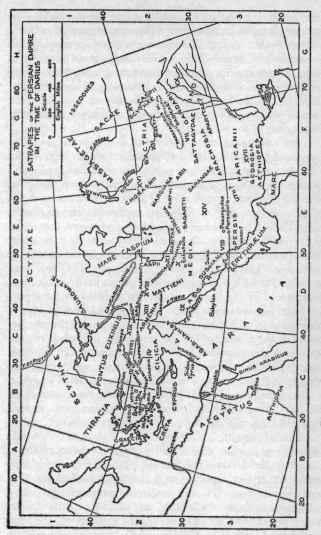

Fig. 54 — Satrapies of the Achaemenian Empire in the time of Darius

statesmanlike policy was essential: each people was to keep its own language, its individuality, its institutions, and its religion, and to enjoy the benefits of the State of which it formed part. But it could be administered only by a Persian delegated by the Great King. The whole Empire was therefore divided into twenty provinces, each under a satrap or 'protector of the kingdom' (Fig. 54). These high dignitaries, usually chosen from the Persian nobility, and even from the royal family, were directly responsible to the King.

It is certain that some satrapies had already been created by Cyrus and Cambyses. Darius established them throughout the Empire, and to forestall any possibility of future disaffection he organized them on a new basis. Next to each satrap he placed the commander-in-chief of the armed forces stationed in the province, who equally was responsible directly to the King. Parallel to these two posts, he created a third, that of the high official whose duty it was to collect taxes. By royal edict, all the provinces according to their resources had to contribute fixed sums annually to the royal treasury. The total sum amounted to 14,500 silver talents, of which nearly a third was contributed by the Indian satrapy. In addition to these payments in precious metals, the satrapies paid dues in kind – horses, cattle, and food. These contributions met the requirements of the Court, which included some thousands of persons, and also provided the upkeep of the armies, whether stationed in the provinces or engaged on campaigns; the satrapy of Babylon alone fed the army for a third of the year.

The satrap was doubled by a secretary who supervised all his actions and provided the liaison between him and the central authority. But control did not stop there: inspectors, called 'the ears of the king', were appointed, who were completely independent and in case of necessity had their own armed force. They travelled all over the Empire, paid unexpected visits to the administrators, and examined their conduct of affairs. This new institution which Darius introduced was much admired by the great monarchs of antiquity, and was adopted by Charlemagne with the object of securing cohesion between the various parts of his empire. Each year he sent out special officials called *missi dominici* or 'royal envoys' to travel through the country and control the local administration.

Darius had set himself a difficult task, for he wished to create a centralized and powerful national state out of a mass of countries, provinces, and lands, which the accident of military success had joined together. The form of government of the time of Cyrus was replaced by an administrative and fiscal organization which still respected national rights. Nevertheless Persia succeeded only in imposing a semblance of unity on the country. The Seleucids, who drew their inspiration from this system, and preserved in this respect a historical continuity, were unable to eliminate the same sources of weakness.

To maintain liaison between the different centres of the Empire and its capitals, Darius created a network of roads, which became so extensive and important that it survived a long time after the fall of the Empire. Intended primarily as an administrative measure, this arterial road system was carefully controlled and elaborately supervised. The new roads facilitated caravan trade and increased its volume throughout the Empire. It is still possible to trace in various sectors the Royal Road that went from Susa, crossed the Tigris below Arbela, passed by Harran and ended at Sardis, whence it was extended to Ephesus. One thousand six hundred and seventy-seven miles long, it was divided into one hundred and eleven post-stations, each with relays of fresh horses for the royal couriers. According to the ancient historians, the caravans took ninety days to travel this road from end to end, while the royal envoys covered it in a week. The old route that linked Babylon with Egypt via Carchemish was improved and connected with another leading from Babylon to Holwan, Bisutun, and Hamadan. As new conquests were made on the eastern frontier of the Empire, this road was extended to the valley of the upper Kabul, whence, following the river, it reached the valley of the Indus. In addition to the great administrative roads, others were built, smaller but no less indispensable, to facilitate the journeys of the royal Court, which was continually on the move. Among these must be mentioned the road joining Susa and Persepolis, of which a part of the stone-paved surface can still be seen near

Bebahan; on this road near Fahlian are the remains of a small
royal pavilion, with stone column-bases, in a pure Susian or
Persepolitan style. Between Fahlian and Bishapur it forks left
and enters the Plateau through the 'Persian Gates'. Another
road crossed Luristan, and linked Susa with Ecbatana, where
the Court used to spend the warm summer months.

The Campaigns of Darius

Owing to the paucity of our sources, the exact limits of the
eastern conquests of Cyrus are not known. It is, however, possible that he reached Gandhara, or the Peshawar district, although the operations conducted by Darius against the rebels
do not seem to have taken his troops farther than the Kabul
region. However that may be, this military action at the beginning of his reign led shortly afterwards to the conquest not
only of the whole district of Gandhara, but also of all western
India and the Indus valley as far as its mouth. At the junction
of the Kabul and the Indus, near the town of Caspatyrus,
Darius built a fleet which, under the command of a Greek of
Asia Minor, Scylax of Caryanda, was given the task of sailing
down the Indus and surveying the way to Egypt. This was an
ambitious scheme for exploring the sea routes which could be
used to link the eastern marches of the Empire to its western possessions. The fleet took thirty months to reach its
goal. This enterprise was a political as much as an administrative measure, and was also probably inspired by the commercial aims that always acted as a stimulus to the plans of Darius.
Subordinate to this was a second scheme for the cutting of a
canal between the Red Sea and the Nile, a forerunner of the
Suez Canal. It is true that Darius was not the first to envisage
this plan, for the Pharaoh Necho had already begun the task of
contriving a connexion between the eastern branch of the Nile
and the Bitter Lakes, with the idea of giving ships direct access
to the Mediterranean from the Red Sea.

While the revolts were being suppressed, Darius had already
become involved in European affairs. The satrap Oroetes, who,
as we have seen, was removed from office by the King, had,
while still in power, done away with Polycrates, the powerful

tyrant of Samos. The brother of Polycrates maintained his right to the succession which Darius recognized and confirmed. This first intervention in Greek affairs may have given Darius a taste for future operations in Europe. Nevertheless, the King did not direct his first campaign west of the Straits against Greece, but against the Scythians of southern Russia. What were the motives that led Darius to undertake this colossal operation in regions about which he probably had less information than Herodotus, who described them half a century later? Without doubt they were substantially the same as those which later led the armies of the Great King to invade Greece. In fact, Darius sought to take the Balkans from the rear and to deprive Greece of building timber for its fleet, the life-line without which it could not exist, the mainstay on which it depended for survival. And since Greece had always imported its wheat from abroad, from Egypt, Libya, and the shores of the Black Sea, now in Persian hands, it may readily be understood that in endeavouring to cut the Straits, through which the Pontic wheat convoys passed, Darius hoped to deal a deadly blow to his future enemy.

The Scythian campaign may perhaps be compared with the tactics of Alexander, who, after his early victories against the Persians, did not drive on towards Iran, but, by the conquest of Syria, Phoenicia, Palestine, and Egypt, executed an ambitious encircling movement, which cut off the Persian Empire from its richest and most productive provinces. Darius probably had other motives in mind. Appreciating the fact that the plains of southern Russia touched on his frontier along the river Jaxartes, he may have hoped once again to take from the rear the nomadic hordes threatening his eastern marches. A successful coup in this direction would also give him control of the countries through which gold passed in transit, for this precious metal was being extracted in the Urals or in Siberia.

In support of this bold and imaginative policy Darius began to take the steps appropriate to its execution. The army intended for this first encounter between Asia and Europe consisted, according to Greek sources, of about 700,000 men. While it was being assembled several maritime reconnaissances were undertaken. Democedes, Darius's famous Greek doctor, was sent with a fleet to reconnoitre the Greek coast, and it is thought that he reached Tarentum. Another force of thirty ships explored the western waters of the Black Sea. The town of Byzantium accepted Persian suzerainty. Holding the Chersonese, Darius was able to begin his campaign.

The army passed over the Straits on a bridge of boats, conquered eastern Thrace and the Getae, and in search of the Scythians crossed the Danube on a bridge built by the Ionians. The King had planned to carry out land operations in conjunction with the fleet, which was to follow along the coast, but owing to the marshes and rivers the army soon lost all contact with the ships and plunged into the interior of the country. Harassed by the elusive Scythians, who disappeared as swiftly as they came, unable to obtain supplies from the 'scorched earth' left behind by the enemy, the army began to suffer, and Darius decided to turn back. Herodotus, describing this campaign, makes no mention of the building of another bridge after the crossing of the Danube, so it is thought that the Persian army did not cross the Dniester.

The Persian Empire thus sustained its first setback; but how serious was it? The loss of 80,000 men was by no means irreparable to a power that could place in the field an army ten times as great. Its gains, moreover, were considerable. Asia had outflanked Europe by taking Thrace, which was incorporated in the Empire, as well as Macedonia, which also recognized the suzerainty of the Great King. In his inscriptions Darius lists among his peoples the 'Scythians living on the other side of the sea', who may be the peoples south of the Danube.

Recrossing the Hellespont, the Persians extended their conquests over the Greek coastal districts, which one after the other fell into their hands. Thus the objectives of the Scythian campaign had been in part attained; a bridgehead had been established and, what was more important, Darius now controlled the commercial centres of the Pontic wheat-trade. Lord of the greater part of the Greek world, he must have realized that the conquest of Greece itself was an inevitable corollary to what had already been achieved.

Greece, though faced by this foreign menace, fell far short of reaching unity. The old antagonism of Athens and Sparta blinded the young democratic party to the strength of the latter, and its policy showed no signs of resilience. Hostile to Sparta, which was strongly anti-Persian, Athens inclined towards recognition of Persian suzerainty, and to this end sent an embassy to Sardis. In the meantime, however, there was a new turn of events in Greece, as a result of which these negotiations were broken off; the democrats and the tyrant Hippias were expelled. Persian diplomacy did not, however, consider itself beaten, and from his capital in Asia Minor the Persian satrap tried to restore the situation and procure the return of Hippias to Athens. For the first time Persian gold appeared in Hellas and, adroitly expended by able and wily Asiatic diplomats, it enabled Darius to interfere in the affairs of Greece. In Athens, however, there was a lively reaction which was the reverse of what had been expected by the Empire. Athens broke with Persia and rallied herself to the opposing camp.

The difficulties encountered by the Persian Empire in its dealings with the European Greeks encouraged the Ionians to raise their head. Knowing the strength of the forces of Greece which seemed to be arrayed against the Great King, and confident in its aid, they decided to throw off the Persian yoke. The Ionian revolt broke out, the tyrants imposed by the Persians were ousted, the 'Ionian league' was re-established and the aid promised by European Greece was proclaimed. There were a few who, like the historian Hecataeus, knowing the power of Persia, thought that Greek arms were unlikely to succeed. But their voices were drowned in the hopeful shouts of the majority. Athens sent reinforcements, and the Greeks seized Sardis, where, however, the citadel held out against them. This first success was short-lived. The Persian army sent to relieve Sardis forced the insurgents to abandon the capital and retreat. Meanwhile war broke out between Athens and Aegina, causing the withdrawal of all the continental Greeks, who were replaced by men from the cities on the European seaboard and Cyprus. Two battles which followed in quick succession, Cypriote Salamis (498) and against the Carians on the river Marsyas (497), proved disastrous for the allies. The revolt was crushed and the Greek towns captured, among them Miletus, which had resisted for two years. At Branchidae the oracle of Apollo was burnt and its treasure, including the statue of Apollo Kanachos, was sent to Susa, remaining there for two centuries until 294 B.C., when it was returned to the Milesians by Seleucus I. A heavy bronze votive offering modelled in the form of a bone and bearing an archaic Ionic inscription was also discovered at Susa and formed part of the same loot. The population of Miletus was carried captive to Susa and finally settled at the mouth of the Tigris. The Persian fleet continued its easy victories. Chios and Lesbos were taken; the young men were made eunuchs and the girls sent to the harems. Byzantium and Chalcedon were also burnt. The Ionians, who had previously enjoyed numerous privileges, were placed under a satrap. The oppressive treatment meted out to them was so terrible that for two centuries the area suffered severely from the consequences. Despite their impoverishment, the inhabitants were forced to pay tribute that was far too heavy for a devastated province. However, after a while this policy was relaxed.

The revolt of the Ionians had been approved of by the continental Greeks, who, as we have seen, had helped them and were to help them again in the future. The time had now come for the Persians to take action against Greece. But since there existed a democratic party which still favoured the idea of accepting the protection of the Great King, Darius judged it more politic to negotiate its return to office. The efforts of the highest officers of a despotic Power were therefore directed to the restoration of democracy in Greece. A fleet of 600 ships left Asia Minor to back up their effort. The Persians hoped that when their intention to take Athens and Eretria was announced the Greek people, faced with this danger, would throw out the conservatives who were in power and place their States under the protection of Darius. But half his ships and at least 20,000 men were lost in a severe storm off Mount Athos, and the operation had to begin again, this time under the command of

a Mede called Datis. He disembarked in Greece and besieged
Eretria; the citizens, although divided into democrats and conservatives, decided to resist, but the town was betrayed into
Persian hands. The Median admiral then committed a grave
error. Instead of trying to reach an understanding with the
pro-Persian element, he burnt the temples, destroyed the town,
and sent all its inhabitants as slaves to Susa. This was a major
psychological blunder, and aroused an outburst of indignation
among all the Greeks who, forgetting their quarrels, and realizing that they could expect no mercy if they were conquered,
resolved to unite in face of the invader. Thus it came about
that when Datis disembarked at Marathon he was met by
the Athenian army, which, not waiting for the arrival of the
reinforcements sent by Sparta, gave battle and won a resounding victory. The Persians were defeated, seven of their ships
were captured by the Greeks, and their fleet, after cruising
along the coasts, withdrew (490). Darius, occupied with a revolt in Egypt, gave up all thought of resuming operations
against Greece. Indeed, shortly after Marathon, Egypt, which
had been heavily garrisoned by troops living off the land, and
in addition had to deliver large tribute and pay taxes, rose in
revolt. Darius, who died in 486, neither had his revenge on the
Greeks nor saw the end of the Egyptian rebellion.

The inhabitants of Eretria, whose sufferings were the price
that the continental Greeks had to pay for their liberty, were
settled near Susa at a place called Arderikka, near a spot where
salt, asphalt, and oil were extracted; we owe the earliest reference to the presence of these minerals in the province of
Khuzistan to Herodotus. There they founded a community,
and when Apollonius of Tyana visited it in the first century A.D.
their descendants still spoke Greek and remembered their origin.

From the Greek point of view, the victory of Marathon was
of capital importance. A small army of men who were prepared
to die rather than to lose their liberty was actually able to defeat
the combined sea and land forces of the Great King. They had
proved that the Persians were not invincible, and it was possible
that in the future a united Greece might successfully withstand
further aggression. From the Persian point of view, this

setback was a moral rather than a material defeat, for the vast resources of men and funds at the disposal of the Empire had still hardly been tapped. More serious was the adverse effect on the maintenance of order in the Empire, especially as regards the Egyptians, who judged this event as a favourable omen for a revolt against the Persians. Taken as a whole, however, Persian power remained unimpaired; indeed, after a series of victories this defeat must have seemed to Darius to be the sort of unavoidable accident that befalls even the strongest of nations and peoples in the course of their lifetime.

The Political and Administrative Achievement of Darius

Alexander the Great, who admired the achievements of Cyrus and Darius, visited the tombs of these two founders of the Persian Empire. Seeing an inscription on the tomb of Darius, he asked that it should be translated. Strabo records that the text read: 'I was a friend to my friends; as horseman and bowman I proved myself superior to all others; as a hunter I prevailed; I could do everything'. Even if the translator gave a free rendering, he nevertheless conveyed what tradition has preserved concerning Darius for whom the phrase 'I was a friend to my friends' was the basis of all personal relationships. Indeed, his written testimony at Bisutun, which is a sort of *credo*, is inspired by this same ideal, and shows that though he was the conqueror of many royal pretenders, he held in high esteem each vassal nation which behaved as a friend. This benevolent imperialism, while reflecting spiritual greatness, did not lack material force, as is shown from Darius's statement that all his subject peoples, and they are enumerated at length, obeyed his orders night and day. Despite the diversity of races, customs, and beliefs, the will of the monarch was universal law from Thrace to the Indus and from the Caucasus to the Indian Ocean.

An empire cannot be constructed without a legal framework, and this Darius did not fail to provide. Scholars who have studied the numerous texts left by Darius in many places, at Bisutun and Persepolis, at Susa and Naqsh-i-Rustam, have recognized a number of parallels between his writings and the ancient code of Hammurabi, which had often been copied and served as a basis for the advisers of Darius.

These official texts, copied on stelae, tablets, or papyrus, were sent to all the main provincial centres of the Empire. Thus fragments of the Bisutun inscriptions have been found written in Aramaic on a papyrus at Elephantine, where a garrison of Jewish mercenaries was quartered, and in Babylonian at Babylon. A tablet found at Susa reproduces, with some variations, the inscription that Darius caused to be engraved on his tomb at Naqsh-i-Rustam:

1. 1–7. A great god is Ahuramazda, who created this earth, who created yonder sky, who created man, who created happiness for man, who made Darius king, one king of many, one lord of many.

2. 7–14. I am Darius the Great King, King of Kings, King of countries containing all kinds of men, King in this great earth far and wide, son of Hystaspes, an Achaemenian, a Persian, son of a Persian, an Aryan, having Aryan lineage.

3. 14–30. Saith Darius the King: By the favour of Ahuramazda these are the countries which I seized outside of Persia; I ruled over them; they bore tribute to me; what was said to them by me, that they did; my law – that held them firm; Media, Elam, Parthia, Aria, Bactria, Sogdiana, Chorasmia, Drangiana, Arachosia, Sattagydia, Gandara, Sind, Amyrgian Scythians, Scythians with pointed caps, Babylonia, Assyria, Arabia, Egypt, Armenia, Cappadocia, Sardis, Ionia, Scythians who are across the sea, Skudra, petasos wearing Ionians, Libyans, Ethiopians, men of Maka, Carians.

4. 30–41. Saith Darius the King: Much which was ill-done, that I made good. Provinces were in commotion; one man was smiting the other. The following I brought about by the favour of Ahuramazda, that the one does not smite the other at all, each one is in his place. My law – of that they feel fear, so that the stronger does not smite nor destroy the weak.

5. 41–49. Saith Darius the King: By the favour of Ahuramazda, much handiwork which previously had been put
   out of its place, that I put in its place. A town by name
   ..., (its) wall fallen from age, before this unrepaired – I
   built another wall (to serve) from that time into the
   future.

6. 49–52. Saith Darius the King: Me may Ahuramazda together with the gods protect, and my royal house, and
   what has been inscribed by me.

We know that Darius attached great importance to the efficient administration of justice, and his laws remained in force
in Iran long after the Empire that he created had passed away.
Herodotus records that 'the royal judges, chosen from among
the Persians, held office until their death, unless they were removed for miscarriage of justice. It was they who judged cases,
interpreted national laws, and were appealed to in all disputes'.
But as was the case in Babylonia, the vanquished peoples retained their own legal system side by side with that of Darius.

The virtue of truth and justice was much emphasized by
Darius, and extolled in several of his inscriptions, together
with an enunciation of nationalism unknown in earlier ancient
oriental empires:

Saith Darius the King: May Ahuramazda bear me aid, with
the gods of the royal house; and may Ahuramazda protect this
country from a (hostile) army, from famine, from the Lie!
Upon this country may there not come an army, nor famine
nor the Lie; this I pray as a boon from Ahuramazda together
with the gods of the royal house. This boon may Ahuramazda
together with the gods of the royal house give to me!

The sentiment of nationalism so keenly felt by the Great
King did not exclude a preoccupation with the welfare of other
countries whose destinies he directed at the behest of his
supreme god. The spirit of the Persian people was imbued with
this love of country; this was remarked on by Herodotus, who
emphasized that no Persian ever prayed to his god for a personal benefit. 'But he prays for the welfare of the king and of

the whole Persian people, among whom he is of necessity included.' This patriotic ideal inspired and developed a national conscience in the fulfilment of the imperial task that was a part of the nation's destiny.

Religion

'Ahuramazda is a great god, he is great above all the gods, he it is who has created heaven and earth, who has created men, and who has loaded with favours the human beings who dwell on it (the earth). He it is who has granted dominion to the king Darius over this wide territory which includes many nations, namely Persia, Media, and the other nations with different tongues, mountains, and plains, on this side the sea, on the other the desert.'

Ahuramazda was thus the great god, the creator of all, the benefactor of every living creature. It was he who by his will directed the actions of the King on whom he had conferred power. It was not in his own name that the Achaemenian King carried his sword so far from his native country; in fulfilling the divine commands the King's acts had to receive the sanction of the great god. It was close subordination. The Persia of the Achaemenians was not a State founded on a religion, as was the case with the Abbasid caliphs. Although Darius derived his power from the god himself, there was in his case no question of being bound down under the weight of a doctrine which became a religion. There was no imperial cult, but the mere fact that the King had been placed on the throne by the will of Ahuramazda gave a sort of unity to the Persian world.

Ahuramazda was not the sole god. Darius repeatedly states this. From Herodotus we learn that the Persians worshipped the sun (Mithra), the moon (Mah), the earth (Zam), fire (Atar), water (Apam Napat), and wind (Vahyu). The inscriptions of Darius and his two successors make no mention of the name of any god apart from Ahuramazda, and it may be that under the Achaemenians a distinction should be made between the official religion and that of the rest of the people. From the time of Artaxerxes II, the official pantheon was enlarged by divinities who are mentioned with Ahuramazda in the texts. These are Mithra, the sun god, god of justice and redemption, who was a very old Iranian deity, and Anahita, goddess of the waters, of fertility and procreation, who shows the influence of non-Iranian cults.

This primitive, polytheistic, Aryan religion, in which all the forces of nature were worshipped, could not remain unaffected by the gods of the Asianic inhabitants of the Plateau. Just as in Greece the Greeks were influenced by the indigenous peoples, so were the Iranians. In the fusion of races, which was on the point of being realized, religion and civilization experienced the same fate.

The Persians worshipped their gods with bloody sacrifices. Herodotus has left a well-known description of these very simple and primitive ceremonies which go back to the distant past of the Indo-Iranian people. No sacrifice could be accomplished without the ministrations of the Magi, a fraternity, probably Median in origin, which held certain political and religious privileges. Their functions were very important under the Achaemenians, who, according to all the evidence, took over this priestly class from the Medes. The Magi accompanied the army to celebrate the sacrifices, they interpreted dreams and took part in the coronation of the new King – a ceremony performed in the temple of Pasargadae; they were also responsible for the education of the young men and were guardians of the royal tombs, as for example that of Cyrus. Very little is known about their origin or their religion, which was not that of the Persians. They formed an isolated group and permitted the marriage of blood relations. Their cosmology recognized two principles, Good and Evil. In contradistinction to the Persians, who buried their dead, the Magi exposed all corpses to be torn by wild beasts or birds of prey.

We know of the tomb of Cyrus where Alexander saw the embalmed body of the Great King lying on a golden couch. From the time of Darius all the tombs of the other sovereigns of this dynasty were cut in the cliff of Naqsh-i-Rustam (Fig. 55). The only example of direct inhumation known was discovered by the French Archaeological Expedition. The body, thought to be that of a woman, had been placed in a bronze

Fig. 55 – Naqsh-i-Rustam: Rock tombs of the Achaemenian kings and fire altar

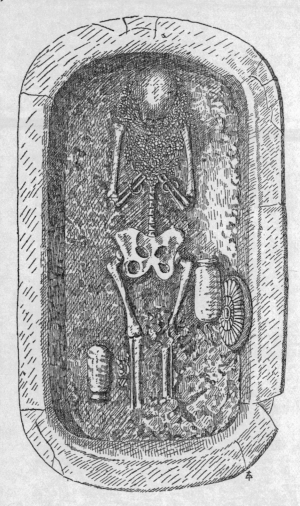

Fig. 56 – Susa: Achaemenian tomb

sarcophagus (Fig. 56), and was decorated with gold jewellery (Fig. 57) and accompanied by rich funerary furnishings which included a silver dish (Fig. 58) and alabaster vases. The Magi were also entrusted with the preparation of *haoma*, an intoxi-

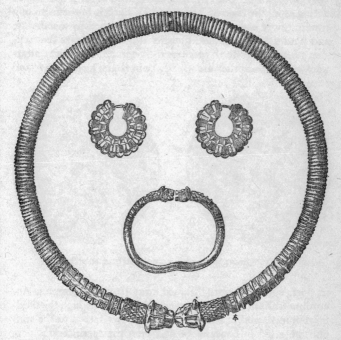

Fig. 57 – Susa: Gold jewellery from the Achaemenian tomb

cating drink made from a plant and used during the Persian religious rituals. The texts discovered in the archives at Persepolis mention it and give details of the profits made from its sale.

Herodotus states that the Persians had neither temples, altars, nor statues of the gods, and from the Greek point of view he was right. The Persians had no temples with altars and statues of the gods where the faithful could worship. Nevertheless they did have temples, and we know of three belonging to the Achaemenian period: one at Pasargadae built by Cyrus, another at Naqsh-i-Rustam in front of the tomb of Darius (Pl. 19a) and probably built by him, and a third at Susa, apparently dating from the time of Artaxerxes II. Each is in the form of a square tower enclosing a single room, reached by a stairway, and here the Magi tended the sacred fire. It appears that religious ceremonies took place in the open air, for all the altars known to us, and they are usually twin altars, have been found

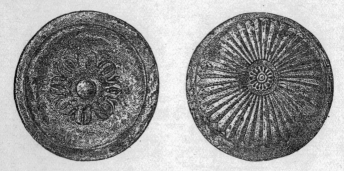

Fig. 58 – Susa: Silver dish from the Achaemenian tomb

in open country, some distance away from the temples. According to Xenophon, these were the places to which the sacrificial animals and chariots drawn by horses sacred to the sun-god were led in procession, and then the sacrifice was performed in the presence of the King.

The Persians also made images of their gods. Artaxerxes II set up statues of Anahita at Susa, Ecbatana, and Babylon and in the other great centres of his empire. All the bas-reliefs above the royal Achaemenian tombs represent the prince sacrificing before an altar with the sacred fire, and above him is a winged disk out of which rises the head and shoulders of Ahuramazda (Fig. 59). The same figure hovers over the bas-reliefs of Bisutun and on certain of the monuments at Perse-

(a) Stone tools from the cave of Tang-i-Pabda (*left*). (b) Siyalk: Carved
bone handle for flint implement (*right*)

(c) Siyalk: Grave of Level I

(a) Rayy: Bowl in red ware

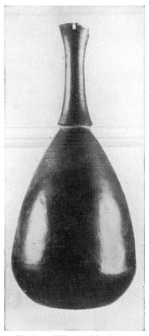

(b) Tepe Hissar: Black ware

(c) Siyalk: Grave of Necropolis B

(b) Stele of Naram-Sin

(a) Bronze statue of Queen Napir-asu

(a) Luristan: Bronze ibex

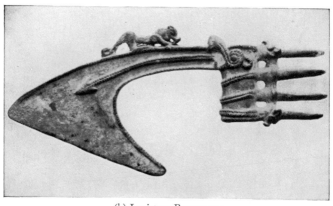

(b) Luristan: Bronze axe

a

b

c

d

e

(a) and (b) Luristan: Piece of harness; (c) Luristan: Bronze axe; (d) Luristan: Bronze terminal of chariot pole; (e) Luristan: Bronze bit

5

(a) Luristan: Bronze rein ring

(b) Luristan: Bronze statuette

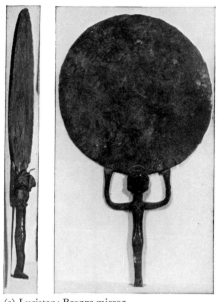

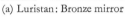

(a) Luristan: Bronze mirror

(b) Luristan: Bronze votive object

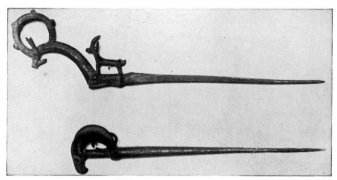

(c) Luristan: Bronze pins

(a) to (c) Luristan: Votive 'pins'

Luristan: Bronze vase

(a) and (b) Sakiz treasure: Gold terminals of furniture

(c) Sakiz treasure: Gold chape of a
scabbard

(d) Sakiz treasure: Gold plaque from a belt

(a) Sakiz treasure: Gold plaque

(b) Sakiz treasure: Gold bracelet

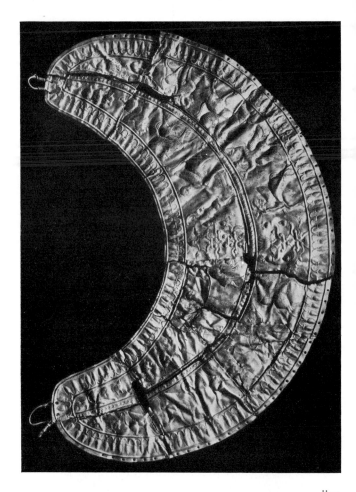

Sakiz treasure:
Gold pectoral

(a) Kalar-dasht: Gold cup

(b) Azerbaijan: Terra-cotta rhyton

(a) Terrace of Masjid-i-Sulaiman

(b) Persepolis: Aerial view

(c) Persepolis: Stairway of the Apadana

(a) Pasargadae: Winged genius (*left*); (b) Bisutun: Bas-relief of Darius (*top right*); (c) Pasargadae: Tomb of Cyrus (*bottom right*)

(d) Bisutun: Darius the Great

Susa: Aerial view

(a) Susa: Lion-griffin in enamelled brick

(b) Susa: Capital from the Achaemenian
palace

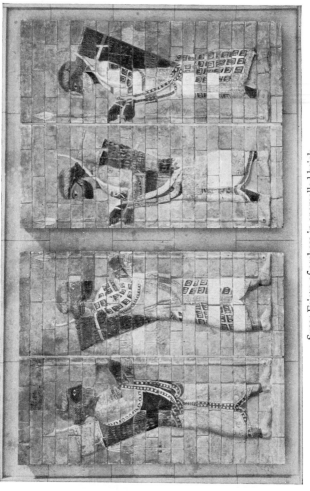

Susa: Frieze of archers in enamelled brick

(a) Naqsh-i-Rustam: Fire temple

(b) Persepolis: Darius giving audience. Bas-relief from the Treasury

(a) Achaemenian bronze vase

(b) Persepolis: Syrian tribute bearers

(a) Persepolis:
Dog in black marble

(b) Persepolis:
Bas-relief
from the Hall of a
Hundred Columns

21

(b) Persepolis: Head of a prince in lapis lazuli paste

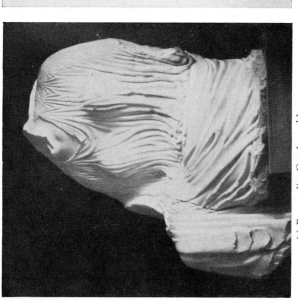

(a) Persepolis: Greek marble statue

(b) and (c) Hamadan (?):
Gold appliqué

(a) Persepolis: Gold plaque

23

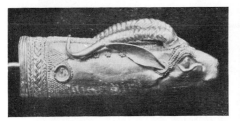

(a) Hamadan (?): Decorated gold handle of a whetstone (*left*).
(b) Gold pendant

(c) Gold wreath of flowers

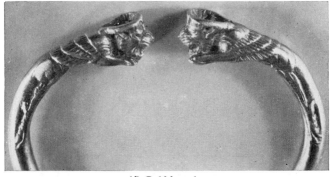

(d) Gold bracelet

(a) to (d) Achaemenian imperial coinage
(e) to (h) Achaemenian satrapal coinage: (e) Mazaeus at Tarsus; (f) Orontes
    at Lampsacus; (g) Pharnabazus at Tarsus; (h) Datames at Tarsus
(i) Persepolis: Elamite tablets

Pompeii: Mosaic representing the battle of Darius and Alexander at Issus

(a) and (b) Persepolis: Bas-reliefs on lintels of a temple below the terrace

(c) and (d) Denaver (?): Head of a satyr (*left*) and of Silenus (*right*) on basins

(a) to (d) Nihawand: Bronze statuettes from the Hellenistic temple

(a) Shami: Bronze head of Antiochus IV (?)
(Each half distorted by a violent blow)

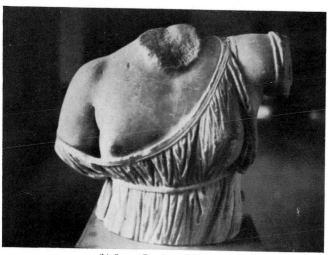

(b) Susa: Greek marble torso

(a) and (b) Susa: Parthian cemetery. Single grave

(c) Susa: Parthian cemetery. Communal grave

Shami: Bronze statue

(b) Shami:
Marble head of a prince

(a) Bust of Vologases III (?)

(b) Susa: Marble head of Queen Musa (?) (Crown inscribed in Greek
with maker's name, ANTIOCHUS. Character of writing dates it to end
of first century B.C. or beginning of first century A.D.)

(a) Susa:
Limestone male head

(b) Hamadan:
Limestone
male head

(a) Bisutun: Parthian bas-relief

(b) Bisutun: Bas-relief of Mithridates II (*left*) and Gotarzes II

(a) and (b) Tang-i-Sarwak: Parthian bas-reliefs

36

Susa: Bas-relief of Artabanus V

(a) Parthian horseman in terra-cotta

(b) Bronze incense burner

(a) Susa: 'Emblema' in terra-cotta

(b) Susa: Parthian figurines in carved bone

Parthian imperial coinage: (a) Phraates IV; (b) Phraataces and Musa; (c) Orodes; (d) Mithridates II; (e) Mithridates II; (f) Gotarzes II; (g) (?) Gotarzes II; (h) Vardanes II

(a) Ctesiphon: Sassanian palace

(b) Bishapur: Fire temple

(c) Bishapur: Votive monument with two columns

(a) Bishapur: Model of the hall of the Sassanian palace

(b) Bishapur: Sassanian palace. Recess decorated
with sculptured and painted stucco

(a) Naqsh-i-Rustam: Investiture of Ardashir I

(b) Bishapur: Triumph of Shapur I

(a) and (b) Bishapur: Mosaics from the Sassanian palace

(a) Bottle of gilded silver

(b) Dish of gilded silver representing a
Sassanian prince hunting

45

(a) Rock crystal goblet

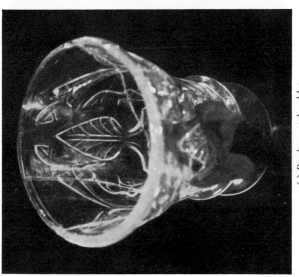

(b) Rock crystal dish

46

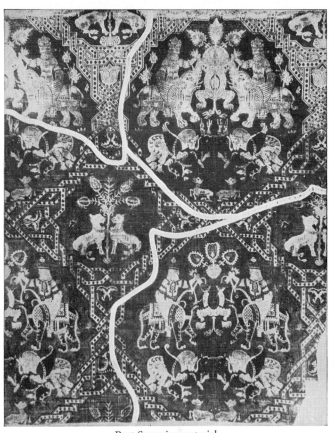

Post-Sassanian material

(a) to (g) Sassanian imperial coinage:

(a) Ardashir I; (b) Shapur I; (c) Shapur II; (d) Bahram V; (e) Yez-degerd II; (f) Chosroes II; (g) Chosroes I; (h) Susa: Sassanian bulla

polis. This was a very old symbol of Egyptian iconography, dating from the time of the creation of the monarchy in that country, and must represent the sky by the out-stretched wings of Horus, the great god. The world was divided: Ahuramazda, the 'wise lord' or 'the sage', reigned in the sky and 'enfolds and protects with his wings the earth and its ruler', the Achaemenian King, his viceroy, who reigned upon earth. Ahuramazda was the supreme god, standing above all others. The Achaemenian religion was not yet monotheistic, but there was already a strong movement in that direction.

During the Achaemenian period the Mazdian religion, re-

Fig. 59 – Image of the god Ahuramazda

formed by Zoroaster, began to spread through the Empire. The date of the prophet is still in dispute. It is thought that he was born in Media but was forced to leave his native province to preach in eastern Iran, where his teaching attracted followers, among whom was a certain prince Hystaspes, thought by some authorities to be Darius's father, the satrap of Parthia and Hyrcania. However this may be, it was from the east that the new religion slowly spread throughout Persia.

The sedentary population of eastern Iran was constantly exposed to the attacks and depredations of invading nomads, and it may be that this state of affairs gave rise to the idea expounded by Zoroaster that the world was ruled by two principles, Good and Evil – the first being a kind of hypostasis of Ahuramazda, the second a malevolent spirit, Ahriman. Ahuramazda

was surrounded by divine assistants, some of whom were probably ancient divinities, worshipped originally in the guise of
natural forces. The struggle between these two spirits, which
stood for an opposition between thought and intelligence, was
to end in victory for the Good Spirit. Thus the dualism was
only apparent, and the Zoroastrian religion was 'an imperfect
monotheism'.

Mankind could not avoid taking part in this struggle, since
it also was divided into good men, the upright and pious, and
evil-doers and atheists. The former followed Ahuramazda, the
latter Ahriman. Each individual was judged after death: the
good went to paradise, while the wicked suffered long punishment. Besides this individual judgement there was to be a general judgement with trial by fire. Man had to avoid and fight
against heresy; he had to be kind to animals, look after them,
and treat them well. Among the wicked were included the bad
judge, the man who neglected his fields, and he who oppressed
others. The good prince fought for his religion, defended his
people, fed the poor, protected the weak. 'Good thoughts,
good words, good deeds, this was the triad which constituted
Zoroastrian ethics.'

The cult was ordered according to strict rules. Blood sacrifices were forbidden, since the beast which fed and worked for
man ought to be venerated. The intoxicating drink, haoma,
was also banned. Finally, the dead could neither be interred,
burnt, nor immersed, for fear of defiling the three sacred elements, namely earth, fire, and water. Bodies had to be exposed
on the mountains or on towers specially built for this purpose.
The bare bones were then placed in ossuaries and deposited in
tombs either built or cut in the rock.

Zoroastrianism was almost contemporary with Buddhism,
and has this in common with the religion that arose in India,
that both were a protest against the cruel practices and bloody
rites of the old Aryan religions. Their fate, however, was not
the same; the first was the work of an aristocracy, while the
second expressed popular aspirations, and this fact is perhaps
one of the reasons for the vast expansion of Buddhism, which
still has hundreds of millions of adherents, whereas the Zoro-

astrian religion is to-day confined to a small community which fanatically defends it.

Language and Writing

The invention of cuneiform writing to express old Persian probably goes back to Teispes, for we have the golden tablet of his son, Ariaramnes. That the Persians at the time of their kingdom in Fars probably wrote on clay tablets seems to be proved by the only tablet we know. Found at Susa, it contains in Old Persian the text of the 'foundation charter of the palace' of Darius. At the moment when this small kingdom was being transformed into an empire, this language and writing were available only to a small minority of the ruling class. It was assumed that non-Persian high officials and satraps did not know the language. The speed with which the Empire was formed made it impossible to create an army of scribes capable of translating Persian into all the other languages. On the other hand, Aramaic had become very widespread since the beginning of the first millennium B.C. The Arameans, who founded several small kingdoms, Damascus, Hama, and Sam'al, spread throughout the Near East as far as western Iran. Under the Assyrians, their language and writing were widely used in commerce and even in conversation. Certain Assyrian bas-reliefs show two scribes, one of whom holds a tablet and stylus for writing in cuneiform and the other a papyrus for writing Aramaic in ink. By the Achaemenian period, Aramaic had become a true *lingua franca* in Asia and was employed, particularly for State business, from Egypt to India, where documents have been found drawn up in that language. The result was that although Elamite was written in Elam and Babylonian in Babylon, all the Persian chancelleries employed Aramaic.

Nevertheless, the Persians must also have written their own language. The use of cuneiform writing was restricted to inscriptions on stone monuments, and fell into disuse. Scribes who knew it became few, and scholars have noticed how many of the cuneiform inscriptions in Old Persian belonging to the last Achaemenian kings contain bad errors, illustrating the lack of skill among the scribes. All the evidence points to the fact that the Persians adopted Aramaic writing in which to express their language. One of the versions of the inscription on the tomb of Darius, unfortunately much damaged, seems to have been drawn up in Persian and written in Aramaic characters. No other evidence on parchment or papyrus has survived. In the cuneiform writing of Old Persian several Aramaic ideograms have been retained, and the same thing must have happened in the transcription of Persian into Aramaic characters; from this in time developed the Pahlavi writing which uses Semitic ideograms. Out of several thousand tablets found in the archives at Persepolis, not one was written in Persian, very few were in Aramaic, and most were in Elamite. This *argumentum e silentio* also lends support to the theory that the Aramaic alphabet was used for writing Old Persian.

The decipherment of the Elamite texts (Pl. 25*i*) shows the manner in which these documents were prepared. The order came in Persian from a high Court official; the scribe translated it into Aramaic and wrote it on papyrus; the text was then passed to a second scribe, who translated it into Elamite and inscribed it upon a tablet. This served as a voucher, for most of these documents are the accounts of the artists and workmen engaged on building the palace at Persepolis.

Art

Gold flowed from all corners of the world into the royal treasury. The Achaemenian prince no longer led the austere life of a soldier, content with a residence that was only a larger edition of that of his subjects. He now required capital cities and palaces that were larger and finer than those built by the most powerful monarchs of Babylonia and Assyria. The magnificence of his splendid residence was intended to dazzle all those who from far and near came to offer gifts or bring tribute. Architecture and ornament alike had to be the measure of his power, his might, and the pomp of his Court.

After residing for a short time in Babylon, Darius chose Susa as his capital, probably in 521 B.C. On the acropolis, where the palaces and temples of the Elamites had stood before they were ruined in the sack of the city by Assurbanipal, Darius constructed a strong citadel. On a neighbouring mound he built his palace and the Apadana, a hypostyle throne room. Farther to the east, and separated from the palace by a broad avenue, lay the city proper, with the houses and villas of courtiers, officials, and merchants. The whole complex was surrounded by a strong wall of unbaked brick, flanked with projecting towers, which can still be traced in the general plan. At the foot of the wall he dug a large moat which, filled with water diverted from the Chahour, surrounded the town and made it an impregnable island. As capital of the world, connected with the sea by four rivers and thronged with kings, princes, ambassadors, doctors, men of letters, and artists, Susa had to be worthy of the role assigned to it by the King of Kings (Pl. 16).

In the ruins of the palace the French Archaeological Expedition found a text in which Darius relates how he carried out this work. As this is one of the finest examples of Achaemenian official literature, we must quote the essential passages.

After invoking the great god, Ahuramazda, Darius says:

THE BUILDING OF THE PALACE

.... This is the palace which I built at Susa. From afar its ornamentation was brought. Downward the earth was dug, until I reached rock in the earth. When the excavation had been made, then rubble was packed down, one part 40 cubits in depth, another (part) 20 cubits in depth. On that rubble the palace was constructed.

And that the earth was dug downward, and that the rubble was packed down, and that the sun dried brick was moulded, the Babylonian people, it did (these tasks). The cedar timber, this – a mountain by name Lebanon – from there was brought; the Assyrian people, it brought it to Babylon; from Babylon the Carians and the Ionians brought it to Susa. The *yakā* timber was brought from Gandara and from Carmania. The gold was brought from Sardis and from Bactria, which here was wrought. The precious stone lapis-lazuli and carnelian which was wrought here, this was brought from Sogdiana. The precious stone turquoise this was brought from Chorasmia, which was wrought here. The silver and the ebony were brought from Egypt. The ornamentation with which the wall was adorned, that from Ionia was brought. The ivory which was wrought here, was brought from Ethiopia and from Sind and from Arachosia. The stone columns which were here wrought – a village by name *Abiradus*, in Elam – from there were brought. The stone-cutters who wrought the stone, these were Ionians and Sardians. The goldsmiths who wrought the gold, those were Medes and Egyptians. The men who wrought the wood, those were Sardians and Egyptians. The men who wrought the baked brick, those were Babylonians. The men who adorned the wall, those were Medes and Egyptians. Saith Darius the King: At Susa a very excellent (work) was ordered; a very excellent (work) was (brought to completion). Me may Ahuramazda protect, and Hystaspes, my father, and my country.*

The importance of this text is far greater than the aim envisaged for it by the Great King. It gives a faithful picture of the Empire and of the demands made by the powerful ruler on his people: to live for him, to work for him, to carry out his least behest, to die for him.

The architecture of the palace was still considerably influenced by Babylonian principles and was also conditioned by the climate. The plan consisted of interior courts which opened on to the rooms and living quarters; these again were surrounded by long corridors that permitted the guards to watch every movement. The walls of unbaked brick were also decorated in Babylonian style with enamelled brickwork representing the faithful immortals (Pl. 18), lions, bulls (Fig. 60), and fantastic beings (Pl. 17b). The throne-room was in the half light, the intention being that the king should not be easily visible. This sense of remoteness was later accentuated, until in the Sassanian period the king sitting in his throne-room was actually separated from his subjects by a long, barely transpa-

* The translation is taken from Kent, *Old Persian Grammar, Texts, Lexicon* (1950), by permission of the American Oriental Society.

rent curtain embroidered with gold and silver thread, and enriched with precious stones.

The throne-room itself, known as the *apadana*, was a hall,
the roof of which was supported by six rows of six columns
nearly twenty metres in height, surmounted by capitals with
protomes of bulls (Pl. 17*a*); on the north, east, and west the

Fig. 60 – Susa: Winged bulls in enamelled brick

hall was surrounded by three peristyles of twelve columns, the
bases and capitals of which were different from those of the
throne-room itself; it was approached by three wide stairways
that have now disappeared. Some of the capitals were simple
imposts, like those at Pasargadae; in others, the protomes
rested on volutes.

The palace at Susa had hardly been finished when Darius decided to build another residence at Persepolis, in his native
country of Fars (Pl. 14*b*). He abandoned Pasargadae, which

had belonged to the branch of the dynasty that reigned before him, and the only remaining connexion with this city was the temple where all Persian kings were crowned until the fall of the Empire.

At Persepolis a great terrace with its back to the mountain, was partly quarried out of the rock and partly constructed of large blocks of stone, joined by iron clamps fixed with molten lead (Fig. 61). The ancestors of Darius had employed the same method for the construction of the platforms on which they built their modest palaces. A defensive wall of unbaked brick followed the contour of the terrace fairly high up on the hillside in order to protect the rear. A great staircase with a double turn gave access to the esplanade, whence two further flights led to the Apadana. This was a replica of that found at Susa, and tablets from the archives of Persepolis give us the explanation. The artists and overseers who had finished their task at Susa were brought to Persepolis to continue their work there. At Persepolis, as at Susa, seventy-two fluted columns supported the cedar-wood ceiling. They were about 65 feet in height and were surmounted by protomes of bulls and horned lions (Fig. 62).

Here also long processions of Immortals sculptured in stone decorate the sides of the staircase (Pl. 14c). They are followed by a line of courtiers, both Medes and Persians. Finally, in two registers, is a procession of subject nations bringing gifts to the king: some lead rare and valuable animals, others carry the products for which their countries were noted, jewellery, vessels, and cloth (Pl. 20b). Achaemenian art shows little interest in scenes from real life. The long files of tributaries on the staircases at Persepolis are only partially an attempt at realism, for their principal aim was to illustrate, on the one hand, the power of the king, and on the other, the diversity of people composing the Empire. It was an art in the service of power and was, above all, decorative. In pursuit of this aim, the artists of the age excelled at animal portraiture (Pl. 21a). The style of the decoration achieved under Darius is marked by clarity, balance, power, and firmness, and translates into stone the very character of his career.

Fig. 61 – Terrace of Persepolis

Fig. 62 – Columns of Persepolis

Near the Apadana (Fig. 65) and at a slightly higher level was
the palace of Darius. Its walls were, as elsewhere, of unbaked
brick and have now disappeared, but the doors and windows
fashioned of wide blocks of stone and surmounted by an Egyptian lintel are still intact. This residence was built on a different

Fig. 63 – Persepolis: Human-headed capital

plan from that of Susa: it was much smaller, and consisted only of a central columned hall, flanked by rooms to right and left and opening on to a portico with wooden columns. This was a Nordic type of house which became the typical dwelling of the Iranians. At one side was a small building, the tripylon, with columns surmounted by human-headed capitals (Fig. 63). Hard up against the mountain lay the Treasury buildings, where two bas-reliefs depict an identical scene: the reception by Darius of a high Court official (Pl. 19*b*).

It has been said that the monumental art of the Achaemenians after achieving its highest point under Darius could create nothing new. This point of view is only partially true, for under Xerxes variations were introduced. Son of the ruler of the Empire and designated as his successor in his father's lifetime, Xerxes translated into stone his intoxication with the power he wielded, though it was not of his winning. In this he resembled the Assyrian monarchs, whom he also imitated by erecting the propylaeum of 'all the nations' on the terrace of Persepolis. This was a massive structure flanked by winged human-headed bulls (Fig. 64), huge replicas of those guarding the entrances in Assyrian palaces. Just as under the successors of Augustus there was a tendency towards the colossal in art, so the reign of Xerxes was marked by an equivalent exaggeration, due not so much to technical progress or to a taste for ostentatious luxury as to the disordered imagination of the king.

In a hall that was even more grandiose than the propylaeum, the 'hall of a hundred columns', he caused the king to be depicted in the window recesses as a hero overpowering monsters (Pl. 21*b*) – a sculpture of imposing dimensions, product of an art that sought to convey force, power, and domination.

There are very few remains belonging to the next period, that of Artaxerxes I. The great hall of Xerxes was not finished in his lifetime, and his son built the south-east entrance. At Susa the palace of Darius was burnt down in the reign of Artaxerxes I, who, like his grandfather, was greatly attached to this capital. Since he could not rebuild this enormous edifice quickly, he built a small palace on the southern edge of the city;

this was restored several times in later periods. The few fragments of sculpture found in its ruins bear a strong family likeness to those he erected at Persepolis.

The age of Artaxerxes corresponds with that in which Phi-

Fig. 64 – Persepolis: Winged bull from the doorway of Xerxes

dias built the Parthenon at Athens, and it is not straining truth too far to believe that the influence of Greek art reached the Iranian Plateau where the Persians were already familiar with Hellenic culture. In the rare examples of Achaemenian art of the middle of the fifth century we can follow how it became more refined and humane, how carving became three-dimensional, and perfection of detail was attained. Although the forms lost their vigour, they seem to have gained in refinement, and after the extravagances of Xerxes they tended towards a greater measure of restraint.

After Artaxerxes I, the monumental art of the Achaemen-

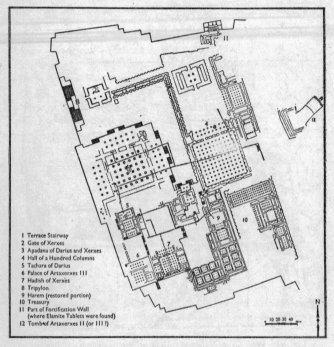

1 Terrace Stairway
2 Gate of Xerxes
3 Apadana of Darius and Xerxes
4 Hall of a Hundred Columns
5 Tachara of Darius
6 Palace of Artaxerxes III
7 Hadish of Xerxes
8 Tripylon
9 Harem (restored portion)
10 Treasury
11 Part of Fortification Wall
    (where Elamite Tablets were found)
12 Tomb of Artaxerxes II (or III?)

10 20 30 40

Fig. 65 – Terrace of Persepolis

ians displayed nothing new. Nevertheless, the princes who followed him never ceased to labour at the adornment of the capital cities; some finished the work begun by their predecessors, others restored what had been destroyed, as Artaxerxes did at Susa, or even built new palaces, as Artaxerxes III did at Persepolis (Fig. 65). But we look in vain for the smallest inspiration of a living art. Within a century Achaemenian art had become quite exhausted.

Greek statuary was much prized by the Achaemenians. Xerxes carried off several statues from Greece in order to transport them to Iran. A magnificent masterpiece of Greek sculpture of the fifth century, representing Penelope(?), was found in the ruins of Persepolis during the excavations of the Oriental Institute of Chicago (Pl. 22a). Plutarch states that there was in the capital a great statue of Xerxes which was thrown down by the soldiers of Alexander; fragments of folds of drapery and a shod foot belonging to a royal statue have been discovered at Susa.

The Persians who had mastered Ionia were captivated by its art, which, even before the Median wars, had spread to Greece itself. The master sculptors of Ionia had a great reputation in the most distant countries; political events uprooted and scattered these craftsmen, who carried their art far from their native land, and Darius acknowledged in his 'Charter' that he did not despise the teaching of the Greeks he had subjected to his rule.

We know nothing of Persian statuary. It certainly could not have rivalled that of the Greeks, for Greek art was founded on a religion that was above all 'a creator of beautiful forms and fine narrative'. Persian religion was too austere to inspire such works as the impassive majesty of a Zeus, the gravity of an Athene, or the beauty of an Aphrodite. To judge from the few statuettes known from this period, recently found in the ruins of Persepolis (Pl. 22b), statuary was confined to representations of the Great King or, perhaps, of some of the more powerful men of his Empire. Achaemenian art, as known to us, was a prisoner of the Court and was deprived of freedom of expression. Nevertheless, it was able to express the magnificence of the age in the variety of forms and the richness of its jewellery and toreutic. Palace doors and valuable furniture were covered with golden plaques in *repoussé* work, depicting real or mythical beings (Pl. 23a–c); plaques were also cast in bronze and worked over with a burin (Fig. 66); and on each of these objects the Achaemenian artist revealed himself as a consummate master of animal portraiture. This is also true of the stone-sculptors and the bronze-smiths who executed such pieces as the support formed of three roaring lions (Fig. 67), or vases with handles in the shape of griffins, also known on the bas-reliefs of Persepolis (Pl. 20a and b). The jewellery, the fine workmanship of which compels our admiration, drew its inspiration sometimes from the animal world, as when on a gold pendant it copied the old Mesopotamian motif of crossed lions (Pl. 24b) or decorated the handle of a whetstone with a gazelle, depicted with powerful realism, the surface studded with granu-

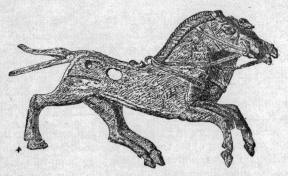

Fig. 66 – Persepolis: Bronze ornamental plaque

lations (Pl. 24a); sometimes from the vegetable world, as in a wreath of leaves and flowers (Pl. 24c); or else it created composite beings like those decorating the ends of a gold bracelet (Pl. 24d). Excavation of the ruins of Persepolis has yielded thousands of fragments of vases of hard stone, some ornamented with heads of ducks or swans (Fig. 68), a motif that was also very popular with the Scythian clientèle. The subjects most favoured by engravers of gems and cylinder or stamp seals were the struggle of the king with animals or monsters, and scenes of the chase, as on the famous cylinder seal of Darius (Fig. 69). Mention must also be made of the engraving on the coinage issued by the King of Kings, which invariably

Fig. 67 – Persepolis: Bronze support

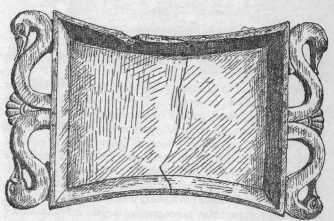

Fig. 68 – Persepolis: Sculptured stone dish

represented the prince as an archer; some of the coins struck by the satraps of the western provinces are real masterpieces (Pl. 25). Weapons, and in particular, ceremonial arms, equalled in craftsmanship and in the decorative value of their subjects the richest Scythian pieces found in the royal tombs of south Russia. For example, the scabbard, probably of precious metal, of the short sword carried by a Median royal official shown on the bas-relief of Darius (Pl. 19b) bears a decoration that was certainly inspired by the best tradition of Scythian art, which, as we know, was a constituent element in Median art (Fig. 70). Also at Persepolis were found a battle-axe and a broken bit for

Fig. 69 – Cylinder seal of Darius

breaking-in wild horses that had probably belonged to the royal garrison (Fig. 71).

The 'Foundation Charter of the Palace' is not only valid for Susa but must also apply to building work at Persepolis and Ecbatana, and indeed gives a picture of the whole of official Achaemenian art. In the cosmopolitan capitals of the Great King of Kings this art, so closely linked with the fortunes of the Empire, also became in itself cosmopolitan. In truth, the Persians could not do otherwise than draw on the achievements of the older Oriental civilizations, for they themselves had passed too rapidly from humble dwelling to palace. In this, did they not act as many other peoples had done before them? Did not the Urartians draw on the Assyrians as well as on the civilizations of Asia Minor or Mesopotamia? And were not the

Fig. 70 – Bas-relief from Persepolis: Sword of a Median officer

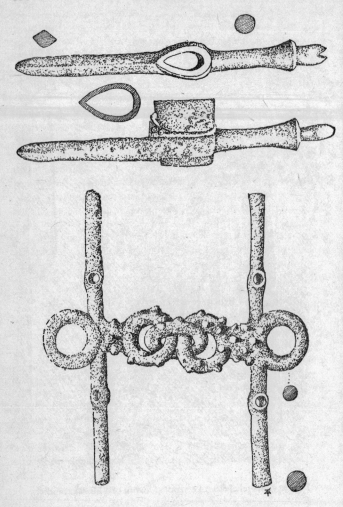

Fig. 71 – Persepolis: Battle axe and bronze bit

Assyrians heirs of Sumero-Akkadian Hurrian and Hittite art? No other people, however, attained a splendour comparable with that of Achaemenian art, even though there is an obvious lack of proportion between the column, the highest known to ancient architecture, and the procession of diminutive figures at its base.

The Persians could not wait for their art to work out its own destiny and reach maturity by a process of slow development. Borrowing from other peoples, they were able to achieve the grandiose, but their art lacked original foundations and contained the seeds of its own decay. Great under Cyrus, it attained its peak under Darius, and apart from the tendencies evident in the time of Xerxes and Artaxerxes, it remained unchanged until its end. This point had already been reached when the fire lit by Alexander destroyed its most magnificent achievements.

Economic and Social Life

The unification of the whole of Western Asia under the Achaemenian crown; the division of this immense area into satrapies with their administration under central control; the creation of land and sea routes linking the different parts of the Empire; a perfectly balanced system of tax collection; the flow of gold into the Government coffers – such were the powerful factors that gave an unprecedented impetus to the economic life of Iran. The introduction of weights and measures and, above all, of coinage (Pl. 25a–h) throughout the Empire stimulated foreign commerce, which greatly expanded owing to certain improvements in the national economy.

Small silver coins had appeared in the seventh century, but a true monetary system, bimetallic in gold and silver, was first introduced by Croesus in Lydia. This quickly spread through Asia Minor and was adopted by Darius in his Empire. The tablets from Persepolis, one group of which consists of wage lists of the men working on the construction of the palace, give a very vivid picture of the transitional period that followed the introduction of money in Iran. Previously wages had been paid in kind: meat, barley, wheat, wine, etc. In the time of Xerxes two-thirds was still paid in kind and one-third in cash. Later in the reign of the same king, payment in kind was reduced to a third only. Thus it took about half a century for money to replace goods and for the new system to become established, despite the fact that from the beginning certain transactions were entirely in cash.

Throughout the country public works were undertaken to increase productive capacity. One of the achievements of the Achaemenian kings was the digging of subterranean canals (*ghanats*) which were of vital importance on the Plateau and in other areas where water was short, such as the Syrian desert or regions of Central Asia. It seems certain that drainage of marshes was also undertaken in the Empire, since this was practised by the Greeks at the same period. Agriculture expanded, and as a result of the wars foreign countries learnt about the useful plants of Iran and started to cultivate them, in particular lucerne, which grew prolifically in the valleys of Media and was an ideal fodder for horses. The Median wars brought it to Greece as fodder for the Persian cavalry, and it was then adopted there. The same wars introduced into Europe the domestic fowl, the white dove, and the peacock, all natives of Asia.

Darius took a personal interest in arboriculture and in the propagation of new species. There is a curious letter of his to the satrap Gadatas, in which he orders him to transplant eastern plants and trees to Asia Minor and Syria: 'I commend your plan', wrote the King, 'for improving my country by the transplantation of fruit trees from the other side of the Euphrates, in the further part of Asia. …' This was not merely the desire of a satrap to gratify the caprice of a prince. It was part of an economic policy, deliberately pursued by the Persian administration with the object of spreading as widely as possible plants that would improve the standard of living for the subjects of the Empire. Thus we learn that at Damascus the Persians tried to plant a type of vine that was highly esteemed at their Court; that they introduced the first pistachios in Aleppo; and that, about this period, the famous nut of Pontus appeared in Greece. It was the Achaemenians who imported sesame into Egypt and rice into Mesopotamia and in pursuing a similar

policy on a large scale the Hellenistic kings were only following the example set by the Persian monarchs.

Being interested in the cultivation of plants, the Persians
were also concerned with the equally vital question of the exploitation of forests. It is not, of course, correct to speak of
scientific exploitation, but there must have been a measure of
planning. We have already seen that cedar of Lebanon and
teak-wood in particular were required for the royal building
projects. Timber was also extensively used for housing and
building boats, war chariots, carts and weapons, and machines
of war. Asia Minor, Crete, and the island of Cyprus were, with
the Lebanon and India, the main centres of the timber trade.
The Empire was as self-sufficient in metals as in timber. Cyprus
yielded silver, copper, and iron; Asia Minor, copper and silver;
and the same metals were also found in Palestine (Edom). Copper and iron came from the Lebanon and the upper Tigris and
Euphrates valleys; the Kerman region yielded gold and silver,
Seistan was noted for its tin and the southern Caucasus for
silver and iron, which came also from the southern shore of
the Black Sea.

Work in the quarries increased as a result of the gigantic
building programme undertaken by the kings to adorn their
capitals; the 'Foundation Charter of the Palace of Susa' in-
forms us that building-stone was quarried in the mountains of
Elam and that lapis lazuli, probably from Badak-shan, and
turquoise and carnelian from the mines of Khorasan were
used.

Hunting and, above all, fishing were much more important
in antiquity than they are to-day. A very large proportion of
the population of the ancient world, both rich and poor, lived
on bread, fish, a little oil and wine. The fisheries of the Persian
Gulf and of the Tigris and Euphrates exported salted, dried,
or cured fish in jars to a considerable distance, and we know
from Herodotus that part of the imperial tribute paid by Egypt
consisted of the profits from the fisheries.

Agricultural production during the Achaemenian period
continued to be based on the large estate worked by serfs attached to the land and bought and sold with it, and also by the

slave brought back from successful wars. Agriculture was the
key industry of the Iranian state, and was considered the
natural occupation of a free man. The small estate existed, but
was probably relatively unimportant in comparison with the
great estates with closed economies. It was above all in Fars,
the country of the master people, exempt from taxes and dues,
that the peasants, being free, owned land. Wheat and barley,
grapes and olives were grown; cattle, sheep, and goats were
raised as well as draught animals, the donkey, mule, and horse.
Bee-keeping was much practised, honey at this period being
used for sugar.

Fig. 72 – Persepolis: Achaemenian pottery

Industry began to develop in the towns although the production of goods by artisan-serfs on the large estates continued. Among the leading industries were the manufacture
of clothing, tunics, trousers and shoes, and furniture, sometimes expensively designed for the use of the rich, who also required gold, silver, and bronze vessels; these vessels of precious metals were no doubt regarded as an investment. Women
adorned themselves with jewellery and used all kinds of cos-
metics. In the poorer homes clay pots (Fig. 72) were used as
substitutes for metal vessels. It must also be emphasized that
as world commerce expanded there was an appreciable rise in
the standard of living in Iran in the Achaemenian period; ac-

cording to the economists the standard was higher in Babylonia than it was in Greece.

With the creation of the Empire, the world entered on a period of great economic prosperity. Commercial relations were inaugurated and developed between countries that had not previously traded with each other – for example, between Babylonia and Greece. As the demand for goods increased, there was a rise in the rate of interest on capital and of prices in general, except for merchandise that was difficult to transport, such as cattle. By contrast, land values fell both in Iran and in Greece.

Southern Europe entered into increasingly close economic relations with western Asia. Previously direct trade seldom went farther afield than it had done in the second millennium B.C. Under the Achaemenians, largely owing to the introduction of coinage, overland as well as maritime trade was extended to far-distant countries. This period is notable for a whole series of great voyages of exploration. As we have seen, Scylax of Caryanda on the orders of Darius undertook a voyage which lasted two and a half years, from the mouth of the Indus to Egypt. Another Persian captain, Sataspes, in the fifth century sailed beyond the Pillars of Hercules (Gibraltar). Greek, Phoenician, and Arab mariners maintained connexions between India, the Persian Gulf, Babylonia, Egypt, and the Mediterranean ports. World commerce spread farther afield, and reached the Danube and the Rhine; its extent is shown by the coin-hoards. India and Ceylon were already exporting spices such as scented barks and pepper. The jars in which wine, oil, drugs, and honey were transported provide evidence of commercial relationships with the west, and have been found in Iran itself.

Luxury goods were still numerous: beads of Egyptian glass, glass rings, amber from the north, textiles from Corinth, Miletus, and Carthage, Attic shields and swords from Pontus. Many artists and craftsmen were needed, and once again we learn from the 'Foundation Charter' that these men took years to complete undertakings on the scale of the palaces of Susa and Persepolis.

The volume of trade in the sixth and fifth centuries B.C. surpassed anything previously known in the ancient East, but its main feature was that, instead of the luxury goods of earlier periods, trade was concerned above all with ordinary, everyday products, household articles, and cheap clothing. Thus the development of industry was increasingly directed to the service of all classes of society in the Empire. It is interesting that by the middle of the sixth century B.C. there was a drop in the price of crude ores: this fall in prices may have been partly due to more economic methods of smelting, and in fact also to greater security, and therefore less costly transport.*

As a result of the introduction of coinage, internal trade probably developed more rapidly than foreign commerce, despite the closed economies of the great estates, provinces, and even of the states incorporated within the Empire. Coinage also facilitated banking activities. In Mesopotamia banking was known as early as the second millennium B.C., but the great invasions at the beginning of the Iron Age, the insecurity of the roads, and the disturbed state of the country retarded its development. The Persian Empire provided the banks with new opportunities; previously banking operations were almost exclusively in the hands of princes or temples, and only rarely in those of private individuals. Under the Achaemenians genuine private banks were established, and their business records have been preserved, like those of the bank of the descendants of Egibi of Babylon – a name identified by certain scholars with Jacob, an Israelite who belonged to the exiled community – which was founded as early as the seventh century. This bank carried on the operations of pawnbroker, floating loans, and deposits; its capital was invested in house property, fields, slaves, cattle, and in the boats that carried the merchandise. Current accounts were operated and cheques were in use. Another bank, that of Murashshu and Sons at Nippur, was founded later. It held leases, dug canals, and sold the water to the farmers; secured monopolies, such as brewing or fisheries, which were farmed out at a profit. Greece followed the example of the oriental banks and similar institutions ap-

* A. T. Olmstead, *History of the Persian Empire*, p. 82.

peared there, particularly in the temples of Delos, Olympia, and Delphi.

The building of roads as well as increased security made for rapidity of transport. At this period a method of road-building was developed that consisted in paving the softer parts of the road, and even of making artificial ruts for wheeled transport. Also from the fourth century dates the invention of shoes for beasts of burden in order to protect their hooves on the rough roads; they were made of copper, leather, or horsehair; the true iron horseshoe was not introduced until the second or first century B.C. Shipwrights designed new vessels which could sail sixty to eighty sea-miles in the day; ships of 200 to 500 tons were already being built, and of 100 to 200 tons for normal navigation on the great rivers, such as the Nile, Tigris, or Euphrates. Ports with quays were also constructed for the first time and fixed buoys were available for the mooring of ships; already ship's papers were in use, and sailors were graded in accordance with their skill.

During the Achaemenian period the first steps were taken in the organization of a national economy. The State levied dues on estates, fields, gardens, flocks, and mines. There was a land tax as well as a tax on industrial production; there were also port dues, taxes on internal trade, and tithes on sales. The taxes collected by Government agents went into the coffers of the satrapies and were then paid into the Treasury. They were used to meet the expenses of the Court, the administration, and the army, but those in charge of affairs had little interest in the development of the national economy, except in so far as concerned the construction of roads and canals, which were also used for military and administrative purposes. In the heart of the Empire the estates and temples continued to be the centre of economic life, although they were no longer monopolies and had less power.

The State nevertheless made an attempt to take an interest in the working class and, so far as the outlook of the day permitted, to regulate both work and wages. As yet there was certainly no question of labour legislation, but there are certain indications of social measures in the tablets from the Treasury at Persepolis in which the wages of each class of workmen were strictly regulated, the pay of a child, woman, or labourer, or skilled artisan being precisely calculated. Furthermore, in order to guard against fraud, the value in money was given of goods used for payments in kind, so that we learn that a jar of wine was worth a shekel, or a sheep three shekels. Even the fees of priests attached to the service of the cult were fixed; thus the magi responsible for the preparation of haoma and of libations received twelve jars of wine a year.

There must have been labour exchanges, for the Persepolis tablets mention that the workmen came from all parts of the Empire. These tablets supplement the information given in the Susa 'Foundation Charter', for they reveal that there was an imperial public works organization. In view of its scope, this organization must have had ramifications in all the countries of the Empire. The construction of towns, building at the Court, and the development of imperial and world trade were responsible for large movements of foreigners in the different parts of the Empire. The Iranians also took part in these migrations, for Babylonian tablets, which made no mention of Persian names in Babylonia before 521 B.C. thereafter list them in ever-increasing number, to such an extent that this movement may be compared to a real invasion of the master people. The administration of the Empire, which involved the army, the judiciary, and commerce, compelled the Iranians to emerge from their isolation on the Plateau and to permeate western Asia.

CHAPTER 4

The Later Achaemenians

*

THE reign of Darius marked the culminating point both of the power of the Empire and of the whole Achaemenian civilization. For nearly a century and a half the Empire lived almost exclusively on what had been fashioned by Cyrus and built up by Darius. It still held firmly together, but in the life of a nation arrested development is equivalent to a sentence of death. Failure to make any further progress and the inability to defend what had been won by the two founders led to the loss of the Empire. It is true that the Empire still experienced periods of prosperity, and even of expansion, which it owed to the few outstanding personalities who subsequently occupied the throne of Darius, and above all to the very skilful conduct of imperial diplomacy; but these transitory gains only aggravated the decline. For more than a century after the reverse suffered by Xerxes in Greece no King of Kings commanded his army in person as Cyrus and Darius had done. Rivalries, intrigues, and struggles were centred round the throne. There were assassinations within the royal house on the accession of each new ruler. So much blood had been shed within the family that on the death of the son of Artaxerxes III, a distant relative, Darius Codomanus, was the only survivor who could be found to ensure the continuity of a royal line which had exercised so powerful a rule over the nations of the world.

The resounding victories of Alexander were not due solely to his talent as a strategist, or to the bravery of the Macedonian soldiers, or even to the driving force which animated the Greeks to liberate themselves from the Persian yoke. The Achaemenian princes who succeeded Darius contributed in no small measure to the reconquest of the world by the Macedonian. They helped to prepare their own defeat, and through their egotism, lack of foresight, political sense, and patriotism, were the architects of their own downfall. It was the fate of the Iranian nation that when there arose a prince who surpassed all others in greatness and courage, as was the case with Cyrus the Younger, his career was cut short almost as soon as it began. None of those who reigned at Susa after Xerxes was capable of the generosity of Cyrus or the firmness and foresight of Darius. They made no effort to tighten the bonds between the ruling people and the many nations brought within the Empire. They sought only after power and domination, placing their gold at the service of corruption and treachery. The basic principles on which the Empire was founded were falsified and undermined. The Empire appeared to stand more firmly than ever before, but the forces of dissolution were at work within. So long as there was no serious external threat, gold could be used as a defence when trouble arose: such wealth could still give the impression of a power as great as that of its early days. Yet, to the amazement of the world, the Empire collapsed under the first blows of a resolute aggressor.

The Iranian people, who had followed their first two leaders with enthusiasm, nevertheless managed to preserve their vitality; being a young nation they were still capable of great exploits, though they did not always find leaders capable of inspiring them to fresh achievement. The fall of the Empire was a violent shock which, however, they were able to survive without suffering disintegration, and, making a slow recovery, they showed how a conquered people could triumph over the conqueror.

XERXES

Xerxes, designated by Darius as his successor, ascended the throne of Persia after twelve years as viceroy at Babylon. One of his first tasks was to suppress the revolt in Egypt begun in the lifetime of his father. This he did with great severity, forcing the Egyptian people to nurse their hatred in secret while awaiting their revenge. He acted with the same brutality towards Babylon, where revolt had also broken out; he razed the walls and fortifications of the city, destroyed its temples, and melted down the golden statue of the god Bel. After this he ceased to use the title of 'king of Babylon', calling himself simply 'king of the Persians and the Medes'. Henceforth the royal confidence was placed only in the ruling people.

Having restored peace in the Empire, Xerxes, whose inclinations were for the luxury of Court life, and who preferred directing his energies to building palaces and monuments, made no effort to continue the war. But fate decreed otherwise. The King, who was easily influenced, yielded to the pressure of the war party, which included Athenian exiles, and, deciding against his own inclination to pursue the policy of his father, he set in motion the formidable war machine forged by Darius. His army was formed of forty-six nations and commanded by twenty-nine generals, all of whom were Persians, for the Medes and Babylonians were allowed to hold only subordinate positions. Xerxes set out at the head of his army against Greece, having decided to make the attack by land rather than by sea. The Phoenicians built a bridge of boats over the Straits, which the army crossed on seven consecutive days. Meanwhile the Great King had placed himself under the protection of the gods, had performed libations, and cast a cup, a sword, and a bow into the waters. Thessaly and Macedonia offered no resistance, and the northern Greeks submitted. Together with the Greeks of Asia and Africa, more than half the Greek world was subject to the King. Already the Athenian democrats were seeking to compose their quarrel with the Persians, but the patriots rallied, formed a league under the leadership of Sparta, and decided to await the enemy at the pass of Thermopylae. In the meantime a storm scattered the Persian fleet supporting the operations; the land army, however, attacked, and found itself faced by the heroic resistance of a handful of Greeks. The battle was bloody and indecisive, and was going against the Persians when treachery turned it into a Persian victory. Attica, abandoned by its inhabitants, was invaded and Athens captured; the defence of the Acropolis by a few rebels ended in a general conflagration which destroyed everything – men, temples, and houses.

Nevertheless the Greeks did not give in: their fleet concentrated on Salamis and determined to defend the isthmus. There, in the sight of Xerxes, seated on a throne placed on rising ground, the Greek fleet destroyed that of the Great King, who lost a third of his forces (480 B.C.). The defeat was not, however, of great importance for the Persians: their army was practically intact, the conquered districts remained in their hands, and the enemy forces opposed to them were insignificant in number. But the impressionable nature of Xerxes, who had witnessed the disaster, ran away with him. The King of Kings lost his head and had the Phoenician admiral put to death, thus provoking his compatriots to desert the fleet, an example that was followed by the Egyptians. Xerxes then departed for Asia, leaving Mardonius in Greece with a third of his troops.

The commander-in-chief decided to change his tactics: entering into negotiations with Athens, he proposed an alliance, autonomy, and the payment of reparations. His overtures met with no success. He then took the offensive and again invaded Attica and Athens, setting fire before withdrawing to everything not destroyed in the previous year. The allies finally managed to form an army which timidly advanced towards the enemy. The two forces met at Plataea (479). Mardonius made the great mistake of taking part in the battle himself and was killed, and his leaderless army withdrew from the field. It was a complete victory for the Greeks; but for the Persians it was no more decisive than Salamis, since two-thirds of the army remained intact in Asia. As ill luck would have it, on the very day the battle of Plataea was fought, a new Greek fleet attacked and burnt the Persian ships which had taken refuge at Mycale near Samos, and this definitely lost the war for Persia.

After this disaster, some of the Ionians joined the Hellenic confederation which exploited its success by passing from the defence to offensive operations. Athens put itself at the head of the Delian League, and each member made its contribution to equipping the army and carrying on the struggle. Finally, on the banks of the Eurymedon (466 B.C.) the Greeks gained a further victory, which deprived the Persians of all the possessions outside Asia Minor bequeathed to them by Darius. The weakness of Xerxes had cost the Empire dear: Europe had thrown Asia back beyond the Straits.

This victory of puny Greece over the colossus of the Persian Empire may at first sight seem astonishing, but on closer study it becomes more comprehensible. The valour of the Greek soldier was certainly beyond question, but his leaders were often incompetent, irresolute, and unworthy of the troops under their command. The defeats suffered by the Persians arose from their own military and diplomatic blunders. The organization of their army left much to be desired: the hundreds of thousands of men composing it were not mustered on the basis of their armed equipment, but on that of their country of origin; there was practically no provision for victualling; the King's men had to live off the country, an impossibility for so large a body of troops. Finally, a considerable number of the ships in the fleet was Ionian, and the Asiatic Greeks in a struggle of this nature were bound to make common cause with their continental brethren. Above all, we are struck by the incompetence of the high command and amazed at the overweening confidence of the advisers of the King, himself a very weak character.

This defeat embittered Xerxes, who gave up all thought of revenge, and never again left his capitals. At Persepolis and Susa he completed the work left unfinished by his father, and busied himself with new buildings in which the inordinate pride of the despot found expression in a style that verged on the colossal.

Modern historians have tried to vindicate this son of Darius. It may be allowed that Greek tradition, which is our only source of information concerning him, inevitably lays too great an emphasis on the destroyer of Athens, and it is possible that his defeats made less impression on his contemporaries than on posterity, although there is evidence that his wars pressed hard on the country, since for nearly ten years all work was stopped at Persepolis by this greatest of all builders. His inscriptions, recently discovered at Persepolis, show him in a new light, not only as the defender but also as the propagator of the official religion. He certainly triumphed over

Egypt and Babylonia and crushed these ancient peoples with the full weight of his terrible power. But he failed to understand that the time was ripe for a change of policy towards the defeated peoples, and that the pretensions of the ruling people to domineer over the conquered in autocratic fashion were out of date. The Persians, who had hardly emerged from infancy and who ruled over people belonging to very old civilizations, should have called on their subjects to take a greater share in the direction of the Empire. But nothing of the sort was done. Hemmed in and oppressed by eunuchs, Xerxes ended his life in tragic circumstances; he was assassinated in his magnificent palace (465 B.C.).

ARTAXERXES I

The accession to the throne of the son of Xerxes, a man of weak character, began with the rebellion of his brother, the satrap of Bactria. This was quickly suppressed, and was followed by the assassination of all the King's brothers. Egypt also rose in revolt, and this time was supported by Athens, in search of wheat supplies which were then difficult to obtain from across the Straits. The first Persian operations against the Egyptians failed; but the arrival of large reinforcements in the end enabled the Persians to defeat the rebels and to dispose of the Athenian fleet in the Nile Delta. At the same time, Persian gold turned Sparta against Athens. This was a serious blow to the latter, then at the height of her power, but a rapid reversal of her policy soon restored the position. Cimon brought about an agreement between Sparta and Athens, and both entered the war against Persia; Citium was beseiged; a successful naval action was conducted near Salamis in Cyprus. The peace concluded after these operations compelled the Great King to relinquish his hold on those Greek cities of Ionia which were members of the League. Persian soldiers could no longer cross the Halys. This was a new and serious setback for the Empire, which, however, once again used its gold to provoke a conflict between Sparta and Athens.

The middle of the fifth century was for Athens under Pericles one of the most brilliant periods in its history. This small country, the founder and leader of the powerful Delian league, enriched by commerce and tribute from its allies, introduced social and political reforms which led to the triumph of democratic ideals.

At Babylon, Artaxerxes followed in the main the policy of his fathers, and although the priests of Bel-Marduk were allowed to carry on their cult, the occupation of the country by the Iranian element was actively encouraged. The King distributed Babylonian land among the Persians and the judges, and the whole of the administration became almost exclusively Persian. The college of the Magi also grew in importance there. The local population, oppressed by the heavy burden of taxation, was ready to rebel at the slightest opportunity. The situation was complicated by the revolt of the satrap of Syria; he was taken prisoner, but the King, with misguided leniency, pardoned him. Losses on the eastern frontiers were added to those on the western marches. Signs of decadence were not, as yet, much in evidence, but they constituted a warning. After the successes won by the allies, the Greeks no longer looked on the Empire as a redoubtable and formidable enemy, and Euripides, who as a writer mirrored the opinions of his age, declared that 'Asia serves as the slave of Europe'. A great change of atmosphere had taken place in the half-century.

Continuing the policy of Cyrus and Darius, Artaxerxes gave Ezra permission to return to Jerusalem with 1,500 of the Jewish families formerly exiled, but the quarrels that arose between them and those of their co-religionists who had never left Palestine compelled the King to intervene, and even to send Nehemiah, his cupbearer and confidential adviser, to settle the differences in the country. He remained friendly towards the Jewish community on condition that its responsible leaders continued to be loyal to the Persian throne. Ezra, in his character as a great founder of Judaism, gave a code of law to the community, and by his far-sighted policy of frank submission to the political power of Persia, enabled the Jewish nation to re-establish itself. In 445 B.C. the temple and walls of Jerusalem were rebuilt and the high priest was proclaimed ruler of Jerusalem and Judaea.

Artaxerxes never led his troops in person. Towards the end of his life he even lost interest in Greek affairs, although they were of vital importance for the prestige of the Empire. Slowly, almost imperceptibly, the work of Darius was breaking up. Nevertheless, the reign of Artaxerxes witnessed an extension of cultural relations between Persia and Greece which explains certain changes in the art of his age. Greek historians and men of science travelled in Egypt, Babylonia, and Iran, and acquired an increased knowledge of the history, religions, and sciences of the East. It was the age in which Herodotus wrote his *History*, and Democritus would probably not have worked out his atomic theory had he not been in contact with Babylonian scholars. The two worlds sought an exchange of knowledge, and Europe, while standing in opposition to Asia, drew on the riches which the latter had accumulated during the centuries, despite the wars, disturbances, and terrible epidemics that had afflicted West and East alike.

DARIUS II

The reign of this Prince was riddled by intrigue and corruption. Persian gold was used to incite Athens against Sparta during the Peloponnesian war. Up to a certain point this was a political success for the Empire, and a revenge for the Median wars. The revolt of the satrap of Sardis, supported by Athens, placed Sparta at the side of the Great King, who delegated to Tissaphernes, the most capable and least scrupulous of the Persian diplomats, the task of crushing the insurrection. He suppressed the revolt with the aid of Greek mercenaries, but the son of the rebel satrap took up his father's struggle. Having signed a treaty with Sparta, the King made war on Athens and retook several Greek cities, forcing them to accept Persian garrisons and to pay arrears of tribute. Shortly afterwards a new treaty recognized the sovereignty of the Great King over the Greeks of Asia. Sparta lost its privileged position, but was compensated with gold.

A revolt in Media was followed by a rising among the Egyptians, who destroyed the temple of the Jews; the Persian administration did not dare to mete out punishment in face of the over-excited state of the native population. The Peloponnesian fleet suffered defeats, and although the King financed replacements, this did not prevent Athens from continuing her successes. Once again, however, Sparta was able, with Persian assistance, to blockade the Straits, and Athens, deprived of its wheat, was forced to capitulate. Gold had won yet another victory.

The palace and Court, where the royal family was rent asunder by intrigue, faithfully reflect foreign policy. Queen Parysatis, supporting her son Cyrus against the official heir, obtained for him the satrapy of Lydia, Greater Phrygia, and Cappadocia, as well as the command of all the imperial troops of Asia Minor. Commanding such power, the young Prince was in a position, if opportunity offered, to use arms in order to gain the succession.

Like his predecessor, Darius II never left his capitals to fight at the head of his troops. It was only towards the end of his life that he directed the campaign against the *Cadusians*, and shortly afterwards he died, leaving the throne to his eldest son, Artaxerxes II.

ARTAXERXES II

The accession of this monarch was marked by an attempt on his life; he escaped the dagger-thrust of his brother Cyrus during the coronation ceremony in the temple at Pasargadae. As the result of the entreaties of his mother, Parysatis, he pardoned his brother, and even allowed him to return to his satrapy, where all Asia Minor with its troops was at his disposal. Shortly afterwards, Cyrus rose against Artaxerxes and set out at the head of a strong army to make a bid for the throne. He almost won a decisive battle in the neighbourhood of Babylon, but, carried away by the impetuosity and rashness of youth, he was killed at the very moment when his weapon struck his royal brother. Artaxerxes ordered the mutilation of the body of this young prince, to whose outstanding courage all the records pay tribute. If he had won the throne he might perhaps have arrested the decline of the dynasty.

Artaxerxes allowed the Ten Thousand Greeks in the army of his dead brother to depart; he executed their leaders by treachery, but was incapable of preventing their return march to Greece across Armenia.

The valour of the Persian soldier was no longer a major factor in imperial policy, as it had been in the time of Cyrus or Darius. It was gold that the skilful and formidable diplomats of the Great King were adepts at manipulating; in a continual stream they poured it into the coffers of the Athenians, Spartans, or of anyone who, by his intrigues, could weaken an enemy or bring him over to the royal camp. On the accession of Artaxerxes, Egypt rebelled and proclaimed its independence; the King was powerless to reconquer it, although he knew that his western satraps would not long remain in subordination if Egypt broke away. Weakened and defeated, Athens was no longer a danger, but Sparta, impressed by the retreat of the Ten Thousand, whom the Great King had been unable to prevent from leaving the very centre of his kingdom, took up arms against the Empire. Agesilaus, the great Spartan leader, carried his sword into Asia Minor, where the satraps, who were quarrelling among themselves, were unable to put a stop to the success of his soldiers. This time, however, Athens went over to the side of the Persian King, and Agesilaus was recalled to Sparta at the height of his success. He remarked, not without bitterness, that he had retreated before 10,000 Persian archers who were not soldiers but images stamped on the coins of the Great King (Pl. 25a–d). This sordid political decision shortly afterwards cost Sparta a serious defeat and its hegemony in Ionia.

While the two great Greek cities, implacable enemies pitted one against the other by Persian gold, were both exhausted by their struggles, the King of Kings proclaimed the 'Peace of the King' from the centre of Persia which he never left: all the Greek towns of Ionia were in his hands; those which opposed him would be fought by land and sea. The Greek ambassadors, before whom this royal decision was read, bowed their heads. That which Darius and Xerxes had been unable to obtain with their formidable war machine the diplomacy of Artaxerxes II had achieved by the unscrupulous use of gold.

The Greeks of Ionia once again became subjects of the Great King. The power of Athens, which under cover of the league had virtually exacted tribute, was ended; ended also was the domination of Sparta, whose protection had proved even more terrible than its taxes, despite the fact that both cities acted in the name of the noble ideal of the liberation of their Asiatic brethren. The Persians reimposed the tribute that had been fixed earlier, and this proved much lighter than the exactions of Athens and Sparta. The Ionian towns were once more included in the sphere of imperial commerce and quickly resumed their activity and former prosperity. The gains of the King did not stop there: his unceasing diplomacy revived the old quarrel between Athens and Sparta. This war, interrupted by a peace and again renewed, was exhausting for both sides. But when the two adversaries finally broke off hostilities, Thebes, supported by Artaxerxes, attacked its former enemies who had made common cause, and smashed them. By the will of the Persian King, the old Hellas lay torn and bruised, for none of the cities had the strength to restore the unity of the country or to re-establish order and peace.

At the very moment when the power of Artaxerxes seemed to have been carried beyond the Straits and the Court of Susa was dictating its orders to the Greeks of Europe, an enormous abscess came to a head in the western provinces of the Empire: the revolt of the satraps. Under the last Achaemenians, the offices of the 'eyes and ears' of the King, which under Darius had been responsible for the control of the satraps, were only a memory. A number of the satrapies had become hereditary offices; and some were so powerful that the King could neither supervise nor control them. Something of the kind happened in Republican Rome with the senatorial legates who were charged with supervising the generals. During long periods of command the leaders of the Roman armies acquired so much power that they threw off their control and ended by nominating their own legates, thus openly proclaiming the weakness of the Senate.

The picture presented by the internal state of the Empire was conducive to pessimism. Taxes oppressed the native populations and drove them to revolt. Egypt, free since the accession of Artaxerxes, had never been reconquered; large-scale operations had been undertaken against it, but had failed lamentably. The Empire slowly disintegrated: Egypt was followed by part of Cyprus, then, one after the other, Phoenicia and Syria proclaimed their independence. The rebel satraps ravaged the country, proof of the decline of imperial administration. There was a rising among the starving peasants and artisans; savagely suppressed, this added to the general unrest. Asia crumbled: Bithynia and then Caria recovered its independence; their example was followed by Lydia, Mysia, Lycia, Pisidia, Pamphylia, and Cilicia; in short, all the countries to the west of the Euphrates were in revolt. The situation within the Empire became increasingly confused, and the danger was general: not only imperial unity but the very life of the King was in peril.

The rebel satraps formed a coalition and issued their own gold coinage, hitherto the exclusive privilege of the Great King. The revolt of the western provinces and the liberation of Egypt deprived the King of half his revenues. Artaxerxes, who had achieved so much diplomatic success in Greece, saw his throne at stake. Only a short time before, the Empire had seemed to recover its unity, but this was only an accident; from lack of cohesion it was on the verge of complete disintegration. Egypt, allied with Sparta and the rebel satraps, marched against the King, its troops under the Pharaoh Takhos moved against Syria, while the rebel satrap, Datames, crossed the Euphrates. The situation was so serious that Artaxerxes himself took over the high command of the army, his son, Ochus, being incapable of arresting the advance of the Greek mercenaries in the service of the rebels. The Empire seemed doomed.

Nevertheless it was saved by the collapse of Egypt following on a rising against Takhos. The Pharaoh deserted his allies and surrendered. His surrender was followed by that of the satrap Aroandre, whom the King pardoned and permitted to retain his office, proof of the weakness of the central power. The treachery of the satraps was accompanied by the growth of armed bands who held up towns to ransom; other cities were torn by struggles between rich and poor. The rebel satrap Ariobarzanes was betrayed by his son and crucified; Datames was assassinated at a meeting of rebel satraps. The threat to the Empire disappeared as rapidly as it had come, but disturbances were still going on when Artaxerxes died. He was a ruler whom none dubbed benevolent, just, or generous, but some spoke of him as unreliable, blood-thirsty, and under the influence of his mother. Throughout his reign, which lasted nearly half a century, he had but one aim, to maintain intact the frontiers of his empire. The task was beyond his powers.

ARTAXERXES III

Fate seemed to offer Persia a last chance of salvation by bringing to the throne a man who, though without doubt cruel and brutal, possessed a will of iron and the authority of a statesman. His accession was steeped in the blood of all his brothers and sisters, to the number of several dozen. Was this too high a price to pay for re-establishing the unity of the Empire, which, faced by one menace after another, was on the downward path and could save itself only by accident? He put down the revolt of the Cadusians with great firmness and also that of the satraps. Athens, which had lent support to some of them, was given a severe warning and under the threat of war withdrew its troops. The King directed his efforts towards the reconquest of Egypt, but his first attempt was a failure. Sidon, allied to Egypt, rebelled. The King burnt the city and its thousands of inhabitants and left it in ruins. A new campaign against Egypt with fresh contingents of mercenaries resulted in total victory. The Pharaoh fled to Ethiopia, its cities were captured and their walls razed; its temples were pillaged, and the priests could ransom themselves only by the payment of enormous sums. The Empire was completely restored. It seemed to be stronger than at any time since Darius.

Greece was hard hit by this rapid revival of Persia. For some time past, patriotic spirits, such as Isocrates, had been appealing to the Hellenes to unite in the struggle against Persia and a new note had crept into their harangues: not only descendants of Greeks were Hellenes but all those who shared in their civilization. The struggle they preached passed from a defence of city states to a conflict between cultures and principles of civilization; but Greece, exhausted by its long wars, lacked strength to realize the unity essential for this new crusade. This was nevertheless achieved in spite of Greece under the compulsion of the Macedonians, a vigorous people of non-Hellenic descent, but of Greek culture. Since 360 B.C. the efforts of Philip of Macedon had been directed to annexing to his kingdom the countries situated north of the Peloponnese, Thrace and Thessaly. He became the dominant personality among the Greeks, and was regarded as the leader who would direct the crusade against Asia 'more prosperous than Europe, where the barbarians are richer than the Greeks'.

But Philip was cautious, and seeing Artaxerxes reconquer Egypt, he preferred to put the enemy on the wrong scent and negotiate with Persia, which was suppressing all revolts, even in Cyprus. In Athens, Demosthenes violently opposed the pro-Macedonian policy, seeing on the contrary the salvation of his country in an alliance with the Great King. When reproached for betraying the Asiatic Greeks, he replied with the hard truth: 'Are we really interested in these Greeks of Asia? Does not each Athenian general demand his "benevolent" contribution?' An Athenian embassy was sent to Susa and an alliance concluded. Secure on the Athenian front, the King dispatched an army which threw Philip out of Perinthus. Only danger could result for Macedonia from this alliance, and Philip decided to finish with Greece, if need be by force. Seconded by his son, Alexander, he won a decisive victory over Athens and its allies, putting an end to Greek independence (338 B.C.). In the same year Artaxerxes was poisoned: in striking down the King the murderer also struck a mortal blow at the Empire, which did not long survive him.

*   *   *

It would be inaccurate and unjust to consider the Achaemenian Persians as conquerors imposing themselves on subject peoples of whom they demanded only blind obedience to their victorious might. It is true that underlying their policy was this imperialism, the desire for power and domination, and the maintenance of subject peoples in a condition of subjection. In their time the world was divided into two very different blocks: the Persian Empire and Greece, each with a civilized and economically balanced life, each with an inclination to extend its way of life to the rest of the world. They were the first to achieve Iranian unity just as they were first to establish the unity of the oriental world, or rather, of the civilized world, the diverse elements of which were brought into a closer relationship than ever before under one political control. The Iranian nation which came into being despite its ethnographical diversity, emerged triumphant from the chaos of languages and civilizations. The Persians not only founded a world empire, but they also achieved a world civilization with a very wide influence.

The composite constitution of this empire should not be regarded as a sign of inferiority: for other great civilizations – for example, that of Rome – followed a like course. The Persians were as successful in administration as they were in their economy and commerce. Recent research has proved that outlying countries affected by Achaemenian expansion were profoundly transformed under their beneficent influence. Thus Chorasmia, as well as other eastern possessions, enjoyed nearly three and a half centuries of peace – a rare event in the history of eastern countries at this period – during which time it experienced real urban and agricultural development. At the same period there grew up an irrigation system of subterranean canals, as in the oases of southern Egypt. Achaemenian art spread far beyond the frontiers of Iran itself: its influence may be discerned in Egypt, Cyprus, on the coasts of the Black Sea, and in particular among the Scythians. The Achaemenians maintained an atmosphere favourable to the development of science, and we know that under Darius a great Babylonian astronomer, Naburimanni, made a study of lunar eclipses and arrived at calculations more accurate than those of Ptolemy and Copernicus; mention should also be made of another astronomer, Kidinnu of Sippar, who towards the end of the Empire discovered the precession of the equinoxes and arrived at an exact calculation of the length of the year, making an error of only seven minutes, sixteen seconds.

Abandoning narrow nationalism, the Achaemenians as a concession to the imperial interest introduced a western tongue, Aramaic, as the official language of their State, and adopted its alphabet. Further, they introduced it to India, where under its influence Kharoshthi the oldest known Indian alphabet was developed. In India, too, Achaemenian art and architecture made their mark: excavations at Patna have revealed that palaces built in the time of the Maurya dynasty reproduced the plan of those at Persepolis. Indian traditions preserve the memory of Persian builders who in popular imagination assumed the aspect of Titans, and this explains the presence of traces of Achaemenian influence in the art of the Maurya as well as in that of Gandhara. Furthermore, it is admitted that from contact between the Persian language and that of the new peoples of the adjacent Indus valley, there arose 'for the use of conqueror and conquered, a sort of mixed dialect of the style of Urdu'.

Tolerant in religious matters and themselves inclining towards monotheism, the Achaemenians were particularly well disposed towards monotheistic peoples, above all the Jews. That the Jewish religion, community, and the very state itself was able to survive and later to become the forerunner of Christianity was in large measure due to the benevolent policy of Achaemenian Persia. Achaemenian religion was not without influence outside Iran. It is considered that the introduction by Artaxerxes II of the cult of Anahita, and the worship of her statues set up in the temples of Susa, Persepolis, Ecbatana, Babylon, Damascus, Sardis, and Bactria, must have helped to unite all the peoples of the Empire in a common cult, the traces of which long remained alive among the people of Asia Minor. Under another aspect, Achaemenian religion, passing by the north-west, penetrated into Cappadocia, and then into Cilicia, where the pirates adopted the cult of Mithra, which in the

Roman army later became the predominant cult. Furthermore, the old Semitic idea of some kind of survival after death was developed by the Persians into a belief in immortality; it penetrated into Jewish doctrines, and through this filter, Zoroastrianism influenced Christian theology.

Technically, as well as in religious and spiritual development, the Achaemenians were prime movers in the transmission of ideas between East and West; they brought together these two worlds and their civilizations, and thus marked out for the future the path to be followed by the Iranian world.

CHAPTER 5

West Against East and the Reaction of the Orient

*

THE assassination of Artaxerxes III threw the political chess-board of the world into confusion at the very moment when a new force, Macedonia, had entered the play. Philip, who had formed a league representing united Greece, assembled a strong Macedonian army, supported by the Greek fleet, against Persia, where the throne was occupied by a young prince, the pawn of powerful eunuchs. Philip himself, how-ever, soon fell victim to an assassin's dagger, a crime in which the Court of Susa was implicated, and was succeeded by his son, Alexander, who, with the enthusiasm of youth, carried on the task begun by his father. On the throne of the Achae-menians, the son of Artaxerxes had been poisoned and replaced by a relative, Darius III Codomannus. This brave man might perhaps have saved his country if it had not been faced, for the first time in its history, by a united Greece, a coalition forcibly imposed, but led by a military genius, at the head of his Macedonian warriors. The great mistake made by Codo-mannus in the pride of his power was to despise the young Alexander and under-estimate the strength of his army.

The struggle that was now joined was fought out in the great tract of territory which extended from Macedonia and the Greek city states as far as Persia itself. Persia was still in full possession of its resources, but on many occasions it must have revealed its weakness to the world, as when its military leaders proved incapable of stopping the retreat of Xenophon and his Ten Thousand Greeks or of preventing Agesilaus from reconquering practically the whole of Asia Minor up to the Halys. Many defeats in the wars against Egypt and the reverses suffered in Cyprus had not helped to raise the prestige of the Persian army among its enemies. There were occasions when a powerful ruler did not know how to use his army or was slow to reach decisions, and when his orders were not carried out promptly. And although the Empire had secured successes in its struggle with Hellas, these must be attributed in large measure to dissensions among the Greeks. For a long time past the courage of Greek mercenaries and the skill of their generals had played a preponderant part in Persian victories. But to each general was attached a Persian noble who, although often incompetent, was the supreme commander, and the resulting disagreements weakened action. Persian domination in most of the countries of the Empire was tolerable; it was a regime which combined firmness with good will. There was little likelihood that Persia would one day attempt to reconquer Hellas, but it could draw on infinite resources in its own defence, and the task of Alexander was by no means an easy one.

Greece was torn between two schools of thought. For one, the subordination of the Greeks of Asia to the Great King was a humiliation. If the Hellenes were incapable of achieving the unity which could give them sufficient strength to liberate their brethren from servitude, what did it matter if it was Hellenized Macedonia which achieved this object? Asia Minor as far as the line from Cilicia to Sinope must be wrested from the empire of the King of Kings. Once liberated, it could be used to settle the fluid mass of mercenaries who were a potential source of trouble, while its flourishing commercial centres would be linked to the West, and so provide new markets for the expanding Greek economy.

To the second school of thought, the Persian yoke did not appear so terrible; the Greek towns of Asia Minor were prosperous and suffered far less than during the short periods of 'liberation' by the Greek armies. The Great King was far away, and his rule easier to bear than the domination of the rough Macedonians was likely to be. The idea that a war of revenge against the Persians might have to be paid for by Macedonian hegemony, and that the unity of Greece might be achieved under a foreign dynasty was more repugnant to them than the domination of Persia. The latter had for a long time offered itself as an arbiter of the Greek people and praise of the might of a powerful ruler as against the unstable power of the masses even found an echo in the teaching of the great philosophical schools of the age.

Macedonia, an agricultural country *par excellence*, had certain features in common with Iran, in particular with Persia, which was the core of the Empire, providing its political direction and its 'military backbone'. As in Iran, the population of Macedonia was divided into tribes and clans; under the authority of chiefs, who were large landed proprietors, lived a free peasantry, and over all stood the King, exercising religious, judicial, and military power. Philip had reorganized the country, united the nation round the throne, and given power to the monarchy. His great achievement was the creation of an army in which the free Macedonians, without severing the links binding them to their tribes, provided the infantry, while the nobility furnished the famous cavalry. In the event of war, it was no longer the nobles who came forward with their troops, but the army of the King, commanded by officers appointed by him. By the time Philip was succeeded by his son the nation, and in particular the nobles forming the *élite* of the army, were ready to follow the youthful hero and under his leadership to perform mighty exploits.

The march of Alexander against the Persian Empire is often spoken of as a crusade, and there are indeed certain analogies between the irruption of the Hellenes under Alexander into Asia and European expansion in the Middle Ages. The later movement was inspired by the noble ideal of liberating the Holy Places. But its driving force was more mundane, and combined the desire of the French barons for territorial conquest with the commercial interests of the Italian maritime republics. Alexander, who was perhaps the only military leader of his age to cherish the pan-Hellenic ideal, placed his expeditions of conquest under the banner of Greek liberation from the Persian yoke. The Macedonian nobility dreamed of conquests for glory and loot, and certain elements among the

Greeks hoped for the extension of their commerce to the rich markets of the Orient.

The young King was aware of the dissensions and internecine struggles dividing the Greeks, but the task left by his father had to be carried on and completed; deeds of glory awaited him, and in spite of the Greeks he set forth as their avenger, though serving above all the interests of his own Macedonia. A harsh warning was given to those Hellenes who had been won over by Persian agents: to ensure their loyalty to the league, which had placed him at the head of the crusade, and to secure his rear, Alexander burnt Thebes, which had assassinated the Macedonian garrison, and sold its inhabitants into slavery. His 'alliance' with Greece brought him in all 7,000 men and a feeble Athenian fleet which, owing to lack of money, he soon disbanded. For a champion of the sacred cause of Hellenism, the support accorded him by the Greek world was indeed parsimonious. With his small army, consisting almost entirely of Macedonians, and a general staff that included scholars, historians, geographers, and botanists, Alexander crossed the Dardanelles by boat at the very spot where Xerxes had not so long before taken his soldiers across on a bridge. Troy was one of the first towns to be captured, and there he sacrificed to the *manes* of the Greek heroes, proclaiming by this gesture that a new war against Asia had begun.

Darius did not take this expedition seriously, for it seemed even more feeble than that of Philip. So confident was he of success that he gave orders for Alexander to be seized and brought to Susa. An army consisting of native soldiery, Persian cavalry, and Greek mercenaries, hardly stronger than that of the Macedonian, was sent to stop him. The Greek commander in the service of the King was more prudent, and proposed that, in order to draw Alexander farther into the interior of the country, the Persian army should fall back, leaving 'scorched earth' behind it, but his advice was rejected. Instead, the satraps sought a battle, imagining that it would be an easy victory, and so furthered the plans of Alexander. The first clash was at the Granicus, where the Persian army was defeated, but it was a very close fight in which the young Macedonian nearly lost his life. The remnants of the Persian cavalry were not pursued, but the Greek mercenaries, surrounded by the Macedonians, were punished as traitors to the cause of the Hellenes and massacred, almost to the last man. The way to Asia Minor lay open.

One after the other, the Greek cities were taken and declared free. But there were some, like Halicarnassus, that wished to remain loyal to the Great King, proof that the Persian yoke did not weigh heavily. Halicarnassus was burnt during a siege. Attempts by the Persian fleet to cut Alexander off from his bases in Europe failed. After he had crossed Asia Minor and reorganized its administration on the tripartite system of command introduced by the Persians, which consisted of a satrap, a general, and a director of finance, Alexander penetrated Cilicia, followed the coast, and met the army of Darius near the Cilician Gates at Issus. Once again an error in tactics proved disastrous for the King of Kings: instead of waiting for the army of Alexander, as he was advised to do by a Macedonian deserter, Darius advanced to meet him. The Persian army was unable to withstand the shock of the Macedonian charge, and Darius, seeing his troops waver, abandoned the struggle and fled (Pl. 26). By rapid marches, Parmenio took Damascus, where he found the Persian baggage-train and royal family; the mother of Darius, his wife, and children fell into the hands of Alexander, who treated them as befitted their royal rank. The troops also seized an immense amount of booty as well as the ambassadors of Sparta, Athens, and Thebes, who had come to treat with the Persian King, thus showing how little the crusade was considered as Greek by the Hellenes.

Alexander had realized the aim of Philip: the Greeks of Asia Minor had been liberated and the western part of the Empire was thus in the hands of a young conqueror who saw fresh deeds of glory awaiting him. He did not go in pursuit of Darius, but decided to secure his rear and postpone his conquest of the eastern part of the Empire. The Phoenician cities surrendered and were occupied. While he was engaged in the capture of Marathos, Alexander received a letter from Darius offering him friendship and alliance and asking that his family should be set free in exchange for a very large sum of money. To this attempt to open diplomatic negotiations Alexander replied with a refusal, and summoned the King to recognize him as overlord. The commander-in-chief of the Corinthian league had become arbiter of the fate of the Great King.

Tyre alone of all the Phoenician cities put up a stubborn resistance, which delayed Alexander for seven months. During this siege he received a second letter from Darius offering him an enormous ransom in return for his captive family, the cession of territories as far as the Halys, and the hand of his daughter in marriage. In the council of his 'companions' voices were raised urging Alexander to accept the offer, but he was already aiming at a universal monarchy in which there was no place for two Kings of Kings, and the message of Darius met with a fresh refusal.

Tyre finally fell, and its destruction was followed by the annihilation of the maritime and commercial predominance of the Phoenicians. Alexandria, newly founded by the Macedonian, replaced Tyre, and the maritime power of Greece that of the Asiatics.

After losing another two months before the walls of Gaza, where Alexander was wounded, the army entered Egypt, encountering no resistance and being acclaimed by the native population, whom hatred of the Persians aroused by the oppressive policy of Ochus drove into alliance with the Macedonians. Alexander visited the temple of Ammon, where the great god announced that he was his son and the oracle foretold his domination of the world. As legitimate Pharaoh, with his chapel in the temple of Karnak, Alexander reorganized the administration of the country, giving a large share in it to the native population, but leaving Macedonians in control of the army. He then turned towards Mesopotamia and crossed the Euphrates and Tigris; Darius, for some incomprehensible reason, made no attempt to defend these two rivers.

With his back to the Persian mountains, Darius prepared for the final defence of his country, gathering the strongest army his means would allow. But before measuring his strength against that of his adversary, he made a third attempt to save

his Empire by diplomacy. Distressed by the death of his wife,
to whom Alexander had given a royal funeral, separated from
the rest of his family, who were still held captive, broken by
military defeat, the King suggested to Alexander that the Euphrates should form the frontier of their two Empires – this
was to be the dowry of his daughter. He agreed that his son
should remain as hostage and offered 30,000 talents as ransom
for his mother and two daughters. He would thus have divided
his power with Alexander, who, as his son-in-law, would have
been associated in his rule. A third refusal by the Macedonian
put an end to these overtures. The two armies met at Gauga-
mela, 'the pasturage of camels', near Arbela in the foothills of
the Assyrian mountains 331 B.C.

Once again, as in the time of Xerxes, the Persian army was
grouped by satrapies, its command taking no account of advances made in the science of warfare, particularly under
Philip. Darius was at the centre, surrounded by his Immortals
and covered by the Greek mercenaries. The records give great
credit to the Persian nobility, whose admirable courage in the
battle was in no way inferior to that of their fathers who had
conquered the Empire. But they knew nothing of the new
military tactics. Their chariotry and elephants had little effect,
the Persian army broke, and Darius fled to Ecbatana, although
his desertion did not end the heroic resistance which was kept
up by formations from eastern Iran far into the night. To all
intents and purposes the war was over. It took Alexander several more years to pacify the Empire, but from this moment a
section of its subjects recognized him as their Great King
of Kings. The loss of the battle reacted on Darius, and his
desertion of the army was tantamount to abdication of his
throne.

The entry of Alexander into Babylon, where flowers were
thrown to him, was a triumph. He retained the Persian satrap
in the city and ordered the rebuilding of the temple of Bel, destroyed by Xerxes. Susa surrendered without resistance, and
an enormous treasure was found in the palace, where the
family of Darius, which had followed the army, was finally installed. The satrap of Susa was also left in his post, but the

commander of the citadel and the treasurer were replaced by Macedonians. The young King was beginning to realize that it would be impossible to govern this great Empire, part of which he had already conquered, with only a handful of Macedonians, and that the Iranian element must be recalled to take its share. By mixing the nations in the army he would prepare for their fusion in the Empire; accordingly he ordered the creation of a corps of 3,000 young Iranians who were to be trained and educated in western military science.

When he left Susa, Alexander was faced with Iran proper, its mountains inhabited by a privileged nation capable of offering stubborn resistance. He met with some opposition, but as there was no concerted action it was not dangerous. By his conduct, attitude, personality, and prestige, Alexander quickly rallied to his person the great majority of Persians. Indeed, he arrived on the Plateau as the successor of Darius. The resistance offered by an army under a satrap at the 'Persian Gates' was only an episode, and Alexander reached Persepolis, where he found another treasure. There was no longer any question of a crusade: Alexander stayed there four months, made various small expeditions to reduce the mountain peoples, and visited the tomb of Cyrus, ordering that it should be left undisturbed. Then, towards the end of his stay, a serious accident caused the royal city to disappear in flames. Did Alexander deliberately order this destruction as a reprisal for the sack of Athens by Xerxes, as some believe? Was it a political and symbolic act by which the Macedonian extinguished the glorious halo of the Achaemenians; or, as others think, was it an accidental blaze, kindled by carelessness during one of the wild drinking bouts sometimes indulged in by the young King with his companions and the women who followed them everywhere?

If political revenge was desired, it was more likely to have been exacted from Susa than from Persepolis. Susa was in effect the great capital of the world, and it was there that all those won over by the Hellenic policy of the Great King came to make obeisance: ambassadors, dethroned kings, and discredited politicians. The Greeks do not seem to have been conscious of the existence of Persepolis, which is not once mentioned in Western sources before the time of Alexander. And why should Alexander destroy his own property? for when he entered Persepolis he was no longer an enemy or conqueror, but the future son-in-law of Darius, the successor of the last Achaemenian, whose tragic death he avenged by the terrible punishment of his assassin. His attitude towards the royal house and Iranian people was unambiguous. In the course of his campaigns he never destroyed a conquered city, nor was it a part of his policy to massacre the vanquished, as had happened before so many times in Iran during foreign invasions. An exception must be made in the case of Persepolis, however, which, according to the Classical writers, among them Diodorus Siculus, Justin, and Plutarch, Alexander destroyed and looted; he is also alleged to have treated the inhabitants with the utmost brutality. Voltaire was right when he said that Alexander had built more towns than other conquerors of Asia had destroyed. He left the Persian administrators at their posts; he attracted the youth of the country, who shared his military glory, and participated equally with the Macedonians in the destinies of the Empire. Not only did he never think of destroying Persian civilization, but, on the contrary, sought to fuse the two worlds of Greece and Iran. When he was at Persepolis all resistance by Darius had ceased, and Iran and the Empire was in his hands; there was no need for him to build the world of his dreams on ashes. Master of Iran, he was 'the last of the Achaemenians'.

Learning that Bessus, viceroy of Bactria, held Darius prisoner and was taking him east, Alexander set off in pursuit. He reached the camp of the fugitives near Damghan and there found Darius stabbed to death by his satrap. Tradition relates that he covered the body of this unfortunate monarch with his mantle and sent it to his mother at Susa. He then continued his march east. After four and a half years of campaigning, his veterans considered that Alexander had attained his objective and demanded to return, but his speech won them over, and they declared themselves ready to follow him still farther. It was at this period that Alexander began to introduce the pomp of the Oriental Court and to clothe himself in the purple of the Achaemenian kings. The Orient had already vanquished its first occidental conqueror.

The occupation of eastern Iran continued; the few disloyal satraps were punished, and most of the others retained in their posts. Everywhere Alexander founded new Alexandrias: at Herat, in Drangiana, in Arachosia, on the southern slopes of the Hindu Kush, the Alexandria of the Caucasus, where he spent the winter of 330–329 B.C. The pacification of the northern borders of the Empire took time, and for two years Alexander was engaged in putting down the revolts of the Sogdians. He also had trouble with his companions, who were jealous of the Orientals, an increasing number of whom were joining his retinue. It is possible that his marriage to Roxana, the daughter of an important chief whom he had made viceroy of Bactria, may have had a political motive: an alliance with the most turbulent elements of this district. He advanced fighting up to the river Jaxartes, to the limits of the settled Iranian world, where he built a line of fortresses and yet another Alexandria, the modern Khojand.

In the spring of 327 B.C. Alexander crossed the Hindu Kush and descended into India. Europe, which before Alexander had ended at the Straits, had pushed its frontiers as far as the Indus. The river that marked the eastern limit of the Iranian Empire was crossed and the victorious army had reached the Hyphasis (Beas) when the Macedonian soldiers informed the King of their refusal to continue the campaign. Fighting and pacifying the Indians, Alexander marched down the Indus, built a fleet, which under the command of Admiral Nearchus was instructed to reach the Persian Gulf, and dividing the army into two groups, one to return by way of Arachosia, the other under his command to follow the coast and maintain contact with the fleet, he gave the order to return. After several months of difficult marching, which cost him dearly in effectives, the two armies joined up near the modern Bandar Abbas, continued to Pasargadae, and finally, in the spring of 324 B.C., reached Susa.

The five years that had elapsed since Alexander's first stay in the great capital had strengthened his resolve to realize the union of the two worlds. The mutiny of his army in India, conspiracy among his closest companions in arms, who were incapable of rising to the level of the aspirations of his genius, determined the young King to push forward with his political policy. He reviewed the corps of the Iranian nobility whose numbers he had continued to increase; he married the daughter of Darius, Statira, gave her sister in marriage to Hephaestion, and united twenty-four of his generals and 10,000 Greek soldiers to Iranian girls at festivities lasting five days.

He left Susa, followed the old royal road to Ecbatana, and thence went on to Babylon – the last tour of this successor of the Achaemenians, for shortly afterwards he fell sick and died in the old capital of the Orient at the moment when everything seemed ready for a new conquest, that of Carthage (323 B.C.).

Alexander devoted the last months of his life to the organization of his Empire. His measures were much influenced by the ideas of the great Achaemenian kings, which, however, he infused with broader and more humane principles. He kept the division of the Empire into satrapies, retained a number of Persian satraps at Babylon, Susa, Paraetakine, in Aria, and in Media, the last being governed by Atropates, who gave his name to Atropatene, known to-day as Azerbaijan. The Macedonian was aware of the weakness of the previous central government that had often proved powerless to prevent the satraps from asserting their autonomy, and to remedy this, he instituted a duality of power by doubling the Persian satrap with a commander of Macedonian troops. All the means adopted by the Achaemenians to maintain the unity of Asia were known to him. The farther he went, the more he felt the need to rely on the conquered people – a policy which the Achaemenians had been very reluctant to adopt. The Greeks and Macedonians could not understand how their King could place them on the same footing as the Iranians; but the loyalty and courage of these peoples won the sympathy of Alexander and the opposition of which he was conscious among his companions and soldiers may have inclined him still further towards his new subjects. He desired to govern in their interests as much as in those of the Greeks and Macedonians. Having conquered Egypt, where royalty was conceived of as divine, and Persia, where the King was a kind of emanation of the god, Alexander, whom Zeus-Ammon had recognized as his son, introduced the deification of his person, not with the aim of becoming the object of an official cult, but as a political measure that should give him a certain authority with the Greek cities. He introduced the *proskynos* or prostration required by the etiquette of the Achaemenian Court from every Persian subject in the presence of the Great King of Kings – a measure directed particularly towards his Oriental subjects.

When his army reached the Indus, only a quarter of the force was Macedonian, the rest being subjects of the Persian Empire. Administrative as well as military necessity required the participation of Persian elements, and Alexander envisaged this as a collaboration, not of victors and vanquished, as the Achaemenians had conceived it, but between equals. This conception goes far to explain the attitude of the Iranians towards their new ruler. They did not feel themselves a conquered nation governed by a foreigner, but remained masters of their country. To convince them of the sincerity of his intentions, Alexander gave them entry to the circle of his companions, receiving into it the brother of Darius and certain nobles. Thirty thousand young men of the best families were educated by Greek teachers, who taught them their language as well as military science; Persian soldiers were incorporated in the infantry.

If the eastern pomp of Alexander shocked the Macedonians, the favours he granted to the Orientals aroused their jealousy, for they thought their own interests suffered. Hence the conspiracies: in 330 B.C. in Drangiana, in 328 in Maracanda (Samarcand), in 327 in Bactria, and in 324 in Opis. The fusion of races and civilizations could be achieved only by a single authority, and these revolts not only left the young King unmoved but never, during the years of his campaigns, seriously imperilled this aim which he steadfastly pursued. It was necessary to give as much to the Iranians as to the Macedonians and Greeks. Towns and colonies were founded not only for the purpose of installing garrisons and overawing the turbulent or unruly population, but also and above all to create a mixed civilization in which the two groups of people could share equally.

The reconstruction of the Empire, which stretched from the Balkans to the Indus, could not be limited to political and administrative measures: ethnic problems had to be dealt with concurrently. The new Great King put into practice ideas that revolutionized previous conceptions of the principles of power. Linking the West to the East and achieving the unity of which the Achaemenians had dreamed, Alexander gave a great impetus to the economic life of a world rid of its divisions. It was hardly possible for a line of policy in this field to be worked out and put into execution during his short lifetime. But, guided by the example of his predecessors, and like them concerned chiefly with military and administrative ends, Alexander paid great attention to lines of communication and, in particular, to navigation, from canal networks to sea routes connecting continents. The voyage of his admiral Nearchus, a repetition of the exploit of Scylax ordered by Darius; the projects for exploring the coasts of Arabia and the Caspian Sea, which he believed communicated with the Black Sea, accorded with these preoccupations. The use of the Lake Habbaniyah as a catchment area, a modern undertaking, had been projected by Alexander with the idea of regulating the Euphrates floods and ensuring the normal working of the canals.

He did not hoard treasure as the Achaemenian kings had done. The wealth found in the capitals of the Empire was converted into silver units of currency, putting an end to imperial, satrapal, or provincial issues. As it was the only coinage in circulation throughout his vast Empire it drew closer the economic bonds between the different areas. Very generous by nature, Alexander freely distributed gifts and rewards, enriching his army and through it all countries, including Greece. The inhabitants of this country found fresh resources open to them within the Empire: impoverished by long wars, Greece saw an opportunity to send its population abroad in search of work and not only as mercenaries in the service of the King of Kings. There is evidence that several ancient cities of Syria and Palestine experienced a revival of prosperity in the time of Alexander, but the majority of Greeks who left their country settled in the towns and colonies founded by the Macedonian, some of which also absorbed the veterans or invalids from the army. The creation of these centres at strategic and economic points attracted a considerable number of Greek merchants who found a large western clientèle among the soldiers and officials, and also before long among the Iranians, who were won over by the way of life of the Hellenes and Macedonians. As trade increased, the old type of commercial centre changed. Roads and canals, intercourse between the towns, made it possible for merchants to penetrate deeper into the various parts of the country, to introduce commercial practices into more and more distant corners of the Empire, and to change the economic character of the region. It seemed that the economic and political union of Iranians and Greeks, strengthened by the prevailing peace and security and based on lofty principles, would have a lasting future. But the death of its founder who by his genius had made such a clean break in the 'chain of historic events' led the world towards other destinies.

THE SELEUCIDS

The Empire of which Alexander the Great laid the foundations did not survive him. The conception of its unity soon disappeared, and for forty years after his death the world was plunged in murderous struggles between his former companions. The commanders of armies or powerful satraps, trained in the hard school of Philip or Alexander in which bravery and daring gained men the highest honours, now aspired to command not armies, but nations. Alexander's ideal of uniting the peoples into a single comity by the renunciation of their nationalism was forgotten. After the battle of Ipsus (301 B.C.) the political organization of the world was stabilized with the formation of three kingdoms: a Macedonian monarchy in Europe; a Ptolemaic monarchy in Egypt; and a Seleucid monarchy in Asia. Of Alexander's successors, Seleucus more than any other was in sympathy with his ideas and the best fitted to

assimilate himself to the Iranian world. He had been made leader
of the cavalry formations of Persian nobles after the capture of
Susa and had transformed them into a homogeneous body
numbering several tens of thousands of warriors. Married to
Apama, a noble Persian, he founded a dynasty in which Iranian
and Macedonian blood was mingled in equal proportions.
Satrap of Babylonia, he finally inherited the Achaemenian Empire shorn of Egypt, Palestine, southern Syria, and certain
parts of the coast of Asia Minor. The only territory he himself
ceded was on the eastern marches, in Arachosia and Gedrosia.
This was given to King Chandragupta of India in exchange for
elephants which he needed for the protection of his western
frontiers. But after his death his Empire began to disintegrate,
a process that continued until its final fall. Founder of two capitals, Seleucia on the Tigris which took the place of Babylon,
and Antioch on the Orontes in Syria, he reorganized the political, administrative, and economic foundations of his Empire,
which he divided into two parts grouped round these two
centres and linked together by a 'royal road'. As long as his
successors remained in possession of the eastern capital the
kingdom could look forward with hope to the future. The capture of Seleucia by the Parthians a century and a half later reduced the Empire to a small Syrian state that was soon absorbed by Rome.

Heirs of the Achaemenians in practically all their possessions
and having very largely adopted the principles of their administration, the Seleucids were compelled to strive for the
unity of their State, notwithstanding the diversity of its peoples
and their heterogeneous civilization. This was an aim their
predecessors had only temporarily succeeded in realizing, and
they themselves were no more successful in the task. They
were faced by the same causes that had progressively weakened
the Achaemenian Empire and led to its unhappy end: the wars
they engaged in with other monarchies, first Macedonia and
Greece and then the Parthians and Rome; the fight they waged
against the separatist tendencies of the various countries included in their possessions; the efforts they had to make to
exact obedience from their satraps; and intrigues at Court and

the rivalries of pretenders, often ending in assassination. Even the use of gold, which opened the door to corruption, was not disdained by the kings of the second century B.C. who bought Roman senators with the object of securing the armed intervention of Rome against their enemies. But for the price of victory, the Romans remained in the country, and too late the Seleucids perceived that they had delivered up the Orient. It is true that, as among the Achaemenians, some of their princes made great and indeed praiseworthy attempts to bolster up the Empire; but they were powerless to arrest the encroachment of the two forces which profited from their weakness: the slow but constant rise of the Iranians and that of Rome, which at the beginning of the second century dealt the Empire a blow from which it never recovered.

Seleucus I associated his son, the future Antiochus I, in his rule and, dividing the Empire, entrusted him with the best provinces, those of the Orient, with Seleucia as his residence. But under Antiochus I (280–261 B.C.) the first signs of weakness appeared, and it is generally considered that Persia became independent. The reign of his successor, Antiochus II (261–246), was marked by serious territorial losses, Bactria beginning to break away and Parthia with Hyrcania seceding about 249–248 B.C.

The King, occupied with wars in the west, was powerless to enforce respect for his authority. The satrapy of Bactria included the northern plain of modern Afghanistan, and its border extended north of the Oxus, the modern Amu Daria. This frontier march had been established to guard against the perpetual danger of Iranian nomads and nearly 20,000 soldiers of Alexander, the sick or wounded, had been settled in newly founded towns in the province. On the death of the Macedonian in 323 B.C. they had risen in revolt, demanding to be repatriated; some were massacred, but enough nevertheless remained to form an armed force in the country. Later a certain Greek named Diodotus, who was satrap of Bactria during the reigns of Antiochus II and Seleucus II, probably assisted by the descendants of these Greeks, gradually made himself independent of his overlords; on Diodotus' death, his son openly

assumed a royal title, allying himself with the enemies of the
Seleucids in about 225 B.C.

Whether it was the remoteness of the Greeks in Bactria –
the most advanced post of the Hellenic world towards the
East – or the foreign menace hanging over this satrapy with a
Central-Asiatic frontier, the fact remains that only in Bactria
were the two peoples, Greeks and Iranians, able to establish a
mutual understanding that proved both firm and lasting. This
association was achieved in spite of the fact that the two parties
represented two different ways of life arising from two different social and economic systems. An agricultural and pastoral
country, Bactria also owed its wealth to its transit trade, for it
linked the West with China on the one hand and with Siberia,
rich in gold, and with southern Russia, on the other. Its markets and bazaars made it an important factor in international
commerce. It was an Iranian country with a feudal society in
which the landed aristocracy lived in fortified strongholds and
managed their estates, and the peasantry also sheltered in fortified villages. It underwent no changes after the arrival of the
Greeks, whose military science brought greater security to its
frontiers. The new masters altered nothing in the economic
structure of the country, but by founding towns and colonies
and introducing a commercial and industrial population they
brought increased wealth from which the Iranian aristocracy
greatly benefited. Thus it came about that the Greeks of Bactria, separated from the Empire by the Parthian revolt and
allied with the Iranians, formed a community which for over
two centuries spread Greek civilization in India and Central
Asia and only succumbed to the flood of a new and formidable
invasion of Iranian nomads at the end of the second century
B.C.

The loss of Parthia with Hyrcania, that is, the districts situated to the south-east and east of the Caspian Sea, followed
within a year or so on that of Bactria, and is to be explained
less by the strength of this semi-nomad people than by the
fundamental weakness of the Seleucid Empire. It was not yet
a reaction of the Iranian world against the foreign element installed in its country. This was to come later, when Iran, roused

by the menace of Rome, regained its national consciousness. It was the Parthians who gave the signal, but it took them over a century to recover Iran from the Greeks and to stabilize their western frontiers on the Euphrates, which thereafter remained in the Iranian world until the Arab invasion. Seleucus II (246–226) attempted to restore the situation in the east. The Parthians fell back before his army, which penetrated the eastern provinces, but a serious revolt at Antioch forced the King to abandon the campaign and return to Syria. The Parthians, a fluid and wary force, returned and won an easy 'victory'. After the death of Seleucus II losses in Asia Minor were added to those in the east. Half a century after the death of the founder of the Empire the imperial lands stretched no farther than the Taurus in the West and Media in the East.

At this critical juncture the throne of Antioch was occupied by Antiochus III (223–187), a prince endowed with fierce energy and a wide political outlook. On his accession, a revolt of the satraps of Media and Persis broke out of the Plateau; the Parthians, allied to the Bactrians, threatened Media. Antiochus crushed the satraps and set out for the East on an 'armed patrol' that was to last no less than eight years. Passing through Cappadocia, he reached Armenia, where King Xerxes recognized his suzerainty and married his sister; he then crossed the whole of Iran from north to south, visited Susa, and returned to Ecbatana to carry on the campaign against the Parthians. Arsaces III fell back before his army and finally submitted and brought tribute. Antiochus advanced towards the frontier of Bactria, where Euthydemus, who had founded a new dynasty in place of that of Diodotus, put up an energetic resistance that was ended by a treaty of friendship and the marriage of his son Demetrius to the daughter of Antiochus. After crossing the Hindu Kush, the Seleucid King met the King of the Maurya of India in the valley of the Kabul and renewed friendship with him. He returned to Persis through Arachosia, Drangiana, and Carmania, visited the western shore of the Persian Gulf with its centres of the incense trade, crossed over to the islands celebrated for their pearl fisheries and returned to Seleucia on the Tigris. There is reason to believe that the interests of imperial trade with the East by land and sea routes had something to do with this lengthy tour. Intoxicated with success, Antiochus decided to attach Macedonia to his Empire and crossed the Straits, but Rome dealt him a fatal blow; he lost the battle of Magnesia and the peace of Apamea (188 B.C.) not only deprived him of his possessions in Asia Minor but imposed on him a crushing tribute.

Antiochus IV (175–164 B.C.) was the last great Seleucid king; by daring initiative he sought to restore the Empire and to save it from disintegration. His military successes in Egypt unfortunately were of no advantage to him; his attempts to weld together the different peoples of his State by a Hellenization 'in depth' were ineffective. Shortly after his death the Seleucids lost Mesopotamia to the Parthians, and a rapid political decline set in which marked the retreat of Hellenism in the Orient. The satraps made themselves independent; petty dynasties and tyrants sprang up everywhere, and the Empire, for all intents and purposes reduced to Syria, consisted of no more than a collection of small countries that were virtually independent. The time had now come for Rome to intervene in the East and, in its turn, to conquer the Greek world. One after the other, the Hellenistic monarchies lost their independence and became vassals of Rome which imposed its will on them and set up a regime that was 'colonial, arrogant, corrupt, cruel, and inefficient'.*

*   *   *

The Seleucid Empire, which included the Iranian world, ancient Babylonia, the Phoenician towns, and the cities of Asia Minor, was as composite as the Empire of the Achaemenians. The first kings were faced with the fundamental task of achieving its unity. The Achaemenians relied for their support on the Iranian people who, spread throughout the Empire and outside Iran, constituted the core of their administration. Alexander the Great, during his brief reign, was able to count on his Macedonians. The Seleucids, however, were not a national

---

* Rostovtzeff, *Social and Economic History of the Hellenistic World*, vol. II, ch. vi, p. 1017.

dynasty sprung from a single people, and it was dangerous for them to rely for their support on an Iranian majority. Nor did they attempt to continue the policy of fusion of races sponsored by Alexander. The solution that commended itself was to extract from this diversity some kind of union which might remain loyal to them. They had to accomplish, in their own way, a task begun by the Achaemenians: they had to unify the land, an immense tract, and to populate it with Greeks and Macedonians. This new population was to form the leaven of the Empire; at the same time it was to act as a liaison between the government and the native peoples; it had to be introduced into the army as well as into the administration, had to settle in the towns and cities, engage in business and cultivate the land. This ambitious project was furthered by a particularly favourable circumstance, namely that Greece was over-populated and suffering from great poverty. Throughout the third century B.C. an almost uninterrupted stream of peoples from south-eastern Europe poured into Syria, Babylonia, and Iran, augmented by elements from Asia Minor and even Syria. To provide for their settlement a vast scheme of urban development was drawn up and put into execution. Military and non-military colonies were created. The Seleucids thus continued and developed the policy of urbanization begun by Alexander, covering the country and in particular Iran – which had first begun to build towns under the Achaemenians – with a great network of settlements, the purpose of which was to defend the country against the nomads, as in Bactria, or to control the turbulent population, particularly in Media. Many were built along the great military road, the main artery of the Empire, linking Seleucia on the Tigris to Bactria, a thousand-year-old route passing through Kermanshah and Hamadan; finally, since outlets to the sea were essential, they founded no less than nine towns on the shores of the Persian Gulf, including Antioch in Persis, the modern Bushire, which replaced an old Elamite town. They also turned their attention to the fertile districts, in particular the triangle formed by the well-watered lands lying between Kermanshah, Hamadan, and Burujird. In the plain of Kermanshah, identified by the soldiers of Alexander with Nysa, birthplace of Dionysus, there were Greek settlements at Denaver and Kangavar; Ecbatana was refounded; farther to the south was built Laodicea, the modern Nihawand, and another town at Khurha, near Arak. The ancient Raga (Rhages), to-day a suburb of Teheran, became Europos; in Parthia, Nysa-Alexandropolis was built, one of the first capitals of the Parthians and even more ancient than Hecatompylos, also a Greek city, so named because it had a hundred gates.

The newly-created towns as well as those that were rebuilt received a mixed population, as in the case of Seleucia on the banks of the Tigris where the greater part of the inhabitants of Babylon were resettled. Little is known of the life of this mixed community, but the administration was everywhere modelled on the ancient type of city with its assembly of the people, its council, and its responsible officials appointed annually. Local cults and traditions were maintained side by side with observances of the Greek religion. As a precautionary measure, the citadel dominating the town was occupied by a garrison and, in the event of danger, the Greeks could take refuge there. The cities were allotted lands, lived on and worked by the peasants attached to them; the peasants themselves, profiting from the more liberal outlook of the towns, were sometimes able to develop their own communities and to group themselves in villages, enjoying a certain measure of autonomy. So long as there was a stream of new colonists, the cities prospered. As colonization gradually slackened and finally came to an end towards the middle of the second century, some of the cities began to decay, and finally lost their Hellenic character.

It is generally believed that most of the colonies were of a military character and were composed of men fit for service who could be called up in an emergency. The colonists were settled in the native villages or allotted land in their vicinity; sometimes they were grouped together in the towns, against an obligation of military service. Each received a plot of land to farm, a house, seed, and cattle. On these lands the soldiers could form themselves into communities and even build towns (*poleis*) with a mixed population, Greek organization, and civic forms. In addition to the Greeks and Macedonians, Iran received mercenaries from Mysia, Cappadocia, and even from Thrace. Greek in mentality and adopting the Greek way of life, this new group of people in Iran provided the dynasty with a support that assured its future, its fortune, and its security.

In the nature of things, this mixed population varied in its attitude towards the king, who was the absolute master and whose edicts had the force of law. The Iranians saw him as the successor of the Achaemenians, whereas for the Macedonians he was the heir of Alexander and for the Greeks the guardian of their property. Antiochus I had already deified his deceased father, and from the time of Antiochus II an official cult of the dynasty was established, the reigning monarch and also the queen being deified. The temples in the leading cities of the satrapies had high priests and high priestesses attached to this cult; thus an edict of Antiochus III, dated in the year 193 B.C. and engraved on a stele recently discovered at Nihawand (Laodicea), orders the establishment of the cult of his wife Laodicea.

The Seleucids adopted the principles of Darius in their policy; they acknowledged the existence of different national groups and at the same time incorporated them in the Empire; but in the end they were forced to revert to the policy of Cyrus and to put up with a relatively lax suzerainty. It is generally thought that the principle of satrapies with two degrees of division was retained in the Empire; that is to say, each satrap was in charge of an administration that functioned almost independently of the central control. The weakness of this form of organization did not fail to make itself felt at the imperial level and the separatist tendency of the satraps and countries, already a menace under the Achaemenians, sapped the strength of the Seleucids. In the end their Empire was reduced to a scattering of petty states which were inherited by the Parthians, who were unable to weld them together. The Greek towns formed islands by themselves.

The Seleucids were nevertheless very successful in their administration of the Empire. The royal officials, well-trained and experienced men, perfected the machinery for supplying the coffers of the State. The taxes on royal lands, on the cities and temples, on the soldiers, the tribes, and on individuals, were levied by an army of professional officials, among whom the Greeks occupied the responsible posts, though Iranians were not excluded. The very flexible fiscal system had been in large part inherited from the Achaemenians, but it functioned with greater precision and regularity and secured an immense income for the king.

All land belonged to the Crown by right of conquest. The temples also held land, and although we know nothing about their estates in Iran, we may assume *a priori* that sanctuaries of the importance of Ecbatana, Kangavar, or Nihawand must have owned great estates with villages in which serfs, and probably also slaves, worked for the upkeep of the throng of priests and priestesses, male and female singers, musicians, temple slaves, and servants. The temples administered very large fortunes which the Seleucid kings, such as Antiochus III or Antiochus IV, did not scruple to pillage when in financial straits, using the pretext that they belonged to them by royal right. Where temples of the goddess Anahita or Nanaia were concerned, the king, as Zeus and consort of the goddess, demanded the dowry.

Other lands were given to members of the royal family, courtiers, officials, and cities, or were sold. As in the Achaemenian period, they were held by the great feudal lords, both Greek and Iranian, but their population of serfs, though tied to the soil, had a certain amount of liberty. These barons were under an obligation to provide the Crown with cavalry if need arose; it seems that within the regular army there was a strong corps of elephants. The Crown also owned estates administered by royal officers and treasury officials. Among the peasantry those working on the lands owned by the towns undoubtedly enjoyed the greatest privileges.

The diverse elements of this new society intermingled in the cities, market-towns, and villages, consisted of a majority of Iranians and a minority of Greeks. The future of the Seleucid Empire depended directly on the success of the settlement of the Greco-Macedonian population in the country. The Seleucid policy, provided a basis for the unification of the country, but did not aim at Hellenizing the Iranians or at forcing them to adopt any particular culture or way of life. Emphasis has rightly been laid on the fact that Hellenization is a modern term and conception, and was unknown to the Greeks. The Hellenization of the Iranians came about quite naturally, as did the Iranization of the Greeks; this happened without any interference or encouragement on the part of the Seleucids. They had no thought whatsoever of creating a Greek or Macedonian state by this settlement of their compatriots in Asia.

The network of cities built by the Seleucids was to unify the Empire. The new urban society superimposed on that of the Iranians ensured a liaison between them and the monarchy. It included high dignitaries, members of the Court circle, and friends and clients of the king. On a lower rung stood the administration and then the merchants. There was also the army, which maintained garrisons in the capital cities and fortified towns. Society presented a similar aspect in the country, where, alongside the great Iranian estates, stretched the lands of the Greek and Macedonian feudal lords and where the houses of the colonists sprang up beside the villages of Iranian peasants. A new aristocracy and *bourgeoisie* were introduced among the old population, emigrants from Greece and Macedonia, teachers, philosophers, and merchants in search of business. The evidence leads us to believe that the Seleucids maintained excellent relations with the upper class Iranians, some of whom, having given proof of their loyalty to the Crown, obtained high office; it would seem that this class of Iranian society was the most Hellenized.

The Greek language had begun to spread in Iran in the time of Alexander the Great, when thousands of young aristocrats entered the cavalry formations of his army while soldiers were incorporated in the infantry. Marriages between Iranian women and Macedonians, many of whom remained in Iran, the founding of colonies, as well as commerce, administration, and justice, all contributed to the replacement of Aramaic, which had been the official language of the Achaemenians, by Greek. The Greek language became in its turn the *lingua franca*, and even under the Parthians continued to be taught in the Greek towns.

As a result a large part of the population of the Plateau became bilingual, like the modern peoples of Kurdistan or Azerbaijan or the tribes of the Baluchis or Kashgais. The urban and also part of the rural population of Iran kept up the use of Greek for centuries, even after the fall of the Seleucid Empire, as is proved by inscriptions on the medals of Parthian kings and also by the parchment of Avroman in Kurdistan which records in Greek a judgement in a case between two Iranians. The two inscriptions known on Parthian bas-reliefs are written in Greek, and those of the first Sassanian kings bear, in addition to Pahlavi-Parthian and Pahlavi-Sassanian, a third version in Greek. Greek was used for all business transactions from Greece to Bactria, and all court cases between Iranians and Greeks were dealt with by Greek judges in accordance with the Greek code. The native people became acquainted with Greek legislation and even adopted it among themselves.

Thus Hellenization came about without compulsion or any special policy, affecting above all the Iranians of the cities and towns; it spread among the upper and middle classes, and also reached the free artisans of the towns, but had far less, if indeed any, influence on the rural population. Hellenization was largely due to the penetration of the Iranian element into the political and administrative life of the Empire; as a result there came into being a mixed society without which Iran would have been no more than a country of Asia inhabited by Greeks. The participation of the Iranian upper and middle classes in the life of the State – the logical result of a policy which did away with barriers between the nationalities – created a kind of solidarity between those who spoke Greek.

Parallel to the Hellenization of the Iranians there also inevitably occurred the Iranization of the Greeks; this was engendered by the frequency of mixed marriages and by the appeal of oriental cults and religious ceremonies in which Greek syncretism found full scope. Some Greeks, while not renouncing their language and institutions, nevertheless passively accepted the Iranian way of life and religion with a consequent weakening of their former intellectual interests.

The great mass of Iranians, the people living in the country,

in the villages and hamlets, remained, however, untouched by
Hellenization; the contrast between urban and rural society
created a gulf between them that was to be a cause of future
antagonism. For the people, a change of dynasty was only a
change of masters, each of whom imposed taxes and exacted
corvées. It would seem that for them the real oppressors were
not so much the officials of the royal administration as the Hellenized *bourgeoisie*; the people became accustomed to seeing
foreigners in their country, but they were hostile to this ruling
class, whose way of life was different from their own, and who
worshipped foreign gods.

Hellenization did not affect all parts of the country equally.
While Media counted a considerable number of cities and
colonies, the outlying regions seemed to have been far less, if
at all, touched by Greek settlement. 'Wherever the Hellenes
were not grouped in autonomous centres and did not mix with
the local Iranian population, they tended to lose their Greek
character.' This seems to have been the case in Persis, which
remained an island where ancestral tradition was best preserved. The records make practically no mention of the founding of new towns in this district, and the archaeological evidence so far recovered appears to confirm this. Since the great
strategic and economic routes did not touch it, this truly Persian land remained outside the admixture of peoples and languages experienced by Iran from the time of Alexander the
Great, and preserved its language, its culture, and its religion
intact. Not far from the ruins of Persepolis was built a city,
Istakhr or 'fortress', which was in time to become the religious
and political centre of the renaissance of true Persia, led at last
by a national dynasty. Below the terrace of Persepolis rose a
temple built on the traditional plan of Iranian sanctuaries; another, farther to the west of Nurabad, was a faithful replica of
the temple built by the Achaemenians opposite their tombs at
Naqsh-i-Rustam. Witnesses to the persistence of Iranian culture, they stood parallel to temples that were Greek in style
and plan, built at the same period in Media at Kangavar,
Khurha, and Nihawand. 'The Greeks formed a unity which
did not absorb the Iranian population. This remained distinct

in the national, social, religious, and cultural life and preserved its characteristics to the end.'

Art

Little is as yet known of the art of this period, which lasted for nearly two centuries from the fall of the Achaemenian dynasty to the conquest of Iran by the Parthians. Objects are rare and monuments few in number. The art of a people can hardly remain unaffected by political weakness and the impoverishment that generally follows. Iranian art was thus affected at this time, and its continuity was inevitably interrupted. Achaemenian art, as we know it, suffered an eclipse, having existed only through the protection of the king and his Court. The little we know of its revival indicates that there was a serious setback.

The art demanded by the king and the Seleucid Court, and also by the bulk of the new inhabitants of Iran, could not, in essence, be Iranian; artists coming from Greece or other parts of the Hellenistic world were chiefly concerned to satisfy the needs of their Greek clientèle. There were also Hellenized Iranians who formed the upper and most wealthy class of Iranian society. Imbued with Greek culture, they adapted their taste to the fashion of the Greek community. Local artists in their employ were also affected by Western influences. They produced works which were neither Greek nor Iranian. Here as elsewhere, it was only an adaptation, a compromise; the form is there, but not the spirit. In this way arose Greco-Iranian art. This was not the only product of the Macedonian conquest; it followed Greco-Syrian and Greco-Mesopotamian art and preceded Greco-Indian or Greco-Buddhist art.

The little that we know of the artistic achievements of the period reveals the existence not of a single art, but of several arts. Like the country and the people, the works of art lack cohesion and reflect the profound upheaval suffered by Iranian civilization. They seem to fall into three categories: (1) Iranian art proper; (2) Greco-Iranian art; and (3) Hellenistic art.

The first group is represented by the architecture of the temple of Nurabad, which, as already pointed out, is a replica of the Achaemenian temples of Pasargadae and Naqsh-i-

Rustam, but smaller, and with certain modifications arising from innovations in the cult itself. The plan of the temple built at the foot of the terrace of Persepolis is also Iranian; its chief importance lies in the decoration of the door-jambs, which, following the tradition of Persepolis, are ornamented towards the inside by two sculptured bas-reliefs. These represent two figures, one holding the sacred fasces (*barsom*) (Pl. 27*a* and *b*). These monuments are primitive work with an incised design on the surface and a deeply cut ground plan. The low relief,

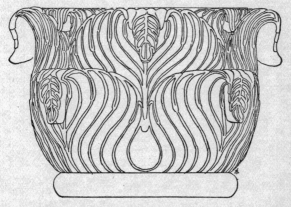

Fig. 73 – Istakhr: Stone capital

the complete absence of any attempt to obtain a play of light and shade, the lack of modelling and the linear aspect of the silhouettes betray the inexperience and timidity of a first attempt. This art did not, however, disappear, and its traces are to be found both in Parthian and Sassanian art.

At present only the remains of three buildings, of which two at least are temples, can be ascribed to the second group. At Istakhr the ruins of an important building of uncertain purpose have yielded an imitation of the Corinthian capital without abacus, which betrays a compromise between the Iranian column and the Greek capital (Fig. 73). At Kangavar, the

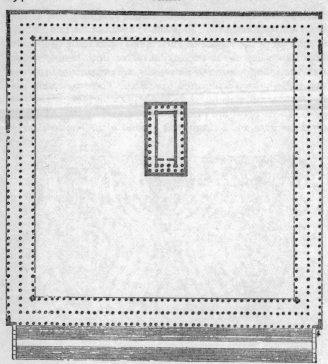

Fig. 74 – Plan of the temple of Kangavar

Fig. 75 – Ruins of the temple of Kangavar

temple is on a Western plan, and is thought to have been built about 200 B.C. The main construction is of great stone blocks in imitation of the terrace of Persepolis, but the columns have Doric capitals surmounted by Corinthian abaci (Fig. 75). Finally at Khurha, where the temple was also built on a Western plan, two narrow plinths are surmounted by a deep, projecting

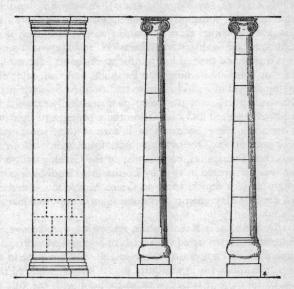

Fig. 76 – Columns of the temple of Khurha

torus. The columns show a great divergence from the classic proportion between height and diameter, an Iranian feature already noticed at Persepolis; their capitals are a bad interpretation of the Ionic style (Fig. 76). Everywhere the conclusion is the same: the Iranian artist was satisfied with the semblance and sought neither to grasp the reason nor to preserve the proportions.

It so happens that most of our information is derived from works of art belonging to the third group, which are the most numerous. It has not yet been possible to determine whether they were actually executed in the country or imported; but they all show the detailed realism characteristic of Hellenistic art. Quite recently accidental discoveries have brought to light four bronze statuettes from the temple of Nihawand (Laodicea) found in the same spot as the stele bearing the edict of Antiochus III of 193 B.C. (Pl. 28a–d). A very fine head of a bronze statue, unhappily damaged, which is attributed to Antiochus IV, comes from an Iranian temple at Shami, near Malamir, in the Bakhtiari mountains (Pl. 29a). It would seem that at this period the fashion was for works of art in bronze, a taste that continued among the Parthians and was, after all, only the revival of an old Elamite tradition. At Susa the little Achaemenian palace of the 'keep' was drastically restored in the Seleucid period and excavation there brought to light no less than ten stone pedestals of bronze statues, some with Greek inscriptions. One of these inscriptions, which belonged to a certain Pythagoras, commander of the Greek garrison at Susa, was discovered in 1852 by Loftus. Also from Susa came a fragment of a female torso in Greek marble and a certain number of small fragments of statues, again in imported marble (Pl. 29b).

At Denaver, near Kermanshah, fragments were recovered of a stone basin decorated with busts of Silenus and satyrs, the companions of Dionysus (Pl. 27c and d). The great plain of Kermanshah, famous in antiquity for its horses, acquired the name of Nysa, a mythical name introduced with the cult of Dionysus by the Greeks in a great number of countries from Greece to India. This well-watered plain, the source of the longest river in Iran, lent itself readily to such an identification. Thus Dionysus was said to have been born in a damp place: one of his synonyms means 'born in the swamp'; he was also the god of wine, and the country is well known for its vineyards. Further, the horse is one of the symbols of Dionysus, which he shares with Poseidon, and both divinities were associated with water and springs. It may be that the Greeks identified this district with the birthplace of their favourite deity, who, according to their tradition, was the first to conquer India; there they may have built a temple to him, and the decorated stone basin may have belonged to it.

Economic and Social Life

The creation of the Empire of Alexander and its transformation into three Hellenistic monarchies, brought about a revolution in the economy of the contemporary world, the most distant parts of which were for the first time so closely linked that the least disturbance in one area had repercussions on another. Never before had the economic situation been so sensitive to political developments or so deeply influenced by them as it was at this period. The circulation of coinage in this immense area now played an exceedingly important part in economic development, and the riches brought by conquest into the world market were so great that the value of gold and silver fell by fifty per cent, an event without parallel in world history, except in the age of the Conquistadors.

The period covered by the reign of Seleucus I and his immediate successors was a particularly flourishing one. An equilibrium, never previously attained, was established between wages and prices, and led to an improvement in conditions of life. The increase of interest rates is indicative of the prosperous state of business and the demand for capital. The gold found by the conquerors in Iran, most of which made its way to Europe, returned in exchange for the products that the country sent to the world markets.

The first disturbances were occasioned by the weakening of the central power and the loss of provinces such as Parthia and Bactria. After a brief recovery which was due to the energetic policy of Antiochus III, there was a return of the crisis, which became catastrophic when Rome, by its brutal intervention in the Orient, changed political conditions there and so brought about a profound economic disturbance. When the Parthians reached the line of the Euphrates, and stabilized their western frontier there, the political and economic centre of the world was shifted to the banks of the Tigris, where it remained for at least four centuries.

The Seleucids were masters of the great intercontinental

routes crossing Iran in the direction of China and India; they
extended and improved them. From the Red Sea to India the
routes were protected by military posts; supplies of water were
organized in the deserts and caravanserais built. The digging
of canals was often financed by capital. Communications and
transport now moved at a greater speed than ever before. Although the Seleucids did not control the route passing to the
north of the Caspian Sea towards southern Russia, they held
the route which terminated on the shores of the Black Sea after
crossing the Caspian and following the rivers Cyrus and Phasis.
For purposes of defence, they sent expeditions to prospect the
country to the north of the Jaxartes and explored the Caspian
Sea with a view to shortening the existing trade routes. They
maintained a large fleet in the Persian Gulf which secured the
connexion with India on the east and the Red Sea on the west.

Once again there was a change in the character of commerce: the marketing of cheap goods, which had formed the
bulk of the merchandise in the preceding period declined in
volume to the advantage of luxury goods and fine wares. A
new factor, Rome, had entered the circuit of world commerce.
Raw materials, such as wood and metals, of which Iran and
India were large suppliers, were in much demand; trade included precious stones and cameos; drugs, exported by India as far
as Brittany; plants, unguents, oils, aromatics, purple dye, attar
of roses; pottery, glassware, textiles, objects of art, papyrus,
and slaves. The introduction of this variegated commerce into
Iran involved the use of new economic methods; there were
new commercial ideas and new bases of exchange.

Iran exported clothing and ornaments, drugs, precious
stones, carpets, seed corn, lead, and pedigree dogs. Its abundant supplies of raw materials favoured its industrial development, in particular the manufacture of textiles, carpets, and
toreutics, for which Iranian artists and craftsmen acquired a
well-deserved reputation. The country also sought to become
independent of certain imported goods, such as papyrus, of
which Egypt had the monopoly; some attempt was made to
grow plants locally or to substitute parchment. Animals replaced men in the mills; the craftsman increased his produc-

tion of pottery and plastic objects, engraving on bone, and chasing; and building, affected by the new trends, also increased.

The Seleucid period is marked by great increase in the cultivation of all kinds of plants; it was the period when, under the influence of the Orient, southern Europe, and in particular Italy, acclimatized a number of new plants and domestic animals, imported from Asia. The defeated Orient subjugated Europe. Cotton, the lemon, the melon, sesame seed, the oriental nut, olives, dates, and figs, the duck, and the Asiatic ox brought about a real agrarian revolution in Italy.

By clearance and drainage of new districts, the Seleucids brought more land under cultivation. The needs of the market demanded rational methods and a scientific approach; agricultural technique developed in such an intensive manner that it was not surpassed until the Middle Ages, not even under Islam. New methods were introduced in the cultivation of the vine, a new plough came into use, a triple rotation of crops was practised, and new techniques were applied in irrigation, forestry, and in the cultivation of orchards and gardens.

The Seleucids weakened the agrarian institutions that had existed in Iran under the Achaemenians, dividing up a number of large estates that had belonged to the crown, private individuals, or temples in order to make gifts, to distribute the land among cities and towns, or to settle military colonists. These changes led to certain modifications in the condition of the peasant, who was called on to live and work side by side with the Greeks from whom he learnt new methods of farming – a cohabitation that lasted for centuries. On other estates, the serfs became something like small-holders. Where the large estate had not been thus parcelled out, the position of the serf was the subject of regulations that to some extent alleviated his condition; the peasants attached to land owned by the cities became practically free. The Seleucids deservedly occupy a high place for their agrarian reforms: their liberation of the Iranian peasant class was a great political, social, and economic achievement.

Consumption of metal, particularly of precious metals,

increased, and the Seleucids imported gold from north-west India, Bactria, Armenia, and the Caucasus. Iran, in its turn, exported iron, copper, and lead, the extraction of which increased in volume, all mines and quarries being State monopolies under the supervision of royal officials.

In social life there was a growing tendency towards greater equality among the inhabitants, particularly in the cities and towns, where a Greek education and a knowledge of the Greek language opened the door to the Hellenized Iranian element which lived alongside the Greeks and was protected by the same legislation. The distinction between descendants of Iranians and Greeks gradually disappeared.

The Seleucid State was a capitalist organism with a powerful fiscal organization. The king multiplied monopolies of raw materials and manufactured goods, and concentrated in his hands practically all the resources of the country. In the opinion of certain scholars, his policy represents the highest refinement of a planned economy known in the new world before the twentieth century. But despite this prosperity the people were ground down by taxes and only a restricted section of society profited from the increase in wealth. This included the king and the royal family, his Court, officials, the holders of concessions and privileges, those concerned in international commerce, and, to a lesser degree, the soldiers settled on the land. With oppressive taxation life appeared to be inexorably harsh, and it is not difficult to understand why man increasingly sought refuge in the ideas of redemption to which so many religions owed their attraction: Christian, Manichean, and Buddhist. Dues and taxes were levied on head, house, beast, field, garden, on birth, marriage, and death. The State needed money for the upkeep of the king and his Court, to maintain the army and fleet, to enable the temples and priests to function and to sustain the arts and sciences. The fiscal organization was centralized; the administration undertook surveys and laid the first foundations of statistics; manufactured goods, salt, perfumes, business transactions, and movement on the great rivers were the subject of regulations. 'The State had an agrarian policy, an industrial policy, a mercantile policy', but in pursuit of these, it lost sight of democratic aspirations and ignored the interests of its subjects.

*   *   *

The European expansion under Alexander and his successors enriched the material culture of Iran to such an extent that several generations were to subsist on its fruits. It left behind a great heritage in administrative organization and in urban development, the principles of the plan of Hippodamus even being adopted by the Sassanian kings, themselves great town-builders. The Greeks laid the foundation of the urban life they succeeded in developing; they created a prosperous industry, intensive agriculture, and a flourishing commerce; they covered the country with a network of roads and communications, encouraged the arts and sciences, and introduced a calendar beginning with a new era. The benefits of these civilizing activities were felt even in distant Chorasmia where recent archaeological exploration has shown that this epoch was marked by the founding of towns and fortified villages, by advances in agriculture, by increased production of manufactured goods and the focusing of social life round 'houses of fire'.

Nevertheless, the Seleucids did not solve the fundamental problem – the political unity of the two different blocs of people; they were unable to promote the proper measure of co-operation between them, a goal that had seemed indispensable to Alexander. The new masters of the country never had a real hold on the Iranians, they did not know how to create a national state, and gave no satisfaction, either political or moral, to the Iranian population. But just as there was no policy of forcible Hellenization, so, on the Iranian side, there was no attempt at open or organized opposition. There is no mention of revolt, sedition or obstruction on the part of the indigenous population, and this in part explains why it took the Parthians over a century to conquer Iran.

The cosmopolitan character of Hellenistic civilization remained foreign to Iran, which preserved its national character and in large measure its social and economic identity. The greater part of the population was never greatly affected by

Hellenism; it preserved its traditional way of life, and continued the pursuit of its own cultural, social, and religious ideals. The people as a whole stood outside the class of society represented by the Greeks and Hellenized Iranians. 'The eternal antagonism between labour and the *bourgeoisie* was aggravated by the national and religious contrasts'.* The city was born, and with it reappeared the old incompatibility between town and country – an incompatibility aggravated for Iran at this period by the opposition that existed between the Greeks on the one hand and the far more numerous Iranians on the other.

It is certain that many of the Iranians who worked with the Greeks and participated in the administration enjoyed similar privileges to the Iranian landed aristocracy. The inhabitants of the towns lived under the protection of the same laws as the Greeks, and some of the peasants even enjoyed a liberty that they later lost under the Parthians and Sassanians. But the Iranian had no desire to become a Greek, and wished only to remain Iranian. He accepted what the foreign civilization had to offer him, but did not wish to be merged or absorbed in it. In fact, the Hellenization of Iran, however widespread it may seem, touched the surface rather than the roots of society. It succeeded 'in substance and in form but did not reach the spirit'. 'The two worlds brought together by conquest were indeed too dissimilar.' This conquest of Iran was a defeat for Hellenism. By contrast it was a peaceful victory for Iran, which emerged materially richer and more advanced, and was able to offer these gains to the new dynasty of the Parthians, a dynasty which, though Iranian in origin, was nevertheless considered foreign by the western Iranians.

* Rostovtzeff, *Social and Economic History*, vol. II, ch. iii, p. 1107.

CHAPTER 6

The Parthians

T HE revolt of the satrap Diodotus and the loss of Bactria were followed within two or three years by the defection of Parthia, a neighbouring province lying farther to the west. It can hardly be correct to regard this as the first sign of Iranian reaction against Hellenism, since neither the people who founded the new dynasty nor the lands in which they had long roamed as nomads had ever been conquered by the Seleucids or formed part of their Empire. It was rather the growing weakness of Seleucid power that encouraged the emergence of the two new kingdoms of Greco-Bactria and Parthia. A Greek and an Iranian dynasty asserted their independence almost simultaneously and threw off the weakened bonds that had united these lands to the distant Seleucid kingdom. But if the cause was identical in each case, the circumstances were totally different.

Such information as we possess about the origin of the Parthians indicates that they belonged to the Parni tribe. This formed part of the Dahae, a great group of Scythian tribes who led a nomadic life in the steppe country between the Caspian Sea and the Sea of Aral. They were horsemen and warriors for whom, according to the ancient writers, to die fighting was the supreme happiness and death from natural causes ignominious and shameful. It is thought that about 250 B.C. two brothers, Arsaces and Tiridates, with their forces under the command of five other chiefs, occupied the district of the Upper Tejen. Diodotus, the new ruler of Bactria, attacked these nomads, but they fled from him and invaded the neighbouring province of Parthia, where they slew the local satrap. Two years later Arsaces fell in battle, but under Tiridates the Parthians occupied the district that to-day forms the Trans-Caspian frontier between Russia and Iran.

Tiridates established his first capital in an impregnable position in the mountains, but shortly afterwards built a second town, named after the founder of the dynasty, Assak or Arsak. There he was crowned king.

Seleucus II attempted to contain this movement and throw back the invaders. On the approach of his army, Tiridates apparently adopted the tactics of the Scythian cavalry and retreated towards his native steppe, but the outbreak of serious trouble at Antioch compelled the Seleucid King to abandon his operations and return in haste to Syria. The Parthians were quick to take advantage of his withdrawal. Tiridates reoccupied the district he had conquered earlier and shortly afterwards annexed Hyrcania, the province skirting the south-eastern shore of the Caspian Sea. In this manner was formed the core of the future Parthian kingdom, which cut off the Seleucid Empire from the Greek kingdom of Bactria. Although it lay between these two States, it had sufficient strength and vitality to maintain its independence and continue its expansion. The neighbouring steppe, inhabited by kinsmen of the Parthians, formed an immense reservoir of man-power, and doubtless the Parthians relied more on this for support than on the goodwill or indifference of the indigenous population, although this was less hostile to them than it had been to the Greek satrap. In the course of the following century, every reverse suffered by the Seleucids and each fresh sign of their weakness was exploited to the advantage of the new kingdom.

It is not known what name the Parthians applied to themselves. The term Parthians, which occurs in western sources, may be the synonym of Parthava, already attested in the time of Cyrus and Darius. Certain Iranian scholars see in it the sense of 'fighter, horseman' – a generic term used by the sedentary population to designate all the nomadic peoples and horsemen who periodically invaded eastern Iran, but which became attached to one of the provinces on the eastern marches of the Achaemenian Empire. This penetration of the Parni into Iranian territory may be regarded as the precursor of the vast movement of Scythian tribes whose invasion a century later overthrew the Iranian State and put an end to the Greco-Bactrian kingdom.

A long reign of thirty-seven years enabled Tiridates to consolidate his power, to build up an army, and expand farther to the west. He transferred his capital to Hecatompylos, a Greek town on the great east–west trade route. Arsak–Hecatompylos and Ecbatana–Ctesiphon – four capitals representing four stages in the progress of a dynasty of nomads which, even at the height of its power, retained the ancient characteristics of the race. The successor of Tiridates, Artabanus I, was not, however, strong enough to withstand the army of Antiochus III when this Prince undertook his 'armed patrol' in the East and won an ephemeral unity for his Empire. Artabanus was defeated and forced to recognize Seleucid overlordship. But his successor, Phriapatius (195 B.C.), took advantage of the defeat inflicted on Antiochus III by the Romans and reconquered the provinces south of the Caspian Sea. The Parthians were not the only people to profit from the Roman policy of weakening and destroying the Seleucid kingdom. Media Atropatene proclaimed its independence, as did Elymais, after seizing the district of Isfahan. Persis may even have preceded them in this movement, while in southern Babylonia arose the new kingdom of Characene. The oriental possessions of the Seleucid Empire disintegrated into petty states jealous of their independence and lacking a common solidarity. They fell an easy prey to the new Parthian power led by Mithridates I, the true founder of the Parthian Empire. His 'liberation' of the dismembered provinces of Iran amounted in effect to a reunion of these lands under a new crown. The policy of Rome had indirectly prepared the way for this ambitious undertaking. Between the years 160 and 140 B.C., Mithridates I forcibly annexed Media, Elymais, Persis, Characene, Babylonia, and Assyria in the West, and Gedrosia and possibly Herat and Seistan in the East. Seleucia, on the Tigris, a powerful commercial centre with nearly 600,000 inhabitants and the greatest city in this part of Asia, does not seem to have feared the Parthian approach to the Euphrates, and there is reason to believe that a compromise regulating the *modus vivendi* was reached between the Parthian conquerors and the Greco-Semitic commercial aristocracy. The Parthians did not place a garrison in Seleucia, but built a vast military camp facing the city on the left bank of the Tigris. This later became the Parthian capital of Ctesiphon (Fig. 77).

The Parthians were nowhere hailed as liberators from the Seleucid 'yoke', a circumstance that may be ascribed to the desire for independence on the part of the petty kingdoms which had but lately thrown off their former vassalage. Certainly the most Iranian of the provinces, such as Media, Atropatene, and Persis, put up a stubborn resistance. Mithridates, however, pursued his course. As restorer of the old Achaemenian Empire he assumed the title of 'Great King', while as earnest of his goodwill towards the Greek communities scattered throughout his new kingdom he introduced on his coinage that of *Philhellene*.

The weakness of the Parthian hold on the newly-won provinces, and the hostility of their populations, both Greek and Iranian, soon became apparent when Demetrius II set out to reconquer the eastern part of his Empire. The Greeks of the cities, in particular those of Seleucia on the Tigris, the inhabitants of Elymais and Persis, and even the Bactrians all hastened to offer him assistance against their new masters. Fortune, however, continued to smile on the Parthians. The Seleucid Prince lost the war and fell into the hands of the Parthian King, who treated him with great magnanimity, installing him in Hyrcania and giving him his daughter in marriage. Mithridates did not deal harshly with his Greek subjects, despite the enthusiastic co-operation they had given to his enemy. This was in marked contrast to his treatment of the territories he had earlier conquered by force, over which he re-established his sovereignty. He meted out particularly severe punishment in Elymais, where, following the example of his 'predecessors', Antiochus III and Antiochus IV, he pillaged and carried off a rich booty from the wealthy temples of 'Athene and Artemis', probably sanctuaries dedicated to the cult of Anahita. He died in 137 B.C., bequeathing to his son, Phraates II, an Empire that stretched from the Euphrates to Herat. The few sources that mention Mithridates speak of him as a monarch possessing many admirable qualities, virtuous, brave, and a good legislator. The part he played in the revival of the Iranian State may be compared to that of Cyrus the Great, whom in some ways he resembled in character.

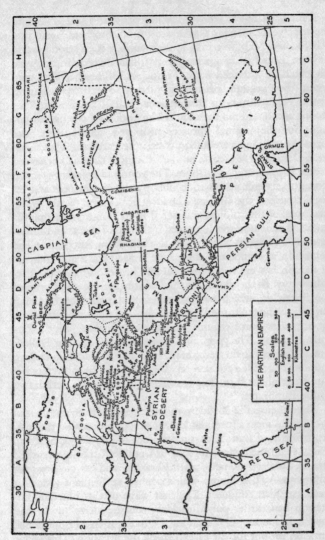

Fig. 77 – Map of the Parthian Empire

A final attempt to recover the lost provinces and to liberate the captive Demetrius was made by his brother, Antiochus VII Sidetes. Marching into Mesopotamia with a strong army, he won three battles against the Parthians, whose forces were no match for a trained army. Antiochus had reached Ecbatana when the weather prevented further operations. Setting up his headquarters in this ancient capital, he dispersed his troops and quartered them on the surrounding towns and villages for the winter. Phraates proposed negotiations. The Greek conditions were unequivocal: the Parthians were to release Demetrius, evacuate all the provinces they had occupied except Parthia, and pay tribute. The young kingdom was saved from this dangerous position only by the carelessness and incompetence of the Greeks. The local population, weary of the exactions of the soldiery quartered in its homes, was ripe for revolt. A rebellion was fomented by Parthian agents and simultaneously Phraates made a surprise attack on Antiochus. The Seleucid was completely routed, he himself was slain, and part of his forces were taken prisoner and incorporated in the Parthian army. In the space of a few months the great victories of the Seleucids, which had promised to restore the tottering Empire, had been turned into disaster, and there was no longer an organized force capable of protecting Syria against a Parthian invasion. The year 129 B.C. was a fateful date for Hellenism. It never again recovered, and the Seleucid kingdom, though it survived for several more decades, lay prostrate before triumphant Iran. The frontier of Europe was withdrawn to the Euphrates.

Nevertheless the Parthians did not march into Syria; instead they had to meet a formidable irruption of nomads on the eastern frontier of Iran. A vast movement of peoples of Scythian origin from the distant regions of Chinese Turkestan reached Iran at the very moment when Phraates won his victory over Antiochus VII, a victory which opened up brilliant vistas for fresh Parthian conquest. The first wave of this nomadic migration had earlier put Mithridates on the alert, but he had fought it successfully. Leaving a governor in Mesopotamia, Phraates set out for the east to check the invasion. This seems to have spread in two directions: one group of nomads pushed straight towards the west by way of Merv, Hecatompylos, and Ecbatana, while the other went south, moving down from Merv to Herat and the rich province of Seistan. At the first onslaught of the enemy, the Greek soldiers of Antiochus, whom Phraates had incorporated in his army, deserted and thereby caused the defeat and death of the King. His uncle and successor, Artabanus II, shortly afterwards suffered the same fate. In Babylonia, the governor left by Phraates proclaimed himself king, and the kingdom of Characene broke away. The West in revolt, the East invaded by nomads, such was the grave situation that faced the Parthian kingdom on the accession of Mithridates II. This ruler was undoubtedly the most remarkable of the line of Parthian princes (c. 123 B.C.). After he had restored order in the West, he turned to the other end of his kingdom, pushed back the frontiers as far as the Oxus by retaking Merv, re-occupied Herat, dammed back the flood of nomads, and made Seistan his vassal. His success was of the first importance, for it saved the Western world from the menace of the Sakae. The Scythians, who but yesterday had been nomads, barred the road to their near relations, and so protected the civilization of Western Asia – a role that Iran had played in the past and was to play yet again in the course of its long history.

The invasion of these nomads from Central Asia swept away the Greco-Bactrian kingdom, and the plains lying north and south of the middle Oxus were occupied by their two great confederations, the Sacaraucae in the west and the Yueh-chi or Tokhari in the east. One group of tribes forming an advance guard slowly moved north towards the Punjab, while another went south towards Sind. At the beginning of the first century B.C. they established kingdoms on the ruins of the last Greco-Bactrians and remained very closely linked, both politically and culturally, with the Parthians.

It is certain that the Indian kingdoms were independent of Parthia. Those of Seistan and Arachosia seem to have acknowledged its overlordship until the beginning of the first century B.C., when they were reunited by Gondophares. This prince, who is thought to have been of Parthian origin, established an empire stretching from Seistan to beyond the Indus.

About 115 B.C. Mithridates received an embassy from the Emperor of China, and the two rulers concluded a treaty designed to facilitate the movement of international commerce in which Iran, as a transit state, formed a vitally important link. Twenty years later Mithridates intervened in the affairs of Armenia and placed his protégé, Tigranes, on the throne. By so doing he inaugurated a new era in the history of that country, whose future fortunes were to remain closely linked to those of Iran. Shortly afterwards Tigranes allied himself with Mithridates Eupator of Pontus who, between 112 and 93 B.C., created a powerful kingdom that included all Asia Minor and bordered on continental Greece and for many years resisted the Roman advance. Faced with this alliance which strengthened the position of Armenia, Mithridates II adopted a waiting policy. When in 92 B.C. the Romans reached the Euphrates, he sent them an embassy with a proposal of alliance. Sulla, knowing nothing of Parthian importance and power, treated the envoy in so cavalier a manner that the Great King took offence and came to terms with the two other oriental princes. Rome was to pay dearly for its contemptuous attitude on the occasion of this first contact with the Parthians.

The parts played by Mithridates I and Mithridates II in the foundation of the Parthian Empire may be likened respectively to those of Cyrus and Darius. The former ruler was responsible for its territorial expansion, while the latter consolidated and organized what had been won. He made Iran into a world power, and its relations with Rome in the West and China in the East show the importance of the position it occupied in the political and economic life of the contemporary world. Mithridates II gave formal expression to the increase in his power by assuming the title 'King of Kings'.

On his death Parthia underwent a period of decadence. During the next thirty years the throne was occupied by a succession of rulers, and the kingdom was so weakened by internecine strife that Tigranes of Armenia, who owed his crown to the Parthians, seized several of their provinces, depriving them of districts as far south as Ecbatana. He added insult to injury by assuming the title of 'King of Kings'. 'The Parthian monarchy, diminished, dismembered, and showing signs of disruption, seemed for the moment to have disappeared from the map of Western Asia.' At this juncture, Tigranes accepted the crown of the Seleucids offered him by the Syrians, who were weary of the strife between the last Seleucid pretenders. The situation was such that it looked as though the Parthian King himself would become a vassal.

Nevertheless, Rome entered into negotiations with Parthia, despite its weakness, and sought to secure its neutrality in the struggle with Pontus and Armenia. Yet there was little change in the Roman treatment of the Parthian King. Lucullus proposed, or perhaps demanded, a treaty. Phraates II agreed, and, even when Lucullus was in difficulties in his war with Pontus and Armenia, he kept faith and made no attempt to invade Syria. Later, when Mithridates Eupator suffered a reverse and in his turn sought an alliance with Parthia, Phraates rejected his overtures and renewed the treaty with Pompey. He was always correct in his attitude towards the Romans, but they in their pride and ignorance continued to show little regard for the people who had kept their pledges so scrupulously. Shortly afterwards Pompey violated the treaty, seized the western provinces of Parthia, intrigued with its vassal princes, and insulted Phraates when he protested. Following the assassination of Phraates, Gabinius agreed, in return for a large sum of money, to assist Mithridates III to seize the throne from Orodes II, but in the end he failed to do so because the Romans accepted the offer of a larger amount from a pretender to the Egyptian throne. The greed of the Roman leaders reached its apogee when Crassus was made proconsul of Syria. The Senate had no wish for war with Parthia, but Crassus, like his soldiers, believed that the conquest of Iran would be an easy victory and yield a rich booty. In the battle of Carrhae, however, the light and heavy Parthian cavalry commanded by Surena, the head of the greatest feudal family of Iran, smashed the Roman army and killed or captured three-quarters of the forces of Crassus, who paid for the disaster with his own life and that of his son

(53 B.C.). The combined Parthian force of heavy cavalry and mounted bowmen carried the day, and proved superior to the Roman army, which had no mounted formations. The battle of Carrhae forced Rome to introduce cavalry into its army, just as nearly a thousand years earlier the first Iranians to reach the Plateau had perhaps induced the Assyrians to introduce a similar reform.

According to tradition the head and arm of the ill-fated Crassus were brought to Orodes II when he was watching the *Bacchae* of Euripides in company with the King of Armenia and the members of his Court. The shock of the Parthian victory opened the eyes of Rome to the real strength of Parthia, a power whose policy was defensive rather than offensive. The eagles of the legions long remained in the Parthian temples, and the prisoners were settled in the oasis of Merv, where a number of them reared families. Rome realized that its statesmen and military leaders had, through their ignorance of the country, made a grave mistake in despising Iran. Once again Iran had forcibly thrown back from its frontiers the Hellenism to which the Romans claimed to be heirs, and for over a century the Euphrates frontier remained inviolate. Furthermore, the western Semites who were hostile to Rome, such as the Jews of Palestine, the Nabateans of Damascus, the Arabs of the desert, and the inhabitants of Palmyra, looked with hope to Persia, where Orodes appeared as a true successor of the Achaemenians. They were to have their revenge with the Parthian horsemen whose coming to defeat the Roman beast was foretold by the author of the Apocalypse. Unfortunately their deliverance was only ephemeral, and the hand of the Roman conqueror weighed still more heavily after the Parthian withdrawal.

The disaster that befell Crassus, like that of Antiochus IV, left Syria exposed to attack, and civil war in Rome impeded the reinforcement of Roman power in the East. Once again the way seemed open for a Parthian advance to the shores of the Mediterranean, but on this occasion it was prevented by the internal state of the kingdom. Surena, whose success had aroused the jealousy of his sovereign, was executed, and Parthia was thus deprived of a capable general. Pacorus, son of Orodes, then an inexperienced youth, invaded Syria at the head of an army that lacked the fighting qualities of the force commanded by Surena at Carrhae, and his short raid met with disaster. Resuming operations in 51 B.C., he overran the whole country, which remained for several months in the hands of the Parthians, who completely disrupted the economic life of the West. But Pacorus was unable to continue operations; falsely accused of fomenting a revolt against his father, he was recalled by Orodes and narrowly escaped being put to death. It is not known why the Parthians remained inactive during the next ten years, nor whether their failure to invade Syria was due to events in the East, to internal dissensions, or to unrest among elements of the Parthian nobility which formed the élite of the army. Whatever the reason, it was not until 40 B.C. that Orodes and Pacorus decided to invade the West, spurred on by Labienus, a former ambassador of Brutus who had entered the Parthian service.

The Persian army was divided between Labienus and Pacorus. The former directed operations towards the north and occupied the greater part of Asia Minor as far as Ionia; the latter marched south, was everywhere acclaimed, and seized Syria and Palestine, where he drove Herod from Jerusalem and replaced him by a national king. The Nabateans accepted the authority of Parthia. Practically the whole of the Roman East was conquered. Labienus remained master of Asia Minor for eighteen months; the war in Syria did not end until 38 B.C., and in face of Roman reinforcements the Parthian army was unable to hold the country. Labienus was killed. Pacorus was the victim of treachery, for he marched against a Roman camp that he had been led to believe was undefended. His heavy cavalry, unsupported by mounted archers, suffered a serious defeat, and he himself was slain. His death was a serious blow to Iran, which lost a brave and energetic leader of undoubted military ability. This last battle proved that the heavy cavalry of the cataphracti was no match for the Roman army in offensive warfare. Nevertheless the invasion was not without results.

The Romans exacted a harsh retribution from the local population and from those princes who had shown too much alacrity in welcoming the arrival of the Persians. Some had to pay heavy tribute; others, like the King of Jerusalem, were put to death. Herod was restored. The aged Orodes was shortly afterwards assassinated by his sons, one of whom, Phraates IV, succeeded him (c. 37 B.C.). Once again the accession of a new ruler was marked by internal strife and struggles between nobles and plebeians, between the partisans of different clans, and between the two great divisions of the Parthian army, the heavy cavalry and the mounted archers. Against the sombre background of the domestic scene there arose the menace of a new Roman invasion. Antony, at the head of one of the most powerful armies ever to undertake operations against the Persians, invaded the Caucasus, subdued the Iberians and Albanians, and made Armenia a vassal state. Having secured his rear, he pressed rapidly forward towards Media Atropatene, intending to lay siege to the capital and leaving his siege-train and baggage wagons to follow on behind. He was impatient to realize the plans of oriental conquest worked out by Caesar a dozen years earlier. But the impression made by the battle of Carrhae had had its effect, and he no longer found it easy to gain allies among the Armenians, the Medes, or the people of Elymais, who hesitated to betray the common cause.

Phraates IV attacked the Roman baggage train with his light cavalry, overcame its escort, and plundered and burnt the siege engines. Deprived of his engines of war and his supplies, Antony was unable to take the strong and stoutly defended fortress. As the season was advancing, he decided to retreat, but in the course of his withdrawal suffered heavy losses from Parthian attacks. Phraates celebrated his victory by surcharging with his name the coins bearing the likeness of Antony and Cleopatra that he had found in the Roman baggage. The following spring Antony recovered the mastery of Armenia, and the next year advanced as far as Media, but the combined action of the Parthians and Armenians deprived him of all his gains, and shortly afterwards he was defeated by Octavian and fell from power.

Roman policy on the eastern question now assumed a different character, and there was a change in Roman public opinion towards the Parthians. Their strength in defence was recognized, and it was realized that the policy of those who sought conquests east of the Euphrates had proved mistaken. Augustus, though he may at first have been attracted by the idea of conquering Asia, changed his mind and sought to reach a compromise. Parthia could never be a menace to Rome; its social organization, frequent palace revolutions, quarrels among the clans, the separatist tendencies of the vassals, and the absence of strong central control made it possible for Rome to adopt a more friendly attitude. This change of policy bore fruit. Phraates IV restored to Augustus the eagles of the legions of Crassus, and later, fearing the menace of assassination that hung over his sons, he sent them to Rome for their protection and to prove to Caesar his goodwill towards the Empire.

Rome began to realize that an *entente* between the two Powers might be advantageous to both parties, if only through the development of commerce. At the same time Rome was anxious to secure the defence of its frontiers, and to this end sought to create buffer states. One was Palmyra on the eastern frontier, the other Armenia, which neither Rome nor Parthia wished to see independent, since for each it was of the highest strategic importance. A compromise was reached when Rome nominated a Hellenized vassal king. Phraates accepted this arrangement, but Parthian public opinion did not forgive the concession, and it cost the house of Mithridates I the throne.

There followed a rapid succession of kings in Armenia, the Roman nominees frequently being deposed and replaced by others more acceptable to Parthia. Despite the friendship between the two empires and the revolts in Armenia, Rome would not renounce its claims to a protectorate over the country. It supported the accession to the Parthian throne of Phraates V, or Phraataces, who poisoned his father, on condition that he renounced his claims to Armenia. The young king was soon deposed by a revolution on the part of the nobility, who requested Augustus to send them one of the sons of Phraates IV from Rome. Vonones I returned, but did not keep

the crown long; his western education made him repugnant to
the Persian nobility and people. He was deposed in his turn,
and shortly afterwards assassinated in Syria, where he had
sought refuge. He was replaced by Artabanus III, descendant
by the female line of the Arsacids, a family closely connected
with Hyrcania which held the crown of Media Atropatene.
The house of Mithridates ceased to reign over Iran. Under the
new dynasty there was a revival of the religious and cultural
life of the country which became more Iranian and nationalist
in character. These developments constituted a setback for
Roman policy, for the Romanized Parthian princes had been
rejected not only in Armenia, but also in Iran.

Artabanus III, who had to face a revolt of Seleucia on the
Tigris that lasted seven years, does not seem to have been able
to consolidate the central power, despite a long reign, and the
close of his life was overshadowed by Roman intrigues. Once
again rival kings contended for power both in Armenia and on
the throne of the Arsacids. A compromise on the Armenian
question was finally reached in the reign of Vologases I. His
brother Tiridates became King of Armenia, but received his
crown at the hands of the Roman Emperor. Rome was anxious
to save its face after a military defeat, and, reverting to the
policy of Augustus, accepted this arrangement. In A.D. 66, the
new King of Armenia, accompanied by his family and escorted
by 3,000 cavalry, arrived in Italy and amid great popular re-
joicing was crowned by Nero. An Arsacid dynasty therefore
ruled over Armenia, where Rome preserved no more than a
feeble pretence of its ancient claims to authority. This arrangement secured fifty years of peace to a country that had long
been torn by the rivalry of its two powerful neighbours, proof
of the firm links binding Parthia and Armenia.

The first signs of a neo-Iranian renaissance appeared under
Vologases I: on the reverse of his coinage is depicted a fire
altar with a sacrificing priest; for the first time the money bore
letters of the Pahlavi-Arsacid alphabet (Fig. 78), and according
to later tradition the text of the Avesta was compiled in his
reign. In order to break the resistance offered by the Greek city
of Seleucia, the Parthian King decided to build the town of

Vologasia, which became a new commercial centre and supplanted the rebel city. Following a serious invasion of the
Alani through the Caucasian passes, the King of Iran proposed
to Rome that their two countries should make common cause
against these nomads who threatened their northern frontiers.
Rome refused, but later changed its attitude when, under the
Sassanians, the menace became more urgent and threatening.

The far-sighted policy of Augustus in eastern affairs was not
pursued for long. Under Trajan a new mood arose in Rome
that paid little heed to the ideas of the great organizer of the
Roman Empire. The question of Armenia and Iran was re-

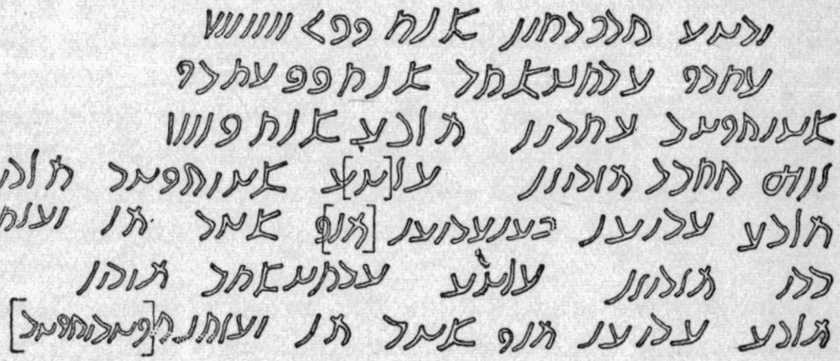

Fig. 78 – Pahlavi-Arsacid script

opened, and solved in a violent manner. Armenia was to be
conquered and made into a Roman province, while Parthia was
to be reduced to vassalage and governed by a puppet king. In
A.D. 114 Trajan imposed his overlordship over the peoples of
the Caucasus, and by this initial success joined the Roman province of Asia Minor to the vassal kingdom of the Bosphorus
without interruption of continuity, so completing the circle of
Roman domination round the Black Sea. He then invaded Armenia where the local ruler yielded up his crown and was assassinated; the kingdom was proclaimed a Roman province.
There was no reaction to these events from Parthia, which had
for several years been distracted by civil war. The following
year Trajan defeated the kingdom of Adiabene and formed it

into another province; he marched down the Euphrates; captured Ctesiphon, the Parthian capital, where the daughter of King Osroes and his throne fell into his hands; then, following the Tigris, he reached the Persian Gulf and perhaps toyed with the idea of the eventual conquest of India. On his return he visited Babylon and offered sacrifices in the chamber of the palace where Alexander had died, thus honouring the great genius whose career he sought to emulate.

But the triumphant career of the Emperor was cut short by a revolt among the countries of the eastern Mediterranean. The Jews of Cyrenaica, Egypt, and Cyprus rose in open rebellion, and the revolt spread to Palestine, Syria, Northern Mesopotamia, and eventually the entire Semitic world. The Parthians profited from the Roman embarrassment to start a partisan war, and this was followed by the rebellion of Armenia. Trajan, who had already begun to make and unmake kings on the throne of Iran, decided to withdraw. On his return march he made an unsuccessful attempt to capture the Parthian fortress of Hatra in Mesopotamia. He died before he reached Rome.

The great victories of Rome had turned to defeat. Despite the weakening effect of continual rivalry between its princes, Iran had once again thrown back the invader. But the capture of Ctesiphon made a deep impression on the Iranians and led to a recrudescence of national feeling. Hadrian, who succeeded Trajan, did not pursue the imperial policy of his predecessor, but was content to maintain the *status quo* and to accept the Euphrates as the frontier between the two empires. Nevertheless the internal affairs of Iran remained disturbed, and the struggle between Vologases II and Osroes lasted for many years. The situation was aggravated by a fresh invasion of nomad Albanians, who penetrated to the borders of Mesopotamia and were halted only by a stout Parthian resistance.

The accession of Vologases II (A.D. 148–92) was marked by an Arsacid revival and the end of the truce with Rome. Having made preparations for his attack, the Parthian King crossed the Euphrates and marched into Syria, where his troops were welcomed by the local population. Another general revolt against Rome seemed imminent. But although Parthia had earlier shown great powers of resistance when faced with invasion, its weakness became apparent when it passed to the offensive. As in the time of Pacorus, two centuries earlier, the army of Vologases III was driven back by the counter-attack of the lieutenants of Antoninus Pius and heavily defeated at Dura. The King sought an armistice, but the Roman troops were soon across the Tigris, Ctesiphon was captured, and the royal palace burnt down (A.D. 165). The capital, which fifty years previously had been delivered by the revolt of the Oriental provinces of the Roman Empire, was recovered as a consequence of a fearful epidemic of plague. This broke out on the frontiers of Iran, and may have been carried by the Roman army, which had marched through Mesopotamia to the banks of the Araxes. It spread throughout Western Asia, Egypt, and Asia Minor, swept across Greece and Italy, and reached the Rhine. The Romans evacuated Babylonia, but kept certain provinces on the Euphrates and maintained their protectorate over Armenia. A new civil war in Rome gave Vologases II hopes of revenge, but he was unable to realize them.

Ctesiphon again fell into the hands of the Romans under Septimius Severus (A.D. 197) and for the third time the Parthian capital was sacked and burnt, although the difficulties the Emperor encountered in the devastated country compelled him to relinquish it again. Taking the route followed by Trajan in his retreat, the Emperor made two attempts to capture Hatra, but was unsuccessful, and retired to Syria. Under Caracalla, the civil war between Vologases V and Artabanus II continued, fomented by the Romans, who once more invaded Mesopotamia. The assassination of the Roman Emperor altered the balance between the two empires. Artabanus V was twice victorious over the Emperor Macrinus and imposed a heavy tribute on Rome. Iran re-established its frontiers on the Euphrates and a Parthian invasion seemed only a matter of time. Thus after two and a half centuries, Roman attempts to reduce Iran to vassalage had ended in failure. The victories of Artabanus V seemed to herald a new era of Iranian expansion towards the West. But this was not to be achieved by the Arsacid dynasty, which proved incapable of expanding their power beyond that of the national framework. It was the Sassanians who, profiting from the favourable circumstances created by the Parthians, had their revenge on Rome and carried the arms of Iran to the shores of the Mediterranean.

THE PARTHIANS AND THE EAST

Information about the Scythian tribes settled in the great plain to the south of the Oxus after the destruction of the Greco-Bactrian kingdom (c. A.D. 128) is confused and obscure. From the end of the first century B.C. there seems to have been a movement of unification among the Kushans, one of the groups belonging to the confederation of the Yueh-chi or Tokhari. In the first half of the first century A.D. the Kushans enter history with their King, Kujula Kadphises, who, after a series of conquests in the course of which he annexed all Bactria, crossed the Hindu Kush, occupied the Kabul district and extended the frontiers of his kingdom as far as the left bank of the Indus, seizing these countries from the last princes of Parthian origin, the successors of Gondophares. In his expansion towards the West, he must inevitably have come into contact with the Parthians, and his coinage seems to indicate that he seized the district of Merv from them, probably fixing the common frontier on the border of Hyrcania. This expansion of the young Kushan kingdom occurred at a time when the vigorous policy of Nero and his advisers was making itself felt as far as the eastern shore of the Caspian Sea. Rome entered into relations with Hyrcania, and the two countries even seem to have concluded a treaty. The economic motive in the agreement was paramount for the Romans, who were apparently anxious to safeguard a route along which trade could move between Rome, China, and India without crossing Parthian territory. The products of these oriental countries passed down the Oxus, crossed the Caspian Sea, were carried up the river Cyrus, and after a portage of five days embarked on the Phasis and so reached the Black Sea. In A.D. 58 Hyrcania became independent of the Parthian kingdom and sent an embassy to Rome. By his annexation of Merv and a probable alliance with the Hyrcanians, Kujula Kadphises controlled practically the whole of the navigable course of the Oxus and reached the Caspian Gates. His successor, Wima Kadphises, continued the work of his father. In the West, he profited from the weakness of the Parthians and their wars with Rome to capture Herat, Seistan, and Arachosia. In the East, he seized all western India and held the mouth of the Indus as well as the western ports of the peninsula. From the time of Augustus and following the discovery of the monsoons, intense maritime traffic sprang up between the Red Sea and India. Merchandise from Egypt and the eastern basin of the Roman Mediterranean was loaded in Red Sea ports, arrived at the mouth of the Indus, went up the river as far as the modern Peshawar, crossed the Hindu Kush and Pamirs in caravans, and, after traversing Chinese Turkestan, reached China. From the beginning of the second century, the Kushans, therefore, controlled the three main stretches of the great 'Silk Road': first, the road of the two seas, the Caspian and Euxine; secondly, the road which passed through Merv, Hecatompylos, and Ecbatana, crossed the Euphrates and so reached the Mediterranean ports; and thirdly, the maritime route between India and the Red Sea. The formation of the Kushan Empire on their eastern confines was a double threat to the Parthians: politically, instead of having the one enemy in the West, Iran became a central empire sandwiched between Rome and the Kushans; economically, the Kushans were, like the Parthians, middlemen in commerce, and since they held stretches of the three trade routes, could divert merchandise to roads that avoided Parthian territory. Rome was quick to seize the double significance of this new empire, and sought to enter into direct relations with its princes. The Kushans, however, even under their great king Kanishka (A.D. 144–73) and his immediate successors, when their empire was at the height of its power, do not seem to have been attracted by the prospect of territorial gain at Parthian expense. The enormous wealth of India, which had not yet been unified under a single power, was much more inviting than the desert regions of eastern Iran, where the frontier between the two States seems to have been stabilized roughly on the line that to-day demarcates the frontier between Iran and Afghanistan. Nevertheless, the war of Kanishka against the Parthians mentioned in Buddhist tradition could only have taken place during the reign of Vologases III, and it may have been caused by a Parthian attempt to recover one of the Iranian provinces annexed by the Kushans. A vague reference in a Syrian text referring to the reign of Vologases IV (A.D. 191–207) speaks of a large army of 'Medes and Persians' who were said to have invaded eastern Iran. Vologases was encircled and at first suffered heavy losses, but his troops rallied and chased the enemy as far as 'the sea'.

It therefore seems probable that relations between the neighbouring empires were not always peaceful. Nevertheless there is reason to believe that the Parthians, who were exhausted by internecine wars and constantly in difficulties with Rome, tried to reduce the tension in the east to a minimum. Their decadence, however, coincided with the ascendancy of the Kushan Empire, which was a constant menace to Iran and threatened to weaken it still further by closing the trade route. The first Sassanians were fully alive to this danger, and the conquest of the Kushan Empire was one of the earliest feats of arms of Shapur I.

ORGANIZATION AND ADMINISTRATION

The rise to power of the Arsacids, who derived their support mainly from a few noble families of the Parni, was a triumph of the northern Iranians over those of the south. This movement represented the supremacy of outer and nomadic Iran over sedentary Iran, which was permeated with the older civilization of Western Asia on to which the conquest of Alexander had grafted Hellenism. The gulf separating these two Iranian societies was too wide to be bridged despite the centuries of Parthian–Arsacid rule. It would seem that in domestic affairs the Iranian population of the country maintained an attitude of reserve, if not at first of hostility, towards its rulers and their entourage. The Parthian kings were conscious of this, and those of them who were in difficulties preferred to seek help from their kinsmen in the steppes to the east of the Caspian, rather than from Persia or Media. The links between these nomads and the Arsacid dynasty were never severed, and this may be one of the reasons why eastern chronicles, particularly those of the Armenians, connect the Parthian family with the Kushan dynasty, which also sprang from Iranian nomads.

The Parthians inherited the decadent Seleucid Empire which had proved powerless to enforce obedience from the numerous kingdoms and principalities that split away from it. They seem to have made little attempt to improve this state of affairs. Possibly they lacked the strength to do so. They did not depose the petty kings and princes, but were content to exact recognition of their overlordship and to make their new vassals render homage and pay tribute. Apart from these demands which established a relatively loose connexion between the dynasty and the vassal states, it is possible that they aroused antagonism in other ways. From the time of Antiochus III, whenever there was a Seleucid attempt to recover the provinces seized by the Parthians, the vassal rulers of these districts were quick to revolt against their Parthian overlord. The Romans replaced the Seleucids, but the situation did not change, and when Lucullus or Pompey crossed the Euphrates the Parthian vassals hastened to embrace the Roman cause. Media put up a long resistance to the Parthians; Hyrcania regained its independence in A.D. 58; Elymais aided Demetrius II and Antiochus VII, and, according to the ancient records, became independent of the Arsacids, and even their enemy, in the time of Artabanus III.

The classical writers list eighteen vassal states of the Parthians, eleven of which were reckoned as *superior* countries and the remaining seven as *inferior* countries. Media, under a dynasty of Arsacid origin, stood second and Armenia, whose kings from the time of Tiridates belonged to the same family, third. Several of these kingdoms, such as Persis, Elymais, or Characene, issued coinage. The rest of the country was divided into satrapies, usually administered by the heads of the great feudal families of Parthia. As they held the position of satrap by hereditary right, there was little effective difference between their status and that of the petty dynasties. There were also the nomadic or semi-nomadic peoples, such as the Kossaioi and the Uxians in the south-west and the Arabs on the western frontier who were, in practice, completely independent. An eastern tradition relates that when he was dying Alexander, wishing to obviate a Persian revenge, divided the country between ninety princes, a measure that led to the political and administrative weakness of the Parthians. Greek cities, such as Seleucia on the Tigris and Seleucia on the Eulaeus (Susa), formed enclaves in the vassal kingdoms and were permitted by the Parthians to retain their Greek organization. Their life underwent little change apart from the fact that they had to obey an Iranian satrap appointed by the Arsacids instead of a Greek satrap. The feudal system of the Parthian kingdom, which resembled very closely that of medieval Europe, was based on seven great families, of which the Arsacids themselves were one – a survival of Achaemenian tradition. On these great feudal families were dependent the petty nobility or knights, while at the base of the pyramid stood the peasantry and serfs. The bonds between the great lords and their small vassals were stronger than those between the nobility and the monarchy. The Parthian crown did not necessarily pass from father to son; the will of the aristocracy carried considerable weight and was expressed through the voice of the council or 'senate' which limited the royal prerogative. Another assembly, that of 'the sages and Magi' was merely a consultative body standing close to the throne.

The great nobility at first formed the strength of the Parthian monarchy, but in the end caused its downfall. The feudal system was not introduced by the Parthians; they inherited it from the Achaemenians and bequeathed it in their turn to the Sassanians, and it persisted, in a modified form, under Islam. Owing to the weakness of the Arsacid kings the feudal nobility was able to concentrate so much power in its hands that the positions were reversed and relations between the Crown and its subjects compromised. Throughout Parthian history, the nobility made and unmade kings, sometimes by constitutional means, sometimes with foreign support, usually that of Rome.

Any prince who attempted to strengthen his position was deposed for his 'atrocities'. The accession of a new ruler almost invariably led to civil war; several pretenders claimed to be 'king', and there was no means of determining who was the legitimate claimant. Those who had lost their throne often took refuge with the nomads or with the Romans, who in that case espoused their cause with their legions.

Iranian society retained its ancient traditions under the Par-

Fig. 79 – Dura Europos: A Parthian cataphract

thians. The noble was a warrior and horseman who spent his time in war or the chase. The Parthians had no regular army. The composition of their armed forces was based on their social organization. Each feudal lord in effect possessed his own army, and in the event of war he and his vassals, free men and serfs, placed themselves at the disposal of the king. At the battle of Carrhae, for example, the cavalry of Surena was mainly composed of his own men. The noble lords furnished the heavy cavalry with iron armour (the cataphracti), with lances and swords, and in a war of manoeuvre this was a formidable force (Fig. 79). The army was also mounted on camels, but the

Parthians never seem to have used elephants in their formations. The lesser nobility furnished the light cavalry (sagittarii), for which the Parthian army was famous. Armed with bows, it was skilled in mobile warfare; the usual tactics were to shower the enemy with a hail of arrows and then to disperse when counter-attacked. At the battle of Carrhae, 1,000 camels loaded with spare arrows accompanied this mounted corps of archers. The infantry played a less important part and was composed of the hill-people and serfs. On the whole, it was a defensive army with no training for a war of conquest. Knowledge of siege engines was comparatively rudimentary and against the strong walls of enemy fortresses the Parthian army proved impotent.

PARTHIANS AND GREEKS

The early Parthians from the time of Mithridates I styled themselves 'Philhellenes' on their coinage. It is probable that this was not an indication of their admiration for Greek culture, but was rather a political measure demanded by the situation they found in Iran. The Iran they had liberated from the Greeks was deeply influenced by Western culture, and although Hellenism had abandoned the field it left lasting traces of itself on Iranian civilization to which it gave a new character. What had nomads of the steppe to offer? What reforms in political, social, and economic life could be introduced by these horsemen who could offer only their valour in war in exchange for the inheritance left by two centuries of Hellenism? Having made themselves masters of Iran, the Parthians found an organized administration in existence, and cities inhabited by strong Greek colonies and the new Hellenized Iranian *bourgeoisie*. The latter class acted as a kind of intermediary between the Parthians and the Hellenes. It collaborated with both sides, guaranteed the administration, undertook the collection of taxes which came mainly from the wealthy trading cities, and, under the control and supervision of royal representatives, was responsible for local government. The city, with its Greek and Iranian *bourgeoisie*, also played an important part in the political life of the country; for public opinion was moulded in the city, and on public opinion the fate of the ruler himself depended.

The Parthian rulers appreciated the situation. The fact that their garrisons did not enter Seleucia, but camped on the opposite bank of the river, was a symbolic gesture, and they maintained this attitude throughout most of their history. 'The Romans and the Parthians owed their Greek character entirely to the existence of the network of Greek colonies.' The Greeks of Iran were a kind of advance post guarding their institutions and their language. For centuries Greek remained the *lingua franca* of diplomacy and commerce, until supplanted by Persian; the Greek script was also adopted by the nomads in Bactria, the later founders of the Kushan Empire, who retained it in use until the eighth century A.D.

The Parthians were fully aware of the value of Greek civilization. It would have been contrary to the interests of the State to destroy the existing order and revert to the conditions pertaining before Alexander or to seek to evolve something new. The Greek cities were therefore left undisturbed and became 'bastions of the wealth and prosperity of the new rulers'. Seleucia on the Tigris, Seleucia on the Eulaeus (Susa), Dura-Europos, Babylon, Uruk, and probably other towns as yet unexplored, preserved their military, agrarian, and commercial character. They were left in possession of their estates and there was no interference in their social and economic organization. They were even allowed to retain their garrisons, their military colonists continued to farm the land, as for example those known from inscriptions at Susa of the first century A.D. They preserved their cults and their educational institutions. Their governors were chosen by the king or the citizens and came from local families; they held office under the satrap; the judiciary, too, was locally recruited. The towns kept their assemblies. In this way the two peoples reached mutual understanding. Yet this harmony was not always perfect, and unrest in some of the great cities, such as Seleucia on the Tigris, shows that there were sometimes violent collisions between the Greek commercial aristocracy and the Iranians and Semites who did not always see eye to eye on their attitude to the existing ruler.

Differences also arose between the city and the Crown, as when, for example, the city of Seleucia openly rebelled against the Parthians and held out for seven consecutive years. On the whole, however, relations remained good. The Parthian governors, their officials and secretaries, all knew Greek. The kings were also familiar with the Greek language, and works of art and the imperial coinage (Pl. 40) prove that they patronized Greek artists and writers and brought them to their Court, particularly during the last two centuries of the first millennium B.C. The benevolent attitude of the Parthians towards the Hellenistic heritage in Iran was of the highest importance for the future development of Iranian civilization. It saved the country from disturbing changes, and by making possible a gradual and progressive absorption of the foreign element, led to the formation of a national culture that found its highest expression in Sassanian civilization.

RELIGION

There are still serious gaps in our knowledge of Iranian religion during the Parthian period. A dynasty that sprang from the peripheral regions of Iran inhabited by Iranian nomad elements must have brought with it primitive cults with worship of natural forces, above all the sun and moon. We know nothing, or practically nothing, about how far the Parthians adopted the religion practised in Iran. Recent research into religious tradition and archaeological excavation deny to Zoroastrianism the preponderant role accorded to it by certain scholars. The Parthians were no more Zoroastrians than were the Achaemenians. Those who support the contrary thesis point to the fact recorded by Tacitus that when Tiridates of Armenia, brother of Vologases I, visited Rome to receive his crown from the hands of Nero, he refused to go by sea for fear of polluting the water, which was a sacred element, but it must be remembered that water was venerated by the Iranians at all periods. This is confirmed by Herodotus, and the divinity who symbolized this element is known to have been Anahita. However that may be, the importance of another passage in Tacitus

(xv. 29) is frequently overlooked. This states that in the course of a 'preliminary' ceremony in Armenia this same Tiridates placed his crown at the foot of a statue of Nero and that he made this symbolic gesture 'after he had sacrificed victims, in accordance with custom'. Bloody sacrifices were thus practised in Iran in the first century A.D. and formed part of the religious rites of the royal family. This was contrary to the precepts of Zoroastrianism, which was strongly opposed to animal sacrifice.

The triad, Ahuramazda–Mithra–Anahita, worshipped under the Achaemenians, seems to have retained its hold on the popular and probably also on the official religion under the Parthians. Although there are no texts to confirm this in Iran, there is written evidence of its existence in Armenia, where the ancient historians refer to cult-places with three altars dedicated to these same three divinities whom they mention by name. This evidence, combined with that from the Achaemenian period, suggests that the two open-air altars found at Naqsh-i-Rustam and Pasargadae, as well as a third standing near the temple tower, were also dedicated to that triad. Worship of the three divinities is also indicated on coins of the princes of Persis, vassals of the Parthians; these coins depict three fires burning on three altars over the roof of a temple tower.

Of these three divinities, the cult of Anahita seems to have occupied the most important position from the time of Artaxerxes II, and under the Parthians it became preponderant. Several of the sanctuaries which Artaxerxes II dedicated to this goddess in the great centres of his empire are known. The cult of Anahita, which had been encouraged by the Achaemenian kings, spread under the Parthians, and all the Iranian temples mentioned in the historical texts were dedicated to this divinity. Tiridates I was crowned in a temple of Anahita at Arsak; at Ecbatana, the summer residence of the Parthian kings, a temple of Anahita was pillaged by Antiochus IV; that at Kengavar was dedicated to 'Artemis', that is to say, Anahita; in Elymais, the two sanctuaries looted by Mithridates I were those of 'Athene and Artemis'; at Susa the goddess worshipped was Nanaia, which is the Semitic name for Anahita, just as

Athene and Artemis are the Greek names. At Istakhr, the ancestors of the Sassanian family were guardians of a temple of Anahita where burnt *Athur Anahit*, or 'the fire of Anahita'; and according to certain scholars, the cult of fire was particularly associated with this goddess. Ardashir I hung the heads of his enemies on the walls of this temple and exposed the skin of Artabanus V, whom he had defeated and killed, in that of Ardeshir Khurra.

Of the Iranian triad, it was Anahita who enjoyed most popularity beyond the western frontiers of Iran, and her cult spread to Lydia, where she was called 'the lady of Bactria', to Pontus, Cappadocia, and Armenia. It was probably even more popular than that of Mithra, which the pirates captured by Pompey took to Rome, whence it was carried by the Roman armies as far as the Rhine and Danube.

Shiz, the great religious centre of Media Atropatene (modern Takht-i-Suliman) and the chief sanctuary of northern Iran, was also dedicated to Anahita. It sheltered a very old community of Magi who, at a period which we cannot determine, seem to have adopted some of the leading ideas of Zoroastrianism while retaining their old traditions and practices. One of these was exposure of the dead, but this custom was not adopted by the Arsacids, for they were buried at Nysa in the mountains bordering the Caucasian steppes in royal tombs like those of the Achaemenians. The practice of exposure does not seem to have been widespread in the Parthian period, for archaeological excavation at Nippur, Kakzu, and Dura-Europos has brought to light Parthian cemeteries in which the dead were buried with their funerary furnishings in terracotta sarcophagi. The coffins were often glazed and decorated with a naked goddess in relief, who is thought to be Anahita. These findings were confirmed recently by our discovery of a great Parthian cemetery at Susa. Among the many tombs found there some had a shaft leading to a funerary chamber (a type of grave that had perhaps survived from the Achaemenian period); others, dug deep into virgin soil, were reached by a staircase leading to a family vault with several chambers and funerary niches. The skeletons were always extended in terracotta sarcophagi. These

were sometimes glazed and had lids with a human face, crudely
rendered, doubtless in imitation of anthropoid sarcophagi, the
fashion for which must have spread from Syria or Palestine
(Pl. 30a and b).

At the end of the first or the beginning of the second century A.D. an important change took place in the burial customs
of the inhabitants of Susa. The individual grave and family
vault were replaced by a communal tomb in which the staircase, funerary chamber, and vaulted roof were built of well
baked brick. The corpse was first laid out on a bench facing
the entrance; after the flesh had decayed, the bones were scattered on two side benches, to the left and right of the entrance
(Pl. 30c). This new method of burial had something in common with the funerary customs of the Magi of the north who
exposed the bodies of the dead on mountains or 'towers of
silence'. In our opinion the graves at Susa may represent a
transitional stage between exposure and inhumation. We do
not know exactly when these changes occurred in the south;
possibly they happened when the female line of the Arsacid
dynasty under Artabanus III ascended to the throne; in Media
Atropatene, where they held sway, Magian influence was prominent, as may be seen from the sanctuary at Shiz, and this
may account for the extension to the south of what appears to
be a variant form of Magian burial.

We can no longer accept the myth which relates that Alexander the Great destroyed the *Avesta*, the sacred book of the
Iranians, written on thousands of skins in letters of gold. Nor
can we place much reliance on the tradition that this book was
drawn up on the orders of Vologases I. The great inscription
of Shapur I engraved on the walls of the fire temple of Naqsh-
i-Rustam is thought by certain scholars to prove that the collection of sacred texts, known as the *Avesta*, was not yet in
existence when this inscription was composed, that is in the
second half of the third century A.D. Our leading authorities on
the subject do not date the invention of the Avesta alphabet
earlier than the middle of the fourth or possibly the sixth
century A.D. The Parthian Arsacids, who like the Kushans,
sprang from the nomad Iranian peoples of Central Asia, were

very tolerant of foreign religions. In Mesopotamia they adopted the cults of the country they conquered, though they modified them or gave them a slightly different aspect. They considered that the foreign gods of the western regions of the Empire were benevolent and protected them, but they do not seem to have encouraged proselytizing among the conquered peoples. Among the many sanctuaries excavated at Dura-Europos, which long remained an advance post of the Parthian Empire, not a single fire temple was discovered, although there was an important Iranian colony in this trading centre.

The tolerance of the Arsacids was particularly evident in their relations with the Jewish people, who regarded the Iranian princes as true defenders of their faith. Having been oppressed by the Seleucids and the Romans, the Jews believed that Iran, which had always been well disposed towards them, was the only Great Power capable of delivering them from the foreign yoke, as it had done once before in the Achaemenian period. The appearance of the horsemen of Pacorus who restored the national dynasty at Jerusalem was greeted with enthusiasm. Under the Parthians there was a great expansion of Judaism in Babylonia. In 20 B.C. a small Jewish vassal state was established on the banks of the Euphrates and remained in existence nearly twenty years. The moral and intellectual life of the Jewish nation with its flourishing schools became centred in this area, in Babylon and the Greek cities, and played a part in the influence exercised by Jewish ideas on Iranian religion. During the great Jewish revolt of the second century A.D., which set all the Roman Orient ablaze, the rebels received aid from the Parthians, a fact which gave rise to the well-known saying: 'When you see a Parthian charger tied up to a tombstone in Palestine, the hour of the Messiah will be near'.

URBAN DEVELOPMENT, ARCHITECTURE AND ART

The Parthians do not seem to have built many towns, and few of their foundations are known. Outside the Plateau the best known sites are Ctesiphon and Hatra in Mesopotamia, and Darabgerd in Iran. Gor-Firuzabad, south of Shiraz, built by the first Sassanian, Ardeshir, while he was in revolt, or preparing to revolt, against his Parthian overlord, may also be considered as belonging to the Arsacid period. The lay-out of these towns is symptomatic of the instability in foreign affairs and unrest at home that prevailed in Iran under the Parthians. They were designed on a circular plan the origin of which went back to an old urban tradition in Western Asia; we may also recall the circular form of the Assyrian military camp. This plan was justified by the situation of these towns; Ctesiphon was first built as a Parthian military camp facing Seleucia on the Tigris; Hatra was a fortress near the frontier between the two empires, and was often used as a base for the defence of Iran against the Roman armies; finally, Ardashir built Gor-Firuzabad at the moment when he was making his daring bid to seize the crown from Artabanus V and had to bear in mind the possibility of defeat and the need to defend himself in a fortified town. He copied its circular plan from the town of Darabgerd where he had previously held an official position; this had been built in the form of a camp, possibly in anticipation of struggles between the feudal families, clans or factions. The state of Iran at this period must in many respects have resembled that of medieval Europe.

No examples of Parthian domestic architecture have yet been found on the Plateau, but we can obtain a fairly accurate idea of its character from remains in the western province of the kingdom. As in the Achaemenian period, there were two basic plans. There was first the house with a courtyard, derived from Mesopotamia, as at Dura-Europos or the palace of Darius at Susa. In contrast, at Assur (Fig. 80), Hatra, and Firuzabad we find the Iranian style of house with an *iwan*, which under the Parthians developed into the triple chamber, the central portion generally being rather larger than the wings. If we except certain modifications, the palace of Ctesiphon is an example of the second style, which became widespread among the Sassanians and survives to this day in Iranian architecture.

Various kinds of building materials were used: walls of rubble with ashlar masonry or of pebbles bonded with mortar were more common than the hewn blocks of stone known at

Hatra. In buildings of the latter type the stonework was decorated with sculpture. At Hatra this included masks (Fig. 81) as well as other motifs. These sculptured stone buildings were derived from Achaemenian architecture and continued under the Sassanians. Rubble or brick walls were decorated with moulded stucco and frescoes. They have been found in Babylonia and Assyria as well as at Kuh-i-Khwaja, an island in the middle of

Fig. 80 – Assur: Parthian palace

Lake Hamun in Seistan. At the latter site the stucco ornament includes the fret, saw-tooth, and overlapping circles. Mural painting apparently became much more widespread under the Parthians, and it is thought that the flatness of the contemporary bas-reliefs may reflect the influence of painting on their execution. The painted panels found at Kuh-i-Khwaja and attributed to the first century A.D. have a purely decorative function and are rich in colour and variety of subject. Among the decorative elements are rectangles with incurving sides, a geometrical framework typical of earlier Assyrian frescoes;

Fig. 81 – Hatra: Parthian palace

the designs within these frames consisted of yellow or violet
acanthus leaves, and also musicians, divinities, and a royal
couple, the free and natural treatment of which seems to prove
that Hellenistic influence was still alive.

No Parthian temples have been found on the Plateau, and
once again it is the outer provinces of the Empire that fill the
gap. To judge from the temples at Hatra (Fig. 82) and Taxila,
on the eastern bank of the Indus (Fig. 83), the plan of the Iranian sanctuary at this period consisted of a square central chamber separated from the exterior by an ambulatory, and was de-

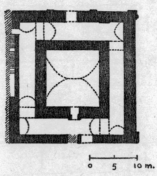

Fig. 82 – Hatra: Plan of the
temple

rived from that of the Achaemenians. The staircase, which in
Achaemenian times had been external, was contrived in the
thickness of the wall and led up to the roof, on which the altars
were situated. Religious ceremonies still took place in the open
near the temple, but the sacred fire burnt on the roof.

In any discussion of Parthian art, reference must be made to
two theories which at first sight may appear irreconcilable.
According to the first, the five centuries of Parthian rule represent a 'pathetically low' artistic level and its works of art give
the impression of a relapse into the unsophisticated state not of
infancy but of senility. The second theory takes the contrary
view, that once Parthian art had freed itself of everything

grafted on to Iranian art by Hellenism, it became national in character and made 'decisive progress'. Under the new impetus, a powerful neo-Iranian movement arose that was no longer contaminated by Greek influence and Iranian tradition, and experienced a renaissance, the effects of which were felt far beyond the frontiers of Iran.

Without appearing paradoxical, it may be argued that the two theories are not fundamentally opposed, since each is interested in a different aspect of the matter. The first considers a work of art from the point of view of its execution; for the second it is above all the subject, the concept expressed by the

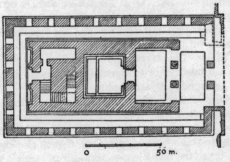

Fig. 83 – Taxila: Plan of the Parthian temple

picture, the intention of the monument, that is important. That phase of Parthian art that corresponds to the transition from Greco-Iranian to neo-Iranian is a melancholy one; the return towards a primitive technique is undeniable, and the decline in workmanship persisted throughout the Parthian period and influenced the early works of the Sassanians. The deterioration in technique was, however, offset by the attempt to revive a native tradition free of all foreign influence. This was a gain on the national plane, though an artistic loss. In the present state of our knowledge it is difficult to establish a precise chronology, but it has been suggested that the change took place during the first century A.D. This seems plausible, but should not preclude the existence of neo-Iranian works in earlier centuries.

So late a date need not seem surprising, for 'slow cultural changes always lag behind ephemeral political regimes with which the initiative must rest'.

A characteristic feature of Parthian art is strict observance of the law of frontality. Since this is not found on official Achaemenian monuments, its origin has been sought everywhere but in Iran itself. Nevertheless it appeared on the Plateau with the first Iranians, for representations of the human head occur on the painted vases of Cemetery B at Siyalk. It therefore dates from the beginning of the first millennium B.C. Not long afterwards it appears in the art of Luristan, where the entire body is shown full face, as in the votive objects on Plate 8 and in many other examples of this prolific art. Although this manner of treating the human form was not favoured by official Achaemenian art, Greco-Parthian carving shows that it continued in use. The convention was retained by the Sassanians, was then taken over by Syro-Mesopotamian artists, and eventually emerged in Byzantine art.

The most important extant monument of the Parthian period is undoubtedly the great bronze statue from Shami (Pl. 31), a district that corresponds to ancient Elymais. The temple in which it was found is near Malamir, which was already an important centre in the neo-Elamite period. Although it was not the capital of the kingdom of Elymais, it was one of its greatest cities, owing to its position on the important trade route linking the Persian Gulf with the district of Isfahan. The remains of the road that led into the heart of the Plateau are still visible; it was partly paved and partly cut into natural rock.

From the same temple a headless bronze statuette (Pl. 32a), was recovered, also the marble head of a prince with diadem (Pl. 32b) and the two fragments of the bronze head of a Hellenistic statue, to which reference has already been made (Pl. 29a). The large number of objects encountered during the excavation of the sanctuary, which yielded many fragments of marble and bronze statues, indicates its wealth. If, as has been suggested, the Hellenistic bronze head belonged to a statue of Antiochus IV, it is possible that the temple of Shami is one of the two sanctuaries pillaged by Mithridates I during his reconquest of Elymais after his defeat of Demetrius II (139 B.C.). If this identification is correct, the works of art found at Shami cannot be later than the middle of the second century B.C. To Greco-Iranian art may perhaps be attributed the marble head of a queen (Pl. 33b) discovered at Susa and thought to be Musa, wife of Phraates IV, which would date this object towards the end of the first century B.C. We are inclined to ascribe to the following century a great head from Hamadan (Pl. 34b), the ancient Ecbatana, where the Parthian kings had their summer palace. This piece of statuary with its inlaid eyes, though executed in a poor quality of limestone, is not without a certain spiritual quality. Finally, the head of a bearded man, also in limestone, from Susa (Pl. 34a) may chronologically bring to an end this group of objects in the round from Parthian Iran. It already shows a tendency towards a flat, linear silhouette, while the rendering of detail by incision connects it with the technique that was characteristic of neo-Iranian bas-reliefs.

These reliefs were far less affected by western tradition. Parthian bas-relief, in so far as it is known to us, shows little change from the work of the *fratadara* of the door-jambs in the temple built at the foot of the Persepolis terrace at the beginning of the third century B.C. (Pl. 27a and b). The oldest Parthian bas-relief known is that of Mithridates II, carved about 80 B.C. at Bisutun (Pl. 35b, left): its rigidity, lifelessness, and ignorance of anatomy emphasize the primitive technique of neo-Iranian art. Beside it is another monument ordered by Gotarzes II to commemorate his victory over his enemy Meherdates, about A.D. 50. This still shows traces of Hellenistic influence in the winged victory crowning the king; despite the 'mechanical' composition of the scene it is not lacking in movement.

The group of bas-reliefs from Tang-i-Sarwak, not far from Shami, is typical of this art, which though inferior in technique has a touch of the majestic, as for example in the scene of the King performing a sacrifice followed by several figures, all shown full face, or in that of the horseman charging with his lance (Pl. 36a and b). The same strict observance of the law of frontality, the same lack of animation in the rendering of detail

by incision (Pl. 35*a*) may be observed in a similar scene of a
prince (?) sacrificing before an altar, on another bas-relief
sculptured on a free-standing rock at Bisutun. To the same
category of monuments we may assign a bas-relief recently
found at Susa, which represents Artabanus V, the last Arsacid
king, handing a ring or crown, the symbol of power, to the
local satrap. Here again we may observe the characteristic
style of Parthian bas-relief, and this monument may justifiably
be considered the latest work of the dynasty (Pl. 37).

Special mention must be made of a small bust of a king in
high relief (Pl. 33*a*), executed in a hard green stone, which on
grounds of size may be classified as a gem belonging to a neck-
lace or crown (height 1¼ inches). The king, shown full face,
wears the Arsacid national head-dress which serves as a frame,
covers up the ears and reaches down to the shoulders. The
front of the head-dress is decorated with a vertical row of
square stones, and across the forehead is a diadem formed of a
double band of horsehair, the ends of which become thicker
and fall on the shoulders. The flaring nostrils, bushy mous-
tache, and long, square-cut beard convey the impression of a
faithful portrait. The realism and calm distinction of its expression rank this small piece among the best examples of Parthian
art. The bust stands out from a plaque, the upper part of which
is shaped like a rounded stele; it bears an inscription in Pahlavi-
Arsacid: 'Arsaces Vologases, King of Kings'. By analogy with
the coinage, this would seem to be Vologases III. A certain resemblance may be observed between this little object and the
busts of Palmyra.

The group of rock or monumental Parthian bas-reliefs just
described is typically Iranian, both in poorness of technique
and in choice of subject. The religious ceremony before a fire
altar, the scene of investiture, mounted combat or the hunt
(Pl. 36*b*, bottom right) were all popular themes in Iranian art
at this period. This art spread far beyond the actual frontiers
of Iran; westwards it penetrated the Iranian frontier posts, particularly Dura, and southern Russia, where similar scenes are
found painted on the walls of Sarmatian tombs. Taken over by
the nomadic Iranians of the Eurasian steppes it spread to the

frontiers of China, where the Han monuments show that Chinese art did not remain untouched by Iranian influence.

Parthian art in its turn drew inspiration from foreign sources. From the nomads it acquired a taste for the flamboyant polychrome jewellery of the Kushans and Sarmatians. Jewellery of this kind was much favoured by the Goths and Germans, and eventually reached the Atlantic coast, where it was adopted by

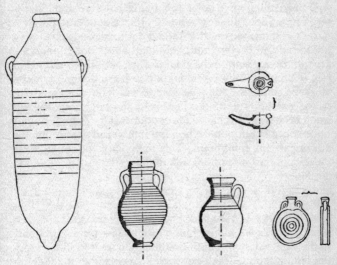

Fig. 84 – Susa: Parthian pottery

the Merovingians. Iran also received from the steppes a vigorous style of animal portraiture, of which we illustrate a fine example on Pl. 38b. This is a bronze incense-burner with a handle in the shape of a magnificent wild beast, whose supple and powerful body bears a marked family resemblance to an animal from the Sarmatian treasure of Novorossijsk.

Finally mention must be made of the work of the potter, who played an important part in daily life. Just as to-day workshops specializing in funerary monuments and objects of piety are to be found near our cemeteries, so in the time of the Parthians

the potter's workshop stood outside the town wall near the
graveyard. We identified several at Susa. These craftsmen
manufactured sarcophagi and funerary urns, the former for
adults, the latter for children; they fashioned vases and cups in
blue or green glazed ware, either for domestic use or as 'pil-
grim flasks' to be placed in the tombs (Fig. 84). They also
modelled figurines of the naked goddess – also known in bone (Pl.
39*b*) – and of mounted horsemen, found in dozens in the ceme-
tary site and probably representing protective deities. We have
already commented on these terra-cotta horsemen, which have
been found in every country through which the conquering
Iranian passed, from Achaemenian Egypt to the Kushan Empire (Pl. 38*a*). Finally a terra-cotta *Emblema* found in a potter's
workshop at Susa must be mentioned. This represented a
naked goddess who presses her breast and catches the milk in
a cup held in the left hand. The workmanship of this piece has
not escaped Western influence, but subject and treatment alike
are oriental in conception. This may represent the goddess
Anahita in the guise of a Greek divinity (Pl. 39*a*).

ECONOMIC AND SOCIAL LIFE

The heritage of Alexander the Great, partitioned between
three Macedonian monarchies which were attacked by Rome
in the west and the Parthians in the east, collapsed after a long-
drawn-out agony. Its fall caused violent upheavals in the countries that had contained it, and of these Asia seems to have
suffered the most. From the middle of the second century B.C.
revolutions and revolts grievously affected the countries of the
Mediterranean basin as well as Iran, and even southern Russia.
Throughout the area there was an economic crisis and fall in
production, while difficulties of exchange and transport were
aggravated by the spread of banditry on the roads and piracy
on the seas. This was a dark age in which war and pillage were
rife. Plundering of caravans and piracy became so frequent
that Rome was forced to put an end to the power of the last
petty Seleucid princes who had degenerated into mere puppet
kings, and Pompey annexed Syria (64 B.C.) in order to scour

this sink of Mediterranean iniquity. The moral crisis was revealed in the unbridled desire of the Roman upper class for self-enrichment, which became an obsession and on occasion involved the Republic in foreign war. The career of Crassus is a case in point.

But in the first century B.C. an intense and growing desire for peace, for which all peoples of the world longed desperately, arose on the Roman frontiers, particularly in Iran. Augustus came to power as this urge for peace reached Rome.

The achievement of the first Roman Emperor in re-establishing world equilibrium, restoring the general situation, and stabilizing prices, was immense, and its consequences were felt in countries far distant from Rome, including Iran. This revival was, however, powerless to save the ancient culture; classical antiquity and Hellenism foundered, and the world began slowly to rebuild itself on new social and economic foundations.

By the second century B.C., Italy was an important economic factor in the Mediterranean basin. Since it was not self-sufficient it became an importer of goods from Hellenistic lands, and its social and economic development led to an ever-growing demand for products from an increasingly wide area. The Roman conquest tapped the riches of the ancient world, and Rome itself became the centre of a vast network of countries stretching from Gaul to Central Asia, China, and India; their highly prized luxury products, silk, spices, ivory, perfume, and precious stones constantly increased the volume of trade, and in exchange Rome exported manufactured goods such as bronze and glass ware, objects of art, wines, oils, and above all gold. In this international trade Iran continued to act as an intermediary between East and West, for many caravans passed along its trade routes. Its role became one of capital importance; within its territory arose centres of specialists in transit trade, middlemen, agents for the various means of transport, caravan leaders, and organizations of boatmen for water carriage. The sending of embassies from China to the Arsacid Court permitted the establishment of direct relations between the two empires, the improvement of the organization of the road system, and the placing of the balance of trade on a sound basis. From the first century A.D. merchandise, after crossing Iran, entered the Kushan Empire; some of it went by way of the Pamirs and Chinese Turkestan to reach the Chinese frontier, some crossed the passes of the Hindu Kush and travelled down from Kabul to India. Never had the states of East and West been so closely linked, nor, before the time of Augustus, had there been so much trade in either direction.

There had been economic links between Iran, Babylonia, and Syria-Palestine since the Achaemenian period, and although the plan of the Roman Emperors to annex Iran and Mesopotamia failed, these links continued to hold, and even became stronger. Iran exported metals, including steel, from China and India, which had a high reputation among the markets of the world at that time; and it is believed that Damascus steel, which was so renowned in the Middle Ages, was of Chinese or perhaps Indian origin. Plutarch calls the arms of the Parthian cavalry the 'Arms of Merv', a town which was certainly only an important intermediary centre for the trade in Chinese steel. Other goods included skins, furs, textiles, worked wood, cattle, birds, rice, saffron, drugs, precious stones, bitumen, and mineral oil. Iran imported papyrus, bronze objects, glassware, pottery, purple dye, and divers metal objects. Internal trade increased in volume and markets were multiplied. Banking was one of the only commercial activities which apparently declined in scope during this period.

Means of transport were improving, the roads had never been so well maintained as under the Parthians, and their kings devoted much attention to their care because taxes raised on goods in transit were a very important source of revenue to the State. The tracks across the desert were provided with wells and caravanserais. In caravan cities like Palmyra, Dura, and Petra houses were built as meeting-places for merchants; documents found at Dura prove the existence of mounted desert police, and attest a belief in tutelary gods for the caravans; they were depicted riding horses or camels. The Parthians ran a postal service, and the relay stations allowed of extremely fast travel; Vardanes on his way to dethrone his brother Gotarzes made a journey of 350 miles in two days. At this period, too, horseshoes first appeared, but it is not known whether they were an invention of the East or West.

The development of crafts and industries is shown by the improvement in the quality and finish of textiles, leather-work, pottery, arms, and glassware, and it is interesting that the same is true of the products manufactured in Rome, which shows how far technical advance kept pace in far distant parts of the civilized world.

There were important changes in the sphere of agriculture. Among the Romans, those who were wealthy and enterprising bought State land cheaply and created large estates or *latifundia*. In Iran the small estate gradually disappeared and was replaced by the large domains of the feudal lords. The peasant and small farmer lost their independence and were increasingly oppressed by the large landed proprietors: officially they remained free, but their liberty was only relative. Agriculture benefited from these developments in the sense that the wealthy landowner was in a position to maintain a good standard of farming and to cultivate the soil scientifically as well as to keep abreast of new techniques which would have been beyond the means of the peasant. This advantage was offset by a partial loss of liberty on the part of the peasant population. As a result of these changes new class distinctions arose in Iran, which split up into a provincial and an urban society, each of which was linked to a particular branch of the national economy and had its own way of life. The price of land rose owing to the security afforded by capital investment, and as a result it became impossible for the small peasantry to keep possession of its holdings or to continue the struggle. Thus the aspect of the country-side was transformed, the greater part being divided between State lands and great estates.

Progress in agricultural science, which had reached a very high level in the Hellenistic period, fell off, but advances were made in the breeding of domestic animals, and particularly of poultry, which was sought for in foreign markets. Following the first embassies sent by China to Iran, lucerne, the vine, the

cucumber, onion, saffron, and jasmine were introduced into
the celestial Empire and began to be cultivated there. In exchange Iran acquired the apricot and the peach from China and
later the silkworm. Cultivation of the sugar-cane imported
from China also began at this period.

Little is known about changes in urban society, but it may
be assumed that the liberal ideas launched by Hellenism and
developed by Rome also affected Iran. There must have been a
certain levelling, as happened in Rome, where a different attitude was adopted towards slaves; enfranchized slaves produced the finest works of art, and those who were reckoned as
'de luxe' slaves succeeded in attaining high office in the State;
indeed some of them even ascended the throne of the Caesars.
In Iran a slave girl given by Rome to Phraates IV became
Queen, and during the reign of her son Phraates V, who subsequently became her husband, she played a leading part in
affairs of State.

The fusion of the Greek and Iranian peoples of Iran continued, and the Greeks founded Greco-Iranian families in
which Greek and Iranian names occur with equal frequency.
It became increasingly difficult to determine the limits of the
lower and upper classes. Impoverished Iranized Greeks could
occupy a lower rung in the social scale than Hellenized Iranians. It followed that society, in which the Greeks occupied the
higher ranks, was divided in accordance with the size of fortunes into the rich, who might include Iranians, and into the
poor, among whom might be Greeks.

Iranian society as a whole experienced an even greater dif-
ferentiation: the great landed proprietors, the courtiers, the
officials, the families who did not belong to the aristocracy,
formed a new nobility, alongside which arose a class of town
and country freemen. In Roman society a similar development
led to a quadruple division into (1) dynasty; (2) church;
(3) honestiores; (4) humiliores. This was reflected in the structure of Sassanian society; (1) nobles and warriors; (2) priests;
(3) scribes and officials; and (4) the working population.

The true character of the Parthian–Arsacids and of the Iran
over which they ruled for nearly four centuries is gradually

emerging as the result of research into their history, religion, art, and civilization. At first it was no more than a conquest by a small and insignificant outlying province of the Seleucid Empire, but gradually it eliminated the traces of dying Hellenism. The Arsacid advance towards the West had its counterpart in that of Rome towards the East. Eventually the two peoples, Iran and Rome, who had divided between them the material and spiritual heritage of Hellenism, came face to face on opposite banks of the Euphrates. The former, claiming to be heir to the Achaemenians and Seleucids, aspired to restore the ancient Empire with its outlets on the Mediterranean. The latter under the Caesars claimed to be heir to Alexander and aspired to the dominion of the whole of Asia including India.

For nearly three centuries Iran stood on the defensive against Rome, all of whose sallies, apart from certain ephemeral successes, were doomed to failure. Iran emerged victorious from the long struggle with the formidable Roman Empire, and perhaps benefited therefrom in that a new branch of the old warlike spirit was infused into it. Under the last of the Achaemenians this martial ardour had been sapped, and hardly any of it had survived under the Seleucids.

The struggle against Rome had other practical consequences for Arsacid Iran. The overthrow of Crassus, the invasion of Syria by Pacorus, the disaster inflicted on Antony, and the concessions made by Augustus proved to the Iranians that they possessed resources capable of resisting the assault of the West and that they could maintain the independence and integrity of their country. A national consciousness, which had played little part in the conquest of Parthia by Arsaces and Tiridates, was slowly reborn. This gradual awakening was perhaps encouraged by the emergence of a new dynasty, and was reflected in the political, religious, and economic life of the nation.

In addition to its struggle with Rome, Parthian Iran had to face the onslaught of nomadic invasions, some of which came from the north-east steppes and others through the Caucasian passes. By resisting these attacks, Iran made a great contribution to the world, since it defended and perhaps saved from destruction the ancient civilization of Western Asia, to which it was one of the heirs. Although exhausted by internal dissension, owing to the absence of a strong central power, Iran nevertheless emerged successful from the contest with foreign enemies on three fronts. By their revival of the Iranian spirit and their successful foreign policy, the Parthian–Arsacids prepared the way for the Sassanians, who were enabled to achieve a national unity and a civilization that was more exclusively Iranian than it had ever been before. 'The sudden renaissance of the Sassanians is a myth.' The liaison between them and the Achaemenians was provided by the Parthians.

CHAPTER 7

The Expansion of Iranian Civilization

*

THE SASSANIANS

THE centre of Iranian revival was the province of Fars, where the Persian tribes had first settled nearly 1,000 years earlier. The Empire passed to a line of national kings who, as descendants of the Achaemenians, claimed that they alone, and not the Arsacids, had the right to the throne. They founded a national state with a national religion and a civilization that was far more Iranian in character than that of the Parthians. They established a central power strong enough to curb the turbulent feudal aristocracy, built up a well-trained regular army, and provided the country with an efficient administration. Thus strengthened, Iran successfully continued the policy initiated by the last Arsacids and became so powerful that the civilized world appeared to be divided between it and Rome.

The Sassanians conducted an active foreign policy and waged war, with intermittent success, on three fronts: against Rome in the West, the Kushans and Ephthalites in the East, and the nomads in the North. The thorny question of Armenia also engaged their attention, but they failed to achieve a final settlement. Over four centuries of war with neighbouring countries, however, eventually sapped the strength of the Iranian people, which was further weakened by internal dissensions. Feudalism, always on the look-out for an opportunity to recover its privileges, revolts of powerful military leaders who coveted supreme power, despotism, violent rivalries centred round the throne, whose authority gradually weakened, and, finally, a class war in the form of a communist movement that shook Iranian society to its foundations and led to bloodshed throughout the land – all these factors contributed to the fall of the Empire at the very moment when, in the eyes of the world, it seemed to be at the zenith of its power. The *coup de grâce* was not, however, delivered by the traditional enemies of Iran, but by the young Arab people who had only just emerged from the nomadic and savage life of the Beduin. Fired with religious fanaticism, they rapidly made themselves masters of the vast Iranian Empire. They found the Sassanian inheritance a valuable training ground, and their military conquest was followed by a long though peaceful struggle from which the Iranian cause finally emerged triumphant.

*　　*　　*

According to tradition, Sassan, the ancestor of the Sassanian dynasty, was a high dignitary in the temple of Anahita at Stakhr. His son, Papak, who succeeded him in this office, married the daughter of a local prince from whom he seized power by a *coup d'état*. He was considered by later tradition to be the real founder of the dynasty, and his accession was the starting-point from a new era (A.D. 208). His suzerain, the Parthian King, refused to recognize the legality of his action, and withheld his consent when Papak wished to secure the succession for his son, Shapur. This caused a breach between the Great King and his vassal that well illustrates the conditions of unrest and anarchy prevalent at this period in Iran, especially in Fars.

Ardashir, the second son of Papak, held a military post at Darabgerd, a provincial town in Fars. On the death of his father, he refused to recognize Shapur as King. A conflict between the two brothers was imminent when the accidental death of Shapur enabled Ardashir to realize his ambition and proclaim himself King of Persis. He reduced to submission all the small princes of Fars, succeeded in uniting the province under his rule, and extended his suzerainty beyond its borders to Isfahan and Kerman. At this point Artabanus V became alarmed at his success and ordered the King of Ahwaz to march against him. But Ardashir defeated this force and shortly afterwards himself took the offensive. He routed the army of the Parthian King in three successive battles and in the final encounter in Susiana Artabanus was killed (A.D. 224). The way to Ctesiphon lay open, and two years later Ardashir was crowned king. Five and a half centuries after the fall of the

Achaemenians the Persian people had regained power, and the new dynasty, as the legitimate successor of the Achaemenians, ensured the continuity of Iranian civilization.

The defeat and death of Artabanus V did not remove all the obstacles that confronted Ardashir in his bid to become the undisputed master of Iran. A powerful coalition was formed against him for the purpose of restoring the Arsacids. The moving spirit was the King of Armenia, Chosroes I, himself a member of the Arsacid family. He opened the gates of the Caucasus in order to bring in Scythian aid and received support from Rome. The powerful King of the Kushans, at whose Court members of the family of Artabanus had sought refuge, also placed forces at the disposal of the coalition. Only one of the great Parthian families, however – that of Karen – joined the movement against Ardashir; all the others hastened to assure the new sovereign of their loyalty.

Ardashir smashed the coalition in a series of battles, and by bribery persuaded some of the allies to abandon what was clearly a hopeless struggle. The Romans and Scythians withdrew, and the Kushan King retired after two years of hostilities. In the end the King of Armenia was left to continue the fight alone. He put up a stubborn resistance and was defeated only after ten years of fighting. Ardashir was now master of an empire extending from the Euphrates to Merv, Herat, and Seistan. After he had reduced his enemies at home to submission, he turned his attention to the consolidation of his frontiers. Conflict with Rome became inevitable. It ended, after several defeats, in the reoccupation by the Persians of the two important fortresses of Nisibis and Carrhae (Fig. 85).

During a reign of nearly fifty years, Ardashir overcame one enemy after another and succeeded in building up a new Iranian Empire. His greatest achievement was to forge the army into a powerful instrument that made possible the realization of his policy. He associated his son, Shapur, in his rule during his lifetime and according to tradition handed over the Crown and retired from active life a few years before his death.

Shapur inherited from his father a state in which Parthian institutions, including the feudal system, were retained but reorganized by the introduction of a high degree of centralization. With a disciplined army and an administration functioning on a new basis, the Empire was firmly established. From the beginning of his reign Shapur directed his attention to foreign affairs. It has been seen that as early as the first century A.D. the formation of a great Kushan Empire on its eastern frontiers constituted a political menace and an economic embarrassment for Iran. It was caught between the Romans and the Kushans, continually involved in the Armenian question and constantly menaced by the nomads who pressed against the Caucasian passes. The young Sassanian Empire may well have felt that a simultaneous war on all these fronts was beyond its strength. An attack on the Kushan Empire, however, held a double attraction, for it had grown rich from foreign trade, and it was against this power that Shapur made his first move. In a long inscription sculptured on the walls of the fire temple at Naqsh-i-Rustam, he records his first success: his victorious army seized Peshawar, the winter capital of the Kushan King, occupied the Indus valley, and pushing north, crossed the Hindu Kush, conquered Bactria, crossed over the Oxus and entered Samarkand and Tashkent. The Kushan dynasty, founded by the great Kanishka, was deposed and replaced by another line of princes who recognized the suzerainty of the Persians and ruled over a state considerably reduced in area.

Having settled the eastern question, Shapur turned towards the West. Here also he was favoured by fortune. He had advanced across Syria as far as Antioch, but was preparing to withdraw after several defeats, when the Emperor Gordian was killed, and his successor, Philip the Arab, hastened to make peace, paying a large tribute to Persia and ceding Mesopotamia and Armenia (A.D. 244). Fifteen years later the war with Rome was resumed and conducted with notable success. Shapur seized an impressive number of Syrian towns, including Antioch. In a great victory near Edessa the Emperor Valerian fell into his hands and 70,000 Roman legionaries were sent into exile in Iran and settled in towns built on the plan of a Roman military camp (A.D. 260). They provided the Empire with specialists, architects, engineers, and technicians who were

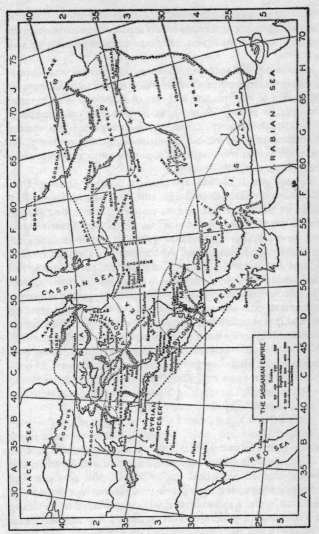

Fig. 85 – Map of the Sassanian Empire

employed on large-scale public works, notably the building of bridges, barrages, and roads which conferred great benefits on the rich province of Khuzistan. Some of their remains are still in use.

Exploiting his success, Shapur ravaged Syria and Cappadocia, but on his return march was attacked and defeated by the Prince of Palmyra and lost part of his booty. This reverse, however, in no way detracted in Persian eyes from the spectacular capture of Valerian; to commemorate his victory Shapur caused five bas-reliefs to be sculptured on the rocks and cliffs of Fars showing the Roman Emperor prostrate at his feet (Pl. 43b, and Fig. 86).

In addition to his military exploits, Shapur completed the internal reorganization of the Empire begun by his father. Possessed of wide interests and an enquiring mind, he commissioned the translation of numerous Greek and Indian works dealing with the most varied questions, such as medicine, astronomy, and philosophy. As the creator of a great empire, he took an interest in Mani and extended his protection to this founder of a 'universal' religion, whose ideas, borrowing from Zoroastrianism, Buddhism, and Christianity, gained adherents in Western Asia among the followers of these three great religions. It is possible that Shapur had a political motive for attaching Mani to his person and encouraging the spread of his religion. But although this great ruler may have had some such idea in mind, his policy was reversed by his successor. Shortly after his death (A.D. 272) Mani was persecuted and finally put to death during the reign of Vahram I, who was almost certainly influenced by the Mazdian priests.

Very little is known about the short reigns of the two sons of Shapur, Hormizd I and Vahram I. A new war with Rome began under Vahram II (A.D. 276–93), and this coincided with a serious revolt in the eastern marches of the Empire. The King's brother, who held the important post of viceroy of Seistan, attempted to seize the throne. He was supported in his rebellion by the Kushan prince, who, encouraged by the laxity of the suzerain power, hoped to regain his independence. Vahram II was therefore menaced on two fronts. The threat

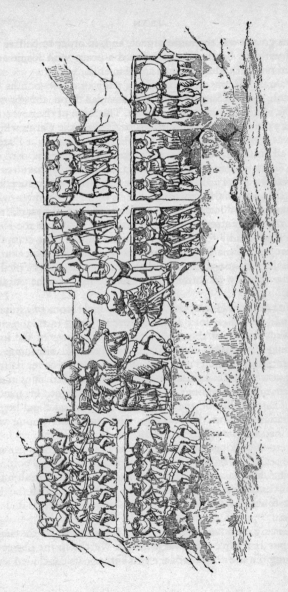

Fig. 86 – Bishapur: Triumph of Shapur I

to his crown was the more urgent, and, in order to be free to
deal with his brother, he concluded a peace with Rome and
ceded northern Mesopotamia and Armenia.

Vahram III was deposed after a reign of a few months by
Narsah, a son of Shapur I, and the Sassanian throne thus passed
to the junior branch of the dynasty. The reign of the new sovereign did not have an auspicious beginning: the war in which
he was involved with Rome ended in disaster, and, like Darius
III, all his family fell into enemy hands. The peace imposed on
him deprived Iran of Little Armenia, the group of provinces to
the east of the Tigris. Never before had Rome made such important gains at the expense of Persia, but it was content with
this success and left the peace undisturbed for forty years. Iran
was no longer strong enough to resist the revival of the Kushan kingdom by force of arms, but attempted to contain the
threat by the marriage of Hormizd II, son and successor of
Narsah (A.D. 303–9), to a Kushan princess, who was a pledge
of the friendly intentions of her family towards the Sassanians.

The death of Hormizd II left the imperial throne to a minor,
Shapur II, whose long reign of seventy years (A.D. 309–79),
proved worthy of those of the first two princes of the line.
During his minority the Kushan kingdom took advantage of
the internal disorders and weakness of Iran to recover its former power, and even made a number of territorial gains at the
expense of its neighbour. But as soon as he attained his majority, Shapur followed the example of his namesake and began
operations against the Kushans. This time their empire was
smashed and its territory annexed to Iran as a new province,
governed by kings chosen from among the Sassanian princes
who resided at Balkh. Cultural expansion followed on political
success, and Sassanian art soon spread to the East through the
door thrown open by the victorious armies. It reached the distant towns of Chinese Turkestan, and even penetrated to
China.

Having removed the threat to his security in the East,
Shapur II resumed the war with the West with the object of
wiping out the disgrace of the two agreements concluded with

the Romans by Vahram II and Narsah which had led to the loss of the greater part of the western provinces. The operations proved protracted: at first they were favourable to the Romans, but later turned to the advantage of the Persians. They were suspended for a time when an invasion of Little Kushans and Chionite Ephthalites threatened the eastern marches. The campaign against these nomads ended in concessions and the invaders settled on Kushan territory as 'confederates' and undertook to furnish troops to the King in his struggle with Rome. A Roman attempt to negotiate a settlement was rejected and the war was renewed. The most brilliant feat of arms in this campaign was the capture of Amida by Shapur II, supported by his new eastern allies. A Roman counter-attack actually threatened Ctesiphon, but when the Emperor Julian was killed in battle the Roman army withdrew, and the subsequent peace restored the disputed provinces to Shapur. Armenia was recovered, but Roman intrigues to place a pro-Roman prince in power there compelled Shapur to take a radical step: just as the Kushan kingdom had been reduced to a Persian province, so Armenia was placed under military occupation and governed by a *marzban* or commander of the frontier marches.

The quarrel between Iran and Rome now assumed a new aspect. The conversion of Constantine the Great and of Armenia to Christianity led to the development of closer ties between Armenia and Byzantium, although a section of the Armenian nobility sought to maintain the old connexion with Iran, whose civilization had so profoundly influenced their country. Armenia, which had long been the cockpit of the Irano-Roman wars, was now torn between two factions of its population, the pro-Iranians and the pro-Romans, and the policy adopted by Shapur did little to calm these passions. When Christianity became the official religion of the Roman Empire, the Christian subjects of the King of Kings inevitably became politically suspect in the eyes of the Iranian authorities, and their persecution stained with blood the rest of the long reign of Shapur II.

During the century following his death there were constant

struggles between the throne, which was occupied by nonentities, and the feudal aristocracy allied with the powerful Zoroastrian priesthood. Despite all the measures introduced by the founders of the Empire to curb their power, the great nobles not only retained certain traditional prerogatives, but actually increased their influence, and certain of the high positions they occupied in the Empire had become hereditary. The royal authority was weakened by their systematic opposition, and finally the King lost the right to name his successor, as had been the custom under the first Sassanian princes. Iran became a monarchy elective in the Sassanian family, which was, as a result, torn by factions supporting rival claimants.

The increase in the power of the nobility began under Ardashir and continued under Shapur III and Vahram IV. It coincided with a fresh attempt to solve the Armenian question. As the result of a compromise with Rome, the two rival Empires partitioned Armenia (A.D. 389), four-fifths of the country passing under the suzerainty of Iran. In the event, Armenia was not long ruled by its own king, for in A.D. 429 it once again became a province administered by Sassanian officials; the same fate befell the area placed under Roman protection. Under these three kings the treatment of the Christians undoubtedly became more tolerant than it had been under Shapur II, but Iranian policy on this question was always closely linked with the foreign situation and the personality of the reigning Prince. Thus there was a radical change in the treatment of the Christians of Iran during the reign of Yazdgard I. This King, who was married to a Jewess, was so well disposed towards them that they called him 'the Christian King'. He convoked a council, installed a *catholicos* at Seleucia and five metropolitans in the provincial towns, and permitted the free movement of clergy throughout the country. But the Christians apparently abused their privileges, and were guilty of violent demonstrations against the Zoroastrian sanctuaries and clergy. In view of this attitude, the King was compelled to revise his policy.

The first clash between Iran and the new power in the east, the kingdom of the Chionite-Ephthalites, seems to have occurred under Yazdgard I. After they had been settled by Shapur

II on Kushan territory with the title of 'confederates', the Ephthalites succeeded in evicting the Little Kushans and formed a powerful kingdom which, towards the beginning of the fifth century, took advantage of Iranian weakness to expand on both sides of the Hindu Kush, whence it threatened India.

On the death of Yazdgard I there was fierce rivalry for the succession between his sons. Vahram V (A.D. 421–38) emerged victorious from this struggle owing to military aid from the Arab prince of Hira, a small vassal state of the Sassanians, west of the Euphrates, where he had been brought up. This intervention by a foreign people in the dynastic affairs of Iran provided a precedent that was followed by others and in the end was one of the causes of the decline of the Empire. Vahram V was the most famous of Sassanian kings, winning renown as hunter, poet, and musician. He was immortalized in many legends which tell of his prowess, and was a favourite subject of the Iranian artist for centuries, even after the fall of the Empire. At home he avoided trouble with the nobles by giving up his prerogatives. Abroad he waged a successful campaign against the Ephthalites that curbed their expansionist ambitions, but was less fortunate in a short war with Byzantium. This had been provoked by renewed persecution of the Christians and ended in an agreement granting them freedom of worship. Once again events led to an *entente* between Rome and Iran. In an earlier treaty concluded between Shapur III and the Emperor Jovian, the two Powers had agreed on mutual defence of the Caucasian passes: the Persian built and garrisoned fortifications, and Roman gold defrayed part of the cost of their upkeep. These northern defences were under continued attack from waves of nomadic Huns who on occasion overran them, as in A.D. 395, when they invaded not only Armenia but also Cappadocia and northern Syria, and even threatened Antioch. Rome was ready to continue this arrangement for mutual defence and to share in the protection of the Caucasian Gates. Under Vahram V a solution was found for the problem of the Christians of Iran; their internecine quarrels led the new Catholicos, with the support of the King, to summon a synod which decided to make the Christian Church of Iran independent of that of Byzantium. Thus suspicion of Christian Iranians, who had in the past been accused of intriguing on behalf of the Romans, was brought to an end.

For a time, indeed, the Christians won the goodwill of Yazdgard II (A.D. 438–59). This King took a particular interest in the question of religion and made a study of all those practised in Iran, but he remained a zealous Zoroastrian and in the end persecuted both Jews and Christians. His attempt to convert Armenia to Mazdaism led to a general rising while he was involved in wars with the Ephthalites, and the Iranian forces were defeated. Yazdgard, however, marched into Armenia, crushed the insurgents and deprived the people of leaders by carrying off to Iran representatives of the great families and of the clergy.

The internal situation of the Empire deteriorated still further under Peroz (A.D. 459–84). For several years in succession, famine ravaged town and country, compelling the King to remit taxes and distribute corn. The land was torn by religious strife: the King continued the persecution of the Jews, while the Christians were divided between Nestorians (who acknowledged two natures in Christ, one divine, the other human) and the Monophysites (for whom the two natures were merged in the unity of his person). In the end the wars undertaken by Peroz against the Ephthalites brought the country to the verge of disaster. The King was defeated and taken prisoner, and regained his liberty only in return for a heavy tribute. He left his son Kavad as hostage while he raised the necessary sum by levying new taxes. Once again he appealed to Rome for assistance.

Byzantium, however, pursued an astute policy towards the Persians. Rome needed Iran as a buffer state to parry the blows of the barbarians whose invasions threatened the eastern frontiers of the Roman Empire; if Iran became too weak the possessions of Byzantium would be exposed to attack. For this reason the Emperor Zeno, according to western tradition, ransomed Peroz when he fell into Ephthalite hands after his defeat. The Persians, however, were always liable to make disastrous raids on the rich provinces of Mesopotamia; but so long as they were embroiled with the barbarians, Mesopotamia was not in danger. It was essential, therefore, to save Persia from too disastrous a defeat, and yet at the same time to instigate and foment its conflicts with the Huns. Indeed, we learn from a Syrian chronicle that the Romans encouraged the Huns in an attack on Peroz in which they forced 'the gates of the Caucasus' guarded by his troops and pushed as far as the Iranian provinces, compelling the King of Kings to mobilize his armies to resist them.

Several years of peace on the Ephthalite front permitted Peroz to restore his financial position and to raise troops for a further attack on these enemies. His advisers sought to dissuade him from the venture, but he remained adamant. In A.D. 484 he attacked the Ephthalites, suffered a fresh reverse, and paid for this ill-fated enterprise with his life.

After his death the eastern neighbour of Iran was no longer a confederate people or a vassal paying tribute, or even an ally. It was virtually the master of Iran. During the reigns of the four successors of Peroz – a period of over half a century – the Ephthalite King not only exacted a heavy annual tribute in cash, but also intervened in Iranian domestic affairs, particularly in the quarrels and rivalries of the pretenders to the throne and in Court intrigues. Thus Balash, who succeeded Peroz, was replaced by Kavad after a reign of only four years. Since the latter Prince had spent his youth among the Ephthalites we may conclude that they had a hand in the events leading to his accession (A.D. 488).

'Every unsuccessful war brings a religious and political reaction in its train.' The task inherited by Kavad was a heavy one – more onerous, indeed, than any that had fallen to the lot of his predecessors. After several years of famine, the wars of Peroz, and his final defeat, the country was on the brink of economic disaster. The vassal states were in revolt and the country was plagued by nomad raids. The northern frontier had to be defended against the invasions of the Huns and tribute had to be paid to the Ephthalites. The need for gold was greater than ever, but the treasury was empty. Kavad sent one

embassy after another to Constantinople, but without any posi-
tive result. At home, he had to choose between the powerful
nobility and the people, the mass of whom followed the Mazdakite movement and demanded far-reaching social reforms to
improve the lot of the disinherited class. He had the courage to
side with the people in order to weaken the power of the
aristocracy.

The Mazdakite movement was based on a religion that had
its own cosmogony and eschatology, derived in the main from
the teachings of Mani. It required of its followers abstinence
and the avoidance of hatred and strife. Its appeal lay in its
social theories, which called for equality in the distribution of
goods. The possessions of the rich were to be given to the
poor, and this applied both to material goods and to women.
In a society like that of the Sassanian Empire, in which the
various classes were in water-tight compartments, where the
plebeian could never hope to raise himself above the station
into which he was born, where the social system was based on
the family, property, and rigid class distinction, the programme
put forward by Mazdak was revolutionary. It has with justi-
fication been described as Iranian communism. Certain scholars
explain it as a reaction of the slaves, of the peasants who had
become semi-slaves, and of the formerly free population of
town and country against feudalism and its 'enslaving' system; as a class struggle which was a protest against the harems
of the nobility in which so many women were incarcerated.

Kavad championed this movement and introduced a number of new laws, some of which apparently dealt with the position of women. He was deposed as the result of a plot, thrown
into prison and tried, but his life was spared, and shortly afterwards he escaped and took refuge at the Ephthalite court. In
A.D. 499 he returned to Iran with an Ephthalite army, deposed
his brother, Zamasp, and regained his throne. From this moment his policy underwent a change. He was forced to continue the payment of tribute to the Ephthalites and to reward
the Ephthalite soldiers who remained in his service; hence-
forward he looked to them for support against his enemies.
The refusal of Rome to pay its promised quota led to the rup-

ture of relations. Kavad invaded Mesopotamia and seized Amida, where he found a rich booty. After concluding an agreement with Byzantium, he renewed the war in the north against the Huns and pursued it intermittently until his death.

In the meantime the Mazdakite movement had resorted to revolution and instigated risings that were marked by excesses, looting of the property of the nobility, the abduction of women, and expropriation of land. After his restoration, Kavad was much cooler towards the Mazdakite leaders, who included a number of converted noblemen. When they opposed the nomination of his son, Chosroes, as his successor, he decided to break with them. A controversy arose in which the Mazdakites were opposed by the Zoroastrian priesthood and the Christian clergy. They were overthrown and massacred, their books were burnt, and their goods confiscated. But although the movement itself was crushed, its ideas persisted and spread in secret. Fifty years later the son of the great khagan of the western Turks placed himself at the head of the poor and disinherited and seized the oasis of Bokhara, driving out the nobles and wealthy merchants. His triumph was, however, short-lived; the revolt was suppressed and its leader savagely put to death. At the beginning of the eighth century the Mazdakite theories seem to have inspired the rising of Khurzad, brother of the Shah of Chorasmia. Having seized power, he meted out harsh treatment to the local nobility, confiscating their possessions, flocks, wives, and daughters, and distributing them among the poor. The King was forced to enlist the help of the Arabs, who under the leadership of Quteiba restored him to power and put an end to the activity of Khurzad.

Kavad, however, was not unaffected by current ideas of social justice, and sought to alleviate the existing state of affairs by fiscal reforms. Death prevented him from putting them into execution, and this task devolved on his successor. During his reign Nestorianism became the only established form of Christianity in Iran, and the Christian Church abolished the celibacy of the priesthood in order to counter Zoroastrianism, which had always opposed this custom.

Under Chosroes I (A.D. 531–79) the monarchy emerged victorious from the long struggle between the aristocracy and people. Its position had never been stronger, and all classes, including the priesthood, recognized the authority of this Prince. One of his first acts was to restore the property seized during the Mazdakite excesses. An extensive legislation regulated the position of the many women and children of the nobility who had been carried off during the disturbances. The State assumed responsibility for the education of the children, and in time they came to form an aristocracy that was attached to the throne in a different manner from the older nobility. Urgent measures were taken to save the countryside: villages were rebuilt, roads and bridges repaired, neglected canals cleaned out, and lost cattle replaced. The Government introduced legislation that reformed the fiscal organization of the Empire. A survey was made of all land, and taxes were fixed according to yield, situation, and type of crop. The tax on the individual was based on the category and class of person. All these reforms were permeated with a new spirit, indicative of the desire of the Crown to introduce more equity into its demands, on which depended the State revenues and the conduct of internal administration and foreign wars.

Reforms were also introduced in the army. Four commanders were appointed for the four divisions of the Empire, in place of the single commander-in-chief. The people were compelled to accept the obligation of military service, and Chosroes created peasant-soldiers. In order to improve the defence of the Empire, subject tribes were settled in the frontier districts, where their role was similar to that of the Roman or Chinese confederates. Strong fortifications were built in the Derband pass to hold the road against nomadic invaders, and a wall, several miles long, was built near the south-east corner of the Caspian Sea, to protect the plain of Gurgan, the 'gap' in the mountain armour of Iran.

Despite the 'perpetual peace' signed with Byzantium, Chosroes invaded Syria in A.D. 540. Antioch was captured and burnt and its inhabitants were transplanted to a new town built on the same plan, near Ctesiphon. Shortly afterwards a peace was concluded, which, in return for increased tribute, left the western frontier unchanged and once more granted freedom of worship to the Christians. In the same year Chosroes felt sufficiently strong to refuse to continue his tribute to the Ephthalites, who were no longer capable of enforcing their will on Iran. Twenty years later, Chosroes formed an alliance with the western Turks and finally smashed the Ephthalite power; its possessions were partitioned between the allies, and the eastern frontier of Iran was re-established on the Oxus. In the north, attacks by the Huns were successfully resisted, and in the south the Empire annexed the Yemen.

The territorial expansion of Iran, its growing strength, and military successes, aroused in Byzantium fear of a new conflict with its old adversary. Rome therefore engaged in large-scale diplomatic activity with the object of forming an anti-Iranian coalition that would virtually encircle the enemy. Ambassadors were sent to the western Turks and other peoples of central Asia who were needed to form the north-east wing of the coalition; approaches were also made to the Abyssinians and the Arabs with the object of strengthening the south-west wing. It was thus hoped to secure the two flanks of the enormous frontier common to the two empires. The attempt was, however, abortive. A clash provoked by disturbances in Armenia provided further proof of Iranian military superiority. Mesopotamia was invaded and devastated by the forces of the King of Kings. While peace negotiations were taking place, the old King died, after a reign of nearly half a century. He was idealized by oriental tradition as a defender of the people, a lover of justice, and a stern yet benevolent ruler. His reign may be considered as the most brilliant period of the Sassanian age, both for its military and diplomatic triumphs and for the achievement of Iranian civilization in art, science, and literature.

His son, Hormizd IV (A.D. 579–90), was an accomplished, intelligent, and learned prince. He sought to continue the policy of his father and to retain his ascendancy over the nobility and clergy, but he was less prudent, and was soon involved in difficulties with these two powerful classes of Iranian society. He tried to strengthen his position by leaning on his Christian

subjects, but this provoked a violent reaction from the Zoroastrian priesthood. The foreign situation also became serious,
for Byzantine policy was at last bearing fruit and the Empire
was simultaneously confronted by enemies on three sides.
Vahram Chobin, one of the outstanding military figures of
his day, won a series of victories over the Huns of the North
and the Turks in the East, but suffered reverses in operations
against Byzantium. Displeased at this turn of events, Hormizd
tried to disgrace Vahram, on which the general, who enjoyed
great popularity among his soldiers, rebelled. This seemed an
auspicious moment for the nobility to depose Hormizd, and
he was taken prisoner, mutilated, and thrown into prison, and
replaced on the throne by his son, Chosroes II (A.D. 590–628).
But Vahram Chobin aimed high; scion of one of the greatest
families of the Arsacid nobility, he aspired to the throne. Supported by his army, he seized the capital and declared himself
king, a crime of *lèse-majesté*, since he was not a member of the
Sassanian family. Chosroes was powerless in face of this *coup
d'état*, but took refuge with the Emperor Maurice, from whom
he obtained troops. With their aid he was able to defeat Vahram, who was assassinated, and to regain his throne. This assistance from Byzantium had, however, to be paid for by an onerous peace: Persia lost practically all Armenia, and the Greek
frontier was extended to Lake Van and Tiflis.

Some years later Chosroes attacked Byzantium, repudiating
his engagements on the pretext of avenging the death of the
Emperor Maurice. The Persian army regained Armenia,
seized Edessa, marched across Cappadocia, took Caesarea, and
reached the Bosphorus near Scutari (A.D. 610). The following
year his Syrian troops captured Antioch, Damascus, and finally
Jerusalem, which they looted for three days; over 50,000 Christians were massacred, and relics, including a piece of the True
Cross, were carried off to Iran. In A.D. 616 the army captured
Gaza and invaded Egypt. It took Babylon (Old Cairo) and
Alexandria, and then marched up the Nile to the borders of
Ethiopia. Iran thus regained frontiers that it had not held since
the time of the Achaemenians. In Asia Minor the Sassanian
general captured Ancyra (Ankara) and besieged Constanti-

nople. This coincided with victories against the Ephthalite vassals of the Turks on the eastern front. These successes were unparalleled in the history of the Empire, which had never appeared more formidable. Never had the Roman Empire seemed so near to disaster.

But the reaction of Byzantium was not long delayed. The new Emperor, Heraclius, launched a vigorous counter-attack, and in a few years had liberated Asia Minor, driven back the army of the King of Kings, invaded Armenia, and penetrated into Azerbaijan, where he seized the most important sanctuary of Iran. Having established contact with his allies, the Khazars, who had crossed the Caucasus, he debouched into the Tigris valley and laid siege to Ctesiphon. Chosroes tried to flee, but was seized by his own people and assassinated. The collapse of the Empire and the tragic death of its sovereign may at first sight appear surprising and incomprehensible, but the reverse side of the picture must not be forgotten: the character of the Great King and the internal condition of the country. Chosroes II was grasping, surly, crafty, and cowardly. He crushed the people beneath the burden of his taxation, sparing neither great nor small. He was prone to suspicion, and dismissed and executed even the most loyal of his servants. Infatuated by pomp, he spent enormous sums on his Court, which included thousands of concubines, servants, musicians, and courtiers. The demand for troops resulted in a serious drain on manpower, and this brought on one of those crises of anaemia that afflicted the people whenever their strength was overtaxed, confounding them at the moment of victory and delivering them into the hands of the enemy.

The advance of the Emperor Heraclius made the Christians politically suspect, and they suffered cruel persecution. Even the elements seemed to conspire against Chosroes, for vast Tigris floods transformed flourishing districts into swamps and caused the collapse of part of the royal palace at Ctesiphon. He fell sick, but although his generals were in revolt he refused to sign a peace with Heraclius. Finally he received the *coup de grâce* from his own son whom he had begotten by the Byzantine Princess Maria.

During the fourteen years between the death of Chosroes II
and the accession of the last prince of the dynasty, Yazdgard
III, no less than a dozen kings succeeded one another on the
throne of Iran. The disappearance of the Great King burst the
dyke of force and cruelty that he had raised against the ambitions of the feudal lords and military leaders. Exhausted by
war, taxation, and other exactions, the country was engulfed
by passions and rivalries. The royal princes became mere
pawns in the hands of rival factions and were crowned only to
be assassinated within a few months. In default of men, women
were placed on the throne, such as the two daughters of Chosroes, Boran and Azarmedukht. The great military leaders,
drawing their support from the army or from Byzantium, also
attempted to seize the throne, although, not being members of
the Sassanian family, they had no right to the crown. In the
end practically all the members of this family were extermin-
ated. When a new king was needed in A.D. 632 a prince of the
royal blood had to be brought out of hiding at Stakhr, whither
he had fled for safety. He was crowned in that city.

By then, however, it was too late to save the situation. The
army, which had contributed so materially to the greatness of
the dynasty, in the end brought about its downfall. The generals treated the provinces of which they were governors as
their own fiefs in a manner that strikingly recalls the independent attitude of the satraps in the last days of the Achaemenian
Empire. The Sassanian Empire crumbled away and disintegrated into a collection of petty states which are precisely enumerated by the Arab historians. No group or individual was
capable of opposing the Arab advance. The new aristocracy
created by Chosroes I was not as yet established and could provide no support for the tottering throne of a discredited family.
Everything foundered under the onslaught of the uncivilized
Beduin.

Although he was an able leader and commanded a strong
army, the Iranian commander-in-chief, Rustam, sustained a
serious defeat at Qadisiyah, near Hira, in Mesopotamia and
lost his life on the field of battle. Ctesiphon was quickly captured, and an enormous treasure fell into the hands of the

Arabs. Resistance continued on the Plateau, and a new army raised by Yazdgard opposed the enemy in the plain of Niha-wand, south of Hamadan. But once again victory went to the Arabs. The King fled with his Court towards the east and, like the last Achaemenian, was assassinated in the neighbourhood of Merv (A.D. 651). The Empire had fallen.

Organization, Administration, Army

A general idea of Iranian social structure may be obtained from original sources that date from the beginning of the Sassanian period. It was a rigid pyramid in which it was practically impossible to pass out of one class into another. At the apex stood the head of the State, the King of Kings. Below him were four groups which increased in size towards the base. These were the pillars of the State, providing its feudal basis and participating in the administration. The first class was composed of the vassals, the great and petty princes, who in return for loyal recognition of Iranian overlordship were left in possession of their thrones. It also included princes of the blood royal to whom was entrusted the government of the great provinces, such as Seistan and Kerman, and of conquered and annexed territories like that of the Kushans. Compared with the Parthian period, the number of these local dynasties declined appreciably under the Sassanians. Indeed, they practically disappeared, particularly on the periphery of the Empire, where, as has been noticed, their role was comparable to that of the federated peoples settled on the Roman frontiers. Their vassaldom was not particularly onerous, but entailed an obligation to furnish troops and protect their territory; in short, they constituted the outer defences of the Empire.

Lower in the social scale came the heads of the seven great families, this number having persisted through the centuries from the Achaemenian period. Their feudal system was inherited directly from the Parthians under whom the power of the nobles had deprived the kingdom of political stability. Although they took over the system, the Sassanians endeavoured to curtail its power. It was in fact diminished during the early years of their rule down to the death of Shapur II, but

increased again during the period of trouble and weakness that
lasted for 125 years up to the accession of Chosroes I. It was
curbed once more by the last two Great Kings. The struggle
of the aristocracy against the throne in defence of its secular
rights was one of the causes of the decline and disappearance
of the Sassanian Empire. Little is known about the prerogatives of these great families. They certainly exercised authority
over entire provinces where the peasants were obliged to pay
them taxes in addition to those demanded by the royal treasury. In return they provided the Crown with military support,
and were under an obligation to levy troops, if necessity arose,
as under the Parthians. Some of these families held hereditary
offices, both civil and military, which must have undergone
certain changes in the course of four centuries of Sassanian
history.

The function of the class designated as 'the grandees and
nobles' was in effect to check the encroaching power of the
great families. It included the high officers of state, ministers,
heads of the administration, and royal officials. The growth
and development of this class introduced a new element into
society, and by relying on it, and on the army, the Sassanian
monarchy was able to reorganize the State and endow it with
a strength that was unknown under the Arsacids.

At the foot of the ladder were the 'free men', the small
landed nobility or 'headmen' of villages who provided the link
between the peasant and the official representative of the central government. These nobles or knights were responsible to
the administration for the collection of taxes which they levied
on the peasants. These last formed the great mass of the population, and, though free *de jure*, were *de facto* reduced to the condition of serfs attached to the soil and sold along with the land
and villages.

Sassanian administration formed another pyramid, at the
head of which stood the grand vizier or prime minister, who
in practice held the reins of power which he exercised under
the control of the sovereign. This high dignitary deputized for
the king during his absence and was responsible for political
and diplomatic affairs, signing treaties and conventions. He

was sometimes given the high command of the army in the field. He was also the head of the 'ministeries' or *divans*, directed by 'secretaries', men highly skilled in drawing up reports, diplomatic treaties, and official correspondence. The administrative duties of the 'secretariat' in the *divans* included the office of the chancellery, and dispatches, appointments, and honours, justice, war, and finance. The last office was of particular importance; it was under the director of taxes, who had at his disposal an army of accountants, tax-collectors, and agents. This was a post of great responsibility, since on it depended the existence and functioning of the State.

The bulk of the revenues in an agricultural country like Iran was furnished by dues levied on the land, augmented by individual taxes. But as so often in antiquity, tax collection gave rise to abuses, and the exactions of the officials often involved the peasantry in debt. This was the case in the Sassanian as well as earlier periods, and, as in Ptolemaic Egypt or second- and third-century Rome, led to serious social unrest. The Sassanian kings made frequent attempts to alleviate the condition of the masses by cancelling outstanding debts or improving the system of payment.

The king was the supreme judge, and those of his subjects who failed to obtain justice had the right of appeal to the Crown. The Iranian people always set great store by right and justice, and an upright judge was highly esteemed. Although there was a *divan* of justice, it was generally the clergy who administered it, since law and ethics were closely linked with religion. Whereas in the provincial towns judicial functions devolved on the priesthood, in the villages they were exercised by the headman or local landowner. It is not known whether there was a written code, but the Zoroastrian sacred books include chapters devoted to law, with a list of crimes against the king, the State, one's neighbour, etc. Ordeal and torture were widely practised, and to judge from the descriptions left by Christian martyrs, were remarkable for refinements of cruelty.

The internal administration of the country continued to be based on the division into provinces or satrapies which were governed by high dignitaries chosen from members of the royal family and nobility or, towards the end, from among the military leaders. The boundaries of the provinces were not always fixed, and the artificial manner in which they were sometimes drawn up often proved detrimental to the efficiency of the administration, which despite its elaborate organization often lacked the flexibility necessary for the promotion of productive activity. The provinces were divided into districts under governors, and subdivided into cantons at the head of which the government appointed petty nobles to whom the village headmen were subordinate. This administrative machinery remained practically intact after the Arab conquest, and its traces may still be found to-day. The main features of the system went back to the Arsacid period, when the feudal aristocracy had already begun to share in the administration. The great achievement of the Sassanians was the creation of a stable bureaucracy which provided the link between the provinces and the central authority to which it was responsible. The Sassanian Empire had been faced at the outset with a country that had split up into a multitude of petty kingdoms. The centralization which it introduced was the foundation of its greatness.

An equally detailed organization regulated Court life. This was governed by a strict and elaborate etiquette. The courtiers were grouped in three classes according to their birth and office. Members of the royal family and the knights of the royal retinue had the highest standing. There were also jesters, jugglers, clowns, and musicians. The last played an important part in Court life and were likewise divided into three grades according to their skill and the instruments on which they performed.

The enormous expenses of the Court, which consisted of several thousand persons, and the costs of the administration, army, and public works, were met by taxes and dues, revenues from Crown lands, exploitation of the State-owned mines, and customs, which, since commercial activities had increased, provided an important part of the receipts. Finally the spoils of war from time to time replenished the depleted treasury of the King of Kings. The disposal of these riches rested with the king. Although the more enlightened Sassanian princes tried to use this wealth for the benefit of the people, the general tendency, as under the Achaemenians, was to hoard it. The royal treasure that fell into the hands of the Arabs at the time of their conquest long remained in the memory of historians.

During the first three centuries of Sassanian rule, the organization and command of the army was in the hands of a commander-in-chief, an hereditary office always held by a member of the royal family. Two high military officers – the adjutant-general and the commander of the cavalry – acted under his orders, and these posts were filled from the great families of the Empire. Chosroes I radically altered this system, and suppressed the office of commander-in-chief. He entrusted the command of the army to four leaders, responsible for the north, south, east, and west of the country, each with a deputy. The object of this measure was to ensure that no one man should control the entire armed force of the State. But in the long run his reform led to even greater evils and, as has been seen, these generals played a disastrous part in the last days of the Empire.

As under the Parthians, the Sassanian army was based on the heavy armoured cavalry furnished by the Iranian nobility. This was protected by the light cavalry of archers formed by the petty nobility. Behind these shock troops came elephants, which the Parthians never used. The rear-guard was provided by the infantry, a mass of peasants, poorly armed and equipped and of little value from a military point of view. Of greater importance were the auxiliary formations of the different vassal peoples on the borders of the Empire who, since the time of the first Achaemenians, had furnished a cavalry that was famous for its fighting qualities. Under the Sassanians this included men of Seistan, Albans, Kushans, and Chionite-Ephthalites. The Armenian cavalry was highly esteemed and occupied a key position in the Sassanian army.

The army was divided into corps formed of divisions which in turn comprised smaller units. Siege warfare had hardly been developed under the Parthians, but received great impetus under the Sassanians, and in this science they were the equals of the Romans. Frontier defence was provided for by the foundation of military colonies composed of warlike subject peoples who had been moved from their original homes. Chosroes I was particularly associated with this policy. The Empire was thus surrounded by a girdle of outer defences furnished by its vassals, behind whom stood the regular Iranian army.

There seems to have been a rich technical literature devoted to military science, but it is known only from indirect sources. There were treatises dealing with the organization of the army in war and peace and instructions on the use of cavalry and care of horses, on how to draw the bow and on victualling the troops. There were chapters dealing with tactics, the treatment of the enemy, the choice of time and place for battle, etc. On the whole, Iranian military science at this period was in no way inferior to that of the Romans.

Religion

According to a late tradition, Zoroastrianism had been preserved in its original form in the province of Fars and was made the official State religion by Ardashir Papakan. Modern research into Sassanian religion, however, has discredited this account, which seems to be at variance with historical truth as it emerges from texts, inscriptions, and archaeological evidence. Undoubtedly the traditional religion was preserved in Fars, but it was the ancient Mazdian faith and seems to have been unaffected by the reforms of Zoroaster.

Artaxerxes introduced into the cult of this religion the worship of Anahita in the form of an image, in imitation of the Babylonian and Greek religions, in both of which worship of images was found. His intention was apparently to introduce a religion that would be common to all the peoples of his Empire. There was a comparable development in Buddhism which, influenced by the Greco-Roman world, encouraged the representation of the form of Buddha.

When the Sassanian dynasty came to power its native province of Fars was thus a centre of the cult of Anahita and of Ahuramazda. The principal sanctuary of Anahita at Stakhr was served by the *herbads* or fire priests, among whom the ancestors of the ruling family seem to have been prominent. As has been seen, both Sassan and his father held important positions in this religious centre: Papak succeeded his father in office there before becoming king, and Ardashir exposed the spoils of his defeated enemies in the temple. The traditional association of the family with this cult continued under Shapur I, who founded a temple in the city of Bishapur. A striking feature of this building is the impressive installation for bringing water from a distance of several hundreds of yards and making it flow round the central chamber. This suggests that the cult of water, of which Anahita was the personification, may have been associated with that of fire.

Such was the religious position in south-west Iran. In the north-east the ancient Iranian faith was centred round the great sanctuary of Shiz. This was served by the ancient fraternity of the magi or *mobads*, who, while preserving the tradition of the priestly caste, had adopted Zoroastrian ideas. Nothing is known of the relations between these two centres. That of the north-east may well have had a wider influence than that of the south-west, but the latter was under the protection of the early princes of the family that had for generations been associated with its cult.

The problem of an imperial religion must have arisen under Shapur I, at a time when the young Empire was winning success in foreign policy and needed to mobilize all its national forces for the struggle with Rome. This may account for the sympathetic interest shown by Shapur in the teachings of Mani, of whom he made a companion.

This prophet was of noble birth, and like Zoroaster, the Buddha, and Jesus, claimed to have been sent by God to fulfil what had been previously revealed. He preached a new universal religion which like Christianity embraced all races and conditions of men. His doctrines were derived from the cults of Babylonia and Iran and were influenced by Buddhism and Christianity.

They were based on the opposition between light and darkness and good and evil. From these two warring elements was formed the world. The spirit of man was light and his body darkness, and the whole of Manichean ethics centred on the emancipation of the soul from the body. When all light and all souls held prisoner by matter were set free and ascended to the sun, earth and sky would collapse and fall apart, but the kingdom of light would endure for ever. The faithful were divided into the 'Elect' and 'Hearers'. The former comprised the clergy, who were vowed to celibacy, ate no meat, and abjured envy and lying. The 'Hearers' were allowed to marry and work like other men, but were commanded to be virtuous, and not to seek after riches. The new religion imposed prayer and fasting, but had no sacrifices or worship of images. The Manicheans practised baptism and communion and received absolution and a remission of sins before death. They rejected Judaism and considered Moses and the prophets to be devils and their god the lord of darkness. In the elaboration of its cosmology their faith was influenced by Gnosticism; its hymns were Babylonian in inspiration; its ideas were those preached by Zoroaster; Jesus was accorded a leading place in the system, and the Trinity and certain parts of the gospels were borrowed from Christianity; its metempsychosis was derived from Buddhism; and the names of its angels were Syrian.

Shapur I conferred great favours on Mani and allowed him complete freedom to preach and make converts. It is possible that the King intended ultimately to make the Manichean faith the State religion. He may also have believed that, having re-established a strong empire, it was the mission of the new dynasty to endow Iran with new spiritual riches and to encourage a religion that was Iranian in origin, a religion, moreover, which owing to its tolerant syncretism could adapt itself to contemporary trends of thought, whereas the cult of Istakhr was losing ground before the great religions, particularly Christianity. The Manichean faith might have fulfilled his expectations, but after his death there was a violent reaction on the part of the Mazdian priesthood, especially among the northern magi, whose leader, Kartir, played an important part in affairs of state under the successors of Shapur I, in particular under Vahram II. The explanation of this reaction is not far to seek. In the east, Buddhism was at the height of its expansion and had been adopted as the State religion of the second Kushan dynasty by the founder, King Kanishka. In the west, centres of Christianity had sprung up in northern Mesopotamia, and Judaism was active in Babylonia. Mazdaism was not only faced with these rival religions on the frontiers of the Empire, but in Iran itself was menaced by the Manichean faith and priesthood. Shortly after the death of Shapur I Mani was tried, condemned, and executed. His followers were persecuted and fled abroad, some to the east, where their teachings flourished in Central Asia, others to Syria and Egypt. In three long inscriptions engraved on the rocks and monuments of Fars Kartir boasts of his persecution of the Christians, Manicheans, and Brahmans. But Kartir disappeared; Narsah, the son of Shapur I, ascended the throne, and there was a change of policy. The Arabs living on the western frontier of Iran had been converted to the Manichean faith, and Narsah needed their support against Rome. There were also many Manicheans in Egypt who were in touch with the followers of Mani in Persia. The goodwill shown by Narsah gained two loyal allies for Iran, and they played an important part in the revolts against Diocletian. It looked as though the Manicheans, and perhaps also the Christians, would be able to regain their influence in Iran. Owing to lack of records, we know nothing of the events that reversed this trend of affairs and encouraged the revival of Mazdaism. Undoubtedly the conversion of Constantine had a great influence on Iranian religious policy. It was followed under Shapur II by the persecution of the Christians, who had become politically suspect, just as the Manicheans were regarded as Persian agents by the Romans. As the result of this development Mazdaism was reinstated, and strengthened its alliance with the throne by the subordination of the spiritual to the temporal.

How far had Zoroastrianism been preserved by the magi and what part did it play in the State religion? Ahuramazda was still worshipped, and the dogmas, with their emphasis on a single divinity, were upheld. At a period when the influence of the great monotheistic religions was spreading, this belief must have proved a valuable defensive weapon in the hands of the *mobeds*. They took over the traditions of the south-west, and, since they could not abolish the old gods, such as Anahita and Mithra, they relegated them to second place. In order not to be outdone by 'the Mediterranean custom of the peoples of the book', it became essential to have a similar weapon and to fix the sacred traditions in writing. This was done in the *Avesta*, which was a collection of oral traditions, some of them very ancient. Certain scholars maintain that this work was compiled in the fourth century, whereas others date it not earlier than the sixth century.* It remains an open question. Equally it is not known to what extent the magi, in addition to performing their 'political and police' functions, also sought to enlighten the new religion by considering philosophy and science. Religious unity followed on political unity. With the support of the temporal power, Zoroastrianism drove out Manicheism and held Christianity in check on the line of the Euphrates, and Buddhism on the Helmand. Just as in the Hellenistic period Iran had been hostile to the cosmopolitanism of Greek civilization, so now there was a revival of nationalism and intense opposition to the international world represented by Rome and its new Christian religion. Zoroastrianism, which had been given the status of an official cult, supported the State in its struggle with Rome and placed the spiritual forces of the nation at its disposal for the defence of the Orient.

Arts, Letters, Sciences

Sassanian art is not the expression of a sudden renaissance, as some would have us believe. Neither is it a delayed manifestation of Greek art, nor the reappearance of old oriental traditions, purged of Western influence. It represents the last phase of an oriental art that had been in existence for four millennia. It was a direct successor of the last phase of Parthian art, which was essentially Iranian in character. It was receptive to foreign influences, but it adapted them to the traditions of its native land, and as the art of a world empire it spread into far-distant countries.

* H. W. Bailey, *Zoroastrian Problems in the Ninth Century Books* (Oxford, 1943).

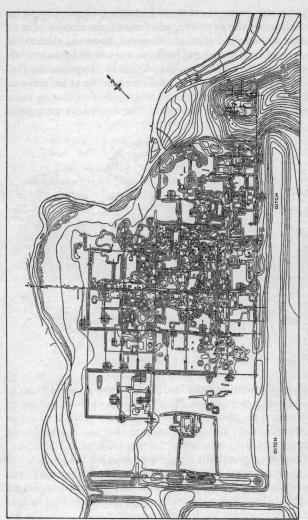

Fig. 87 – Plan of the town of Bishapur (*after A.P. Hardy*)

As we saw earlier, the town of Firuzabad, founded by Ardashir before his rise to power, was built on the circular plan so popular among the Parthians. Shapur I, however, abandoned this style of architecture and built the town of Bishapur according to the western traditions established by Hippodamus (Fig. 87). It was rectangular in plan, followed the lie of the ground, and was intersected by two arterial roads that met at right angles in the centre of the town. The Sassanians were great

Fig. 88 – Taq-i-Girre

builders of towns, and the historical sources record urban development in most reigns. No other plans of Sassanian towns have been recovered, but those of towns in which the Iranian kings settled their Roman prisoners are known. Shapur I built such a town at Gundeshapur, between Dizful and Shushtar. Its ruins have practically disappeared beneath the plough, but the plan was based on a great rectangle, curiously reminiscent of a Roman military camp. The same arrangement was noticed by the writer at Eivan-e-Karkha near Susa, where Shapur II is said to have settled his western prisoners.

Sassanian architecture was strongly influenced by national

traditions, and carried on those of the Parthians. Buildings of well-dressed stone remained in fashion up to the end of the third century A.D., and one of the palaces at Bishapur was built in this style. The stone blocks were adorned with historical reliefs that depicted the king charging on horseback or standing figures. The Sassanian period was thus familiar, at any rate at the beginning, with architectonic relief. Buildings in the same style, which goes back to the palace of Hatra, are the small *iwan* of Taq-i-Girre, on the road from Baghdad to Kermanshah (Fig. 88), the temple of Bishapur (Pl. 41*b*) and the tower of Païkuli, which may have been a fire temple. Special mention

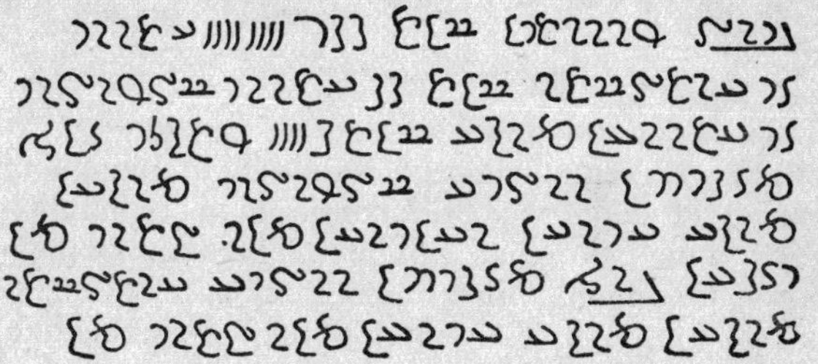

Fig. 89 – Pahlavi-Sassanian script

must be made of a votive monument with two columns set up in the centre of Bishapur and identified by the inscription (Fig. 89) as part of a statue of Shapur I. This piece is Syro-Roman in inspiration, but adapted to Iranian conventions. In the foreground we can still see the pedestal for the royal statue, flanked by two small fire altars (Pl. 41*c*); the position of the inscription on one of the columns is typically oriental.

The most usual building material, however, was rubble and plaster. The palace of Firuzabad was built of these materials. It has semi-circular vaulting above the *iwans* and a cupola on a square plan (Figs. 90, 91). The lay-out shows a happy combination of reception rooms and private apartments which in Achaemenian architecture were separate. The same material was used for the palace of Shapur I at Bishapur, where the

Fig. 90 – Palace of Firuzabad

great hall with central cupola had four *iwans*, giving a cruci-
form plan (Pl. 42*b*). Baked brick continued in general use, particularly in the Babylonian provinces, where part of the royal
palace of Ctesiphon, with its arched audience chamber, still
stands (Pl. 41*a*). A typical example of the use of unbaked brick
is the town wall of Stakhr, thought to be earlier than the Sassanians (Fig. 92). These round towers seem to have enjoyed
great popularity in the East from the imperial Roman epoch.
They occur at the fortress of Bishapur and at Taxila, in north-

Fig. 91 – Palace of Firuzabad: Restored façade

west India, in the town of the second century A.D. built by
the second Kushan dynasty.

Certain modifications were introduced in religious architecture. The central chamber of the fire temple on a square

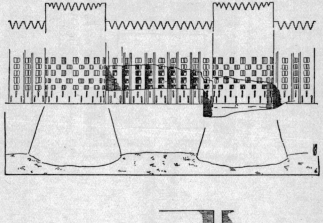

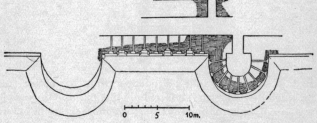

Fig. 92 – Istakhr: Town wall of mud brick

plan was enclosed by four corridors. The temple excavated by
the writer at Bishapur (Pl. 41*b*, Fig. 93) is the most imposing
from the point of view of size (height of walls: 14 m.). At the
side of the temple at Firuzabad stood a tower, on top of which
a fire was lit during open-air ceremonies (Fig. 94). These ceremonies generally took place round pavilions that were open on

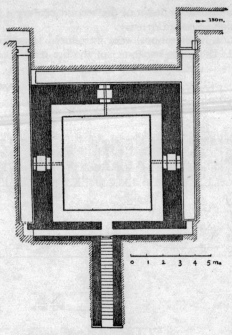

Fig. 93 – Bishapur: Plan of the fire temple

all four sides, with four pillars supporting four arches surmounted by a cupola. The sacred fire that burnt in the temple
was used to light the braziers that stood under the dome before
the worshippers.

Palace and house walls were constructed of brick or rubble
and decorated with sculptured and painted stucco to hide the
unpleasing surface. In the oldest palace built by Ardashir at
Firuzabad, decorative treatment was restrained and confined to
the 'Egyptian grooving' (Fig. 95) used on the doors and recesses of the palace at Persepolis. But under the second King,
Shapur I, there was a sudden change in the style of stucco ornament. In his palace at Bishapur, built shortly after his victory

over the Emperor Valerian, the great audience chamber had sixty-four recesses (Pl. 42*a*) covered with sculptured stucco, the decorative elements of which show strong Syro-Roman influence and include the fret, lanceolate designs, and acanthus leaves. Later the designs were further elaborated by representations of animals, plants, hunting scenes, and even royal portraits. Towards the end of the Sassanian period stucco decoration even influenced sculpture in stone, as in the grotto of

Fig. 94 – Firuzabad: Tower with fire altar

0   1   2 m.

Fig. 95 – Firuzabad: Stucco decoration from the palace

Taq-i-Bustan (Fig. 96) or on the stone capitals of the royal pavilions (Fig. 97).

We learn from the historical records that Sassanian palaces had painted decoration and that at Ctesiphon there was a fresco representing the capture of Antioch. None of these monuments has so far been recovered, but the recent discovery by the writer of a mosaic pavement in the *iwan* of the Bishapur palace partly fills the gap, since the mosaicists are known to have worked from painted cartoons. Some of the mosaic panels represent portraits, and out of twenty-two of these no two are alike – proof that at this period the artist sought to convey an individual likeness (Pl. 44a). With the exception of a few heads in profile, all are shown three-quarters face; this seems to have been the most popular pose in Sassanian art and may have been due to Syro-Roman influence. Alternating with the portraits of men and women are larger panels on which we may see a Court lady fanning herself, courtesans, with long robes and crowns of flowers, holding bouquets (Pl. 44b), or a naked musician playing a stringed instrument. As in the paintings of Dura-Europos, these tableaux are decorated with architectonic motives of Hellenistic inspiration.

The Sassanian kings encouraged the tradition of rock bas-relief known in Iran from the third millennium B.C. More than thirty of their reliefs are sculptured on the rocks of the Plateau,

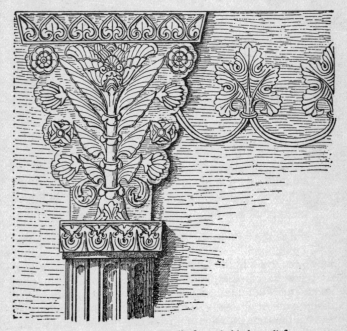

Fig. 96 – Taq-i-Bustan: Detail of a capital in bas-relief

the majority in Fars, the native province of the dynasty. None is religious in character: the subjects include the investiture, triumphs, victory over the enemy, the chase, and the king with members of his Court or family, and illustrate the many

Fig. 97 – Bisutun: Capitals from an unknown building

influences that affected Sassanian monumental art during the four centuries of its existence. The earliest phase is known from the bas-relief of Firuzabad, which represents the victory of Ardashir over Artabanus V. This still shows Parthian influence and has the same flat relief and rendering of detail by incision. A little later in the same reign the modelling shows greater depth. This is particularly noticeable in the investiture scene of the king and Ahuramazda, the composition of which is in the traditional heraldic style of the East. The god gives the prince the beribboned ring, the symbol of royalty. Both figures are shown on horseback, and their steeds respectively trample underfoot the Parthian King defeated by Ardashir and the evil spirit Ahriman, the adversary of Ahuramazda (Pl. 43a).

From the time of Shapur a new way of rendering drapery was introduced as the result of Western influence. Whereas in the earlier style the human form beneath the dress had been ignored, the drapery is now moulded to the body. In imitation of Roman decorative bas-relief, the Iranian artist began to compose complete scenes, grouping a number of figures round the prince who occupies the central position, as on the bas-relief depicting the triumph over Valerian at Bishapur (Fig. 86). Nevertheless the composition never conveys a feeling of unity. This is very apparent in a circular relief from Bishapur, depicting another triumph, in four registers (Pl. 43b). It betrays the influence of Roman bas-relief, particularly Trajan's column. But on the Roman monument the spiral was used to reproduce on marble the unrolling of two *volumina* or manuscripts and the account of the military exploits of the Emperor is unfolded in natural sequence. The circular and concave bas-relief of Shapur I, however, is no more than a series of registers, having no connexion one with another or with the central scene, the whole being limited to a single episode and strictly defined subject.

The art of Sassanian bas-relief reached its highest point under Vahram I, and his scene of investiture at Bishapur is the most lively and expressive work achieved by Iranian artists. The standard remained high under Vahram II, but from the fourth century the modelling became flat and uninspired and detail was again rendered by incision. Towards the end of the period, the hunting bas-reliefs from the grotto of Taq-i-Bustan (Fig. 98) show that the art was strongly influenced by painting.

Sassanian bas-relief has often been compared to Roman decorative relief, and there is some truth in the contention.

Nevertheless there are fundamental differences between the
two, for they are the products of different worlds and contrasting artistic concepts. Whereas Roman relief was subordinate to architecture and of limited dimensions, the human figure
in Sassanian art was often more than life-size. Roman relief
sought to interpret an historic event by a continuous picture
in which truth and allegory were happily blended. Sassanian
relief also was often inspired by an historical event, but it concentrated on one outstanding incident, and confined itself to
that alone. In the West relief was a moving film, in the East a
'still' of the most representative scene. Thus a victory was
portrayed by a representation of the king or the god on horseback trampling the fallen enemy; or by the king overcoming
a mounted enemy in single combat. The outcome of the battle
is never in doubt and the dramatic moment is omitted. This
treatment of the subject is strikingly similar to the scene of the
king killing monsters on the Persepolis sculptures. Although
Sassanian relief preserved the static dignity and tranquillity of
the Achaemenian, nevertheless it also imitated the vigorous
Parthian combat and hunting scenes. Its aim was to create a
subject that would remain unchanged irrespective of the king
with whom the monument was identified; practically the only
difference is the crown, which varied in shape from reign to
reign. There are also marked differences in composition between the two arts. The background of a Sassanian scene never
suggests the surroundings in which the event took place; in
accordance with oriental tradition the king is always taller
than his companions, and when several figures are shown they
are always in single file, with the result that, as in Achaemenian art, they remain isolated. The group is non-existent in Persian bas-relief. Undoubtedly the artist adopted certain Western
principles, such as the rendering of dress, modelling, high relief, and a more natural expression, but Sassanian relief remained essentially Iranian, and is characterized by symmetrical
composition, strict antithesis, and a heraldic style. It is differentiated from Western bas-relief by its character and its hidden
meaning, for in Iran the representation of a victory was a kind
of magic that secured power and glory for the prince.

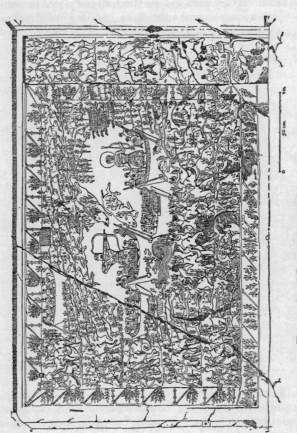

Fig. 98 – Taq-i-Bustan: Bas-relief depicting a royal hunt

Very little is known of Sassanian funerary art. At this period
the dead were exposed on 'towers of silence'; when only the
bones remained they were wrapped in cloth and placed in ossuaries which were deposited either in cavities dug in the mountain side or in special mortuary chambers. Many fragments of

Fig. 99 – Bishapur: Ossuary in sculptured stone

baked brick ossuaries have been found in Russian Turkestan,
dating from the end of the Sassanian period. Only two stone
ossuaries have so far been found in Iran. One from Bishapur
(Figs. 99 and 100) is decorated in bas-relief. The sculpture is
much worn; there is practically no modelling, and the figures
stand out as a flat mass from the background. By analogy with
the baked brick ossuaries these bas-reliefs probably represent
Mithra, on a chariot drawn by winged horses, Zervan, the god

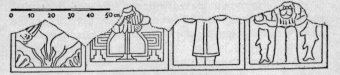

Fig. 100 – Bishapur: Ossuary in sculptured stone (detail)

of fire, and the goddess Anahita; these three deities probably formed a triad in the Mazdian pantheon.

Sassanian toreutic is better represented by a considerable number of decorated plates, cups, and bottles, the favourite subject of the design being the royal hunt. The prince is shown mounted on horseback and clad in rich garments and an elaborate crown. He pursues his quarry at the gallop and shoots the animals down with arrows. The scene is treated in a conventional manner and is similar in conception to those of the rock bas-reliefs (Pl. 45b). That this is not an actual hunt is shown by the dress of the prince, the flowing ribbons, the crown which could never have been worn when galloping, and the number of animals surrounding the hunter. It is a picture with a hidden meaning which by a kind of magic secures success for the king in his hunting exploits and gives him courage to meet lion, tiger, or boar. It is a representation of the 'royal huntsman'. Other subjects portrayed are an investiture (Fig. 101a), the king seated on his throne (Fig. 101b), and a banqueting scene, another popular theme. To the last group belong a number of bottles decorated with dancers or servants

Fig. 101 – Representations of princes in Sassanian goldwork

(Pl. 45*a*). Plates are engraved with real (Fig. 102) or fantastic animals. The most beautiful and effective pieces from the point of view of technique seem to have been executed in the third

Fig. 102 – Sassanian silver cup

and fourth centuries; later examples were often little more than copies of earlier works.

Rock crystal, a stone that had been highly prized from earliest antiquity, remained popular with the Sassanian artist. Few objects of this material have survived, and it is probable that it was being replaced by products of the glass industry. The most famous object of rock crystal is the centre medallion of the gold cup from the Treasury of St Denis, now in the Cabinet des Médailles in Paris. This represents a Sassanian prince seated on a throne supported by winged horses (Fig. 103). A dish from the Treasury of St Mark in Venice, ornamented with the demi-palmettes that occur so frequently in Sassanian stucco decoration (Pl. 46*b*) and a goblet with floral design (Pl. 46*a*) may be attributed either to the Iranian workshops of the period, or to craftsmen influenced by them.

Fig. 103 – Medallion in rock crystal on the gold cup from the treasure of Saint Denis
(*Bibliothèque Nationale, Paris*)

There are thousands of Sassanian intaglios in museums and private collections, and they are still used by people who cannot sign their names. Some carry a portrait of the owner with his name and title in Pahlavi, but the majority have animal or floral motifs or symbolic designs whose significance still escapes us. Pl. 48*h* shows a *bulla* of unbaked clay of the fourth century (?) found in the Sassanian level at Susa. It was attached by a ribbon to an official document, probably of parchment, and was signed by the important person whose bust is shown, and countersigned by an imperial officer whose official seal simply bears an inscription in Pahlavi.

As the result of its geographical position between China, the producer of silk, and Rome, the largest consumer of this precious material, Iran acted as a transit country for the trade in raw and woven silk. The great Sassanian kings were anxious to develop this branch of the textile industry in Iran, and following their Syrian conquests, they deported whole communities of weavers and settled them in the Iranian provinces, notably in Khuzistan. Rock sculptures, such as those of Taq-i-Bustan,

Fig. 104 – Bas-relief of Naqsh-i-Rustam:
Ardashir before Ahuramazda

give us an idea of the Sassanian materials on which designs similar to those on stucco decoration and in toreutics were embroidered in silk. Medallions with animals, hunting scenes, particularly the exploits of Vahram Gor, and symbolic subjects adorn the few fragments from this period which are still preserved. During the first millennium A.D. there was a brisk trade in relics from the East, and the richest and most beautiful materials were used for covering the remains of saints. As a result, the churches and cathedrals of Europe still possess fragments of Sassanian or post-Sassanian cloth which would not normally have been preserved in the soil of Iran. The tradition of using funerary cloth and the manufacture of such material did not end with the advent of Islam, and cloth occasionally found in post-Sassanian tombs shows how iconography persisted through the ages (Pl. 47).

The more vigorous an art, the greater its influence abroad and its chance of survival, even on foreign soil. Sassanian art radiated over an area stretching from China to the Atlantic; its influence was particularly great in the West, where it inspired medieval art.

Fig. 105 – Church of Vic (Indre): Adoration of the Magi. French religious art of the twelfth century

The church of Germiny-des-Prés, near Orleans, was built on the plan of a fire temple, and its walls are decorated with frescoes in which occurs the tree of life of the Taq-i-Bustan grotto. This is not an isolated case. The stucco decoration on the tomb of the Abbess Agilberta, who died in 665 and was buried in the crypt of the church of Jouarre between Paris and Chateau-Thierry, is another example. The king, as the emanation of the god on earth, is represented in Sassanian art as enthroned in glory and surrounded by a brilliant Court. This picture provided Byzantine artists with a model for Christ triumphant surrounded by a Court of angels, apostles, prophets, and evangelists. In the

Fig. 106 – Gold jug from the so-called treasure of Attila

sculptures and frescoes of the old French churches the artist reproduced, probably without understanding its significance, the gesture of the raised right hand with bent index finger, which was a sign of respect among the Sassanian nobles (Figs. 104 and 105). The goldsmiths of Central Europe imitated the designs of Sassanian toreutic, but probably understood them

Fig. 107 – Centre motif of a gold jug from the so-called treasure of Attila

as little as we do. Magnificent examples of such work are the two gold pieces from the so-called treasure of Attila, attributed to the eighth to ninth centuries (Figs. 106 and 107). Sassanian art also inspired the painters of the frescoes in the Buddhist sanctuaries in Central Asia (Fig. 108) and the weavers of Egypt and Byzantium. But the 'true heir of Sassanian Iran' was Islam, and wherever it went it carried the forms created by Sassanian art.

The national literature that had been handed down from one generation to another by oral tradition was replaced under the Sassanians by a written literature that was read by the aristocracy and courtiers. Certain sections of the *Avesta*, the source of all knowledge, contained passages treating of medicine in which the precepts of Hippocrates were adapted to the teachings of Zoroastrian religion. The translation of foreign works, Greek, Latin, and Indian, began under Shapur I and flourished

Fig. 108 – Buddhist frescoes from Ming Oï
(Chinese Turkestan)

under Chosroes I in whose reign there was a real Iranian renaissance. The broad-minded and tolerant attitude to religion shown during the 'century of Chosroes' was in marked contrast to the intolerance of the Christian Church of Byzantium, and Greek philosophers who had suffered persecution in Greece were attracted to Iran, where they found a welcome at the Court of Ctesiphon. Western ideas penetrated Iran and were blended with those coming from India. They inspired the most enlightened spirits of the age, such as the great Court doctor, Burzoe, who deals in his writings with society, ethics, and religion. Tracts or books of precepts were popular among the reading public and appeared in large numbers, but unfortunately not all of them have survived. They deal with wisdom, charity, kindness, the duty of the rich towards the poor, the advantage of honest poverty over selfish and unjust riches. This freedom of thought threatened to undermine the influence of the Zoroastrian priests who fought a losing battle against the new ideas. The records accuse them of heresy and greed, and even disloyalty, for in an attempt to counter the influence of the great contemporary religions, the orthodox church revived and laid stress on its monotheistic principles. But the reform was introduced after the conquest by Islam and was too late to save the national religion.

Economic and Social Life

The national economy continued to be based on agriculture rather than trade. Although the Sassanian period ended in the collapse of the ancient order, the administration and people by their efforts made notable cultural and political advances. Revenue increased, and there was a more equitable distribution of goods. In both the Roman and Sassanian Empires a process of levelling took place that affected every aspect of life and human activity, and in this respect this part of the ancient world was undoubtedly in advance of southern, central, and northern Europe.

In commerce, Sassanian coinage of silver and copper, more rarely of gold, circulated over a wide area. The bill of exchange appeared during this period, and Jewish banking circles in Babylonia and analogous Persian institutions played a leading part in its circulation. The bill had been known since the second millennium B.C., but its use had been limited, and in effect it was no more than the recognition of a debt fixing the date of repayment. In the Sassanian period it became a legally recognized title-deed. The banks of the Empire run by Iranians or Jews employed a highly developed system of monetary exchange by writing. How many financiers and bankers know, for example, that the word 'cheque' or the term *avaliser* come from the Pahlavi language and were invented by the Iranian banking institutions of this remote age? The Christian traders of Syria borrowed the bill from Iran, and introduced it into the West, where it was in use from the Merovingian period.

More money was in circulation in the towns, as is shown by the great number of silver dirhems found in Iran and neighbouring countries (Pl. 48a–g). In the rural districts, however, the wages of the peasant, soldier, and official, and even the taxes were paid in kind – a custom that persisted in certain countries down to modern times. Foreign trade, however, was already conducted entirely on a monetary basis. This continued to expand, and the chief commodities handled were valuable merchandise and luxury goods demanded by the Court and wealthy aristocracy. The levying of dues and taxes in kind enabled the Government to build up large stocks of essential goods from which their agents supplied the market; the reserves could also be used in time of famine to alleviate distress.

Never before had commerce been subject to such strict control. In order to deal with the increased traffic, the State was forced to organize stations, caravanserais, and water supplies along the roads, rivers, and canals. Officials specially allocated to this service inspected the frontier posts and sea-ports. The State also established monopolies, of which the most important seems to have been that in raw silks from China. Silk was woven mainly in the Syro-Phoenician workshops, but a rival industry was established by the Sassanian kings on Iranian territory, and the workshops of Susa, Gundeshapur and Shushtar were famous for their products. Luxury china and glassware from the Syro-Palestinian and Alexandrian workshops were imported into Iran; there was considerable trade in textiles and clothing. Amber came from the Black Sea; papyrus was still bought, but was increasingly replaced by parchment; the use of paper was not introduced from China until the Islamic period. There was a transit trade in spices from China and Arabia, and nard and pepper were exported from Media. International trade encouraged the growth of colonies of merchants, particularly Jews and Syrians, who established themselves as far afield as India, Turkestan, Brittany, and the Black Sea. The exporting houses became more specialized, and confined their dealings to corn, cattle, and manufactured goods. The distinction between the exporter and the trader dealing with the home market was accentuated, with the result that middlemen increased in number. On the whole, however, there was no marked expansion of foreign trade, the reason probably being the growth of State interference in business and the consequent restrictions on freedom of exchange.

In internal commerce there is evidence in Babylonia, and therefore by analogy in Iran, that the merchants and the country pedlars who depended on the traders in the great centres became more specialized. Banking activity was limited, and was confined almost entirely to commerce, banks coming into play only in the event of a bad harvest or at the time of tax payment. This did not prevent the State from taking an increasing interest in the working of credit institutions, and it imposed controls that were so well organized that they remained unchanged for many centuries and survived down to modern times.

Production improved and expanded, particularly in the silk and glass industries, and this also was marked by a greater degree of specialization. As the result of its monopolies the State became a producer and ran its own workshops. It also intervened in certain private industries, notably those that directly concerned the Court, army, and administration; it supervised the prices of raw materials, and the wages and organization of the workers. New tendencies thus arose, which finally crystallized in the medieval guilds.

The great landowner had his own labourers, carpenters, blacksmiths, weavers, bakers, and millers, his oil-press and water-mill; the last coming into general use in the fourth century. Agricultural production expanded and innovations were introduced such as the cultivation of the mulberry and the breeding of silkworms which were of great importance in view of the great demand for silk. The great estates belonging to the State and nobility continued to be exploited by the old methods. Improvements could be introduced only on State lands, for there was too little economic liberty to encourage private enterprise.

But although the national economy as a whole appeared to prosper, the lot of the peasant deteriorated. The enlightened attitude from which he had benefited in the Hellenistic period was a thing of the past. Down-trodden, dependent, and uneducated, he was attached to the soil, the property of the State, a great noble or a temple, except in a few cases when he preserved a more or less precarious independence. As the great landed proprietor became increasingly powerful, so the small landowner was driven by fear of economic crisis and State encroachment to seek his protection. His responsibility for levying taxes on behalf of the State further increased the number of people under the great man's control. Although the collection of taxes and dues was thereby facilitated, the State became dependent on the feudal lords, and its attempts to limit their influence were abortive. In the end the power of the nobles became so great that the king was financially and militarily dependent on them.

Iran was not the only country to suffer from this disequilibrium. Throughout the Roman Empire, in Italy, Gaul, Egypt, and North Africa, agricultural magnates sprang up. Chosroes I sought to curb this growing ascendancy of the nobility by radical reforms and the creation of a peasant army. The Sassanian measures influenced Rome and were copied by the Emperor Heraclius, who also formed a class of peasant soldiers, but his reforms came too late to withstand the assault of the foreign enemy.

The great estate developed into a closed enterprise. Most of the land was on lease and worked by an army of peasants who produced everything required by the owner, corn, oil, wine, fruit, and meat. Wages and rents were paid in kind, and the circulation of money in the rural areas fell very low. The landlords no longer lived in the towns, but settled on their estates in fortified strongholds from which they directed the cultivation of the land in a rational and bureaucratically organized manner. Their castles were managed with all the luxury the age had to offer, and the nobles had their own garrisons to defend them, their families, friends, and retainers against the threat of revolt. A stable but somewhat inhumane economic system based on agriculture grew up in the world, and in certain areas remained in existence for centuries. A new civilization also arose in response to these changed conditions and in time spread from the country to the town. Iran, like Rome, evolved a form of feudalism which was more effective than that of earlier periods. 'The enslavement of the free peasantry was compensated for by the creation of a feudal élite ... by a feudal revolution which later affected all the countries of Europe and Asia and took over the agrarian institutions of the ancient world.' This revolution produced the medieval Arab, Slav-Russian, and Mediterranean forms of feudalism in which the culture of the ancient world was preserved.

The fiscal system of the State was without mercy. Reviving Hellenistic tradition, it burdened the land and the individual with exactions that were beyond human capacity and extorted payment by force. Indirect taxes levied by customs, octrois, and tolls further increased the pressure on the people. All those who were not members of the privileged class were obliged to render all kinds of service. They had to build the royal palaces, furnish materials and skilled labour, maintain the posting-stations, provide quarters for the army, and pasture the royal herds. The peasant had to provide his horses for the post, the caravan leader his pack animals, the waggoner his cart, and the boat-man his boat. The State bought produce at prices lower than those ruling in the market, and in spite of royal measures to stamp it out, official corruption was rife.

The State needed money. The royal lands and workshops provided for the needs of the Court and army, and the surplus was sold. Individual liberty was subordinated to the will of the State and disappeared for nearly a millennium. The exchequer was insatiable; the administration and the army both required enormous sums of money; the fortifications on the frontiers were costly; the expenses of the fleet and of the envoys sent to foreign Courts with royal presents had to be met. In times of disaster and famine the State had to provide relief for the victims and destitute. Large sums were allocated for expenditure on cultural projects such as the building of schools and colleges; the amenities of the towns were improved and canals

and water supplies provided. Although one can hardly speak
of a 'Sassanian peace', the urban population expanded and
new towns sprang up in all parts of the Empire, with the result that settlements became less isolated. This was especially
the case in the fertile plains that had long been cultivated or
had been brought under cultivation by the enlightened policy
of the Great Kings. Khuzistan and Seistan, in particular, derived great benefit from this urban development.

The fiscal reforms of Chosroes I were concerned less with
the general welfare than with the interests of the exchequer,
and the state of oppression and ignorance in which the people
lived drove them to revolt. This was nothing new in the ancient world, which had already experienced upheavals in
Egypt, Greece, and Rome. But whereas the revolutions that
shook the Hellenistic world were the work of slaves and deb-
tors, the Mazdakite movement was different in character; it
had a social as well as an economic basis, and for this reason is
called communist. The misery of the people did not stop them
from reflecting and resenting the prevailing social injustice.
They found sympathizers among the noblest spirits of the age,
such as Burzoe, physician to Chosroes I, who wrote: 'Our age
is decadent everywhere'. The civilization of the Sassanian State
might dazzle the eye and its armed force seems omnipotent,
but its social structure was rotten, and this delivered the country
into the arms of the conqueror. It proved powerless against the
Arab invader.

*   *   *

In the third century A.D. the world, from Spain to China, was
in a critical state. Rome was suffering from a political, social,
and economic crisis from which the country was rescued only
by the advent of Diocletian. Iran was beset with political and
religious crises, and the Arsacid dynasty, which had reigned
for nearly five centuries, was overthrown and replaced by the
'national' dynasty of the Sassanians. There were political
troubles in the Kushan Empire, and the dynasty which had
reached its highest point under Kanishka disappeared after the
conquest of Shapur I.

Sassanian civilization was the culmination of the thousand-year history of the Iranian nation, and represented its highest achievement. Except for the Far East, the world, after the disappearance of the Kushan Empire, was divided between Rome and Iran. The latter was no longer, as under the Parthians, a partner standing on the defensive but an adversary of equal if not superior strength. Nationalism was now stressed in every aspect of life. The State was based on an interrelated aristocratic society, with its roots in the country. The royal house, the nobility, and the clergy provided the foundations of the kingdom; it was a structure that aroused the admiration of Arab historians, who regarded it as a model of political science. The nobility held the land, enjoyed certain hereditary prerogatives, and elected the king. Their lives were occupied in hunting, feasting, and the delights of the harem; polygamy was widely practised, although women had certain rights. With time, the refinements of life became more evident; the soldier and huntsman developed an interest in literature and writing; chess, tennis, and polo became popular sports; music, singing, and the arts were cultivated. The Court set the fashion in dress, devised jewellery to please its tastes, and made progress in the gastronomic art. It was a brilliant society that reflected a cultured and luxurious civilization. Between the Court and the lower classes there was an unbridgeable gulf; the class formed by the citizens, artisans, and merchants was politically weak; and the mass of the people belonged to the peasantry, whose servile condition accorded ill with the precepts of the Zoroastrian Church.

The role of the Sassanian kings differed little from that of the Roman Emperor, who devoted his life to preserving the patrimony represented by the old culture of the ancient world. Like Rome, Iran was surrounded by barbarous and primitive peoples, against whom its kings raised barriers with varying success. On the whole, however, the Sassanians were successful rulers, and they remained in popular memory as the most powerful princes of the world.

The superiority of the Iranians may be seen in government and administration, in warfare, in the refinement of their art, in their dress, bearing, and manners. Once again the influence of Iranian art and religion spread beyond its frontiers. It would seem that as the result of its contact with Mazdaism, Buddhism adopted the principles of dualism in the fight between the Good, in the person of the one Buddha, and the army of Evil, led by Mara, and it is tempting to see in Maitreya the character of Mithra, the divine saviour of the Mazdians. The Manichean faith spread to Turkestan and China and through Syria and Egypt to North Africa, where St Augustine was one of its followers. When it was persecuted in the East it established itself in Asia Minor, spread to Armenia and reached Thrace (tenth to eleventh centuries). The Levant trade carried it to southern France, where it gave rise to the powerful sect of the Cathari. The Nestorian Church, the only official Christian sect in Iran, also reached China. Religious ideas that had sprung up on the soil of Iran thus spread as far as France in the West and China in the East.

Although Sassanian art may appear different from that of its predecessors, it was essentially composed of old oriental elements. A comparison with contemporary Western art shows that the differences are more striking than the similarities, and such affinities as can be observed are entirely superficial. Although it was the culmination of a long evolution, it had enough vitality to influence the art of neighbouring peoples. During its best period it inspired Roman architects and designers to introduce new forms into Byzantine art, and the Slav tribes who had only just emerged from their forests tried to copy it in their first artistic attempts. It crossed the eastern frontiers of the Empire and, entering the service of a foreign religion, laid the foundations of Irano-Buddhist art, which eventually spread from Afghanistan to China.

The civilizing activity of Sassanian Iran manifested itself in other ways also. For centuries Iran had maintained friendly relations with the Indian State of the Gupta, which finally achieved a national unity and inaugurated a period of renaissance in Hindustan. Towards this State Iran acted as an intermediary for the transmission of Western values. During the 'golden age' of Indian civilization the friendship and economic and cultural exchanges between the two countries brought India into contact with Western ideas and introduced her to Western medicine, astronomy, geometry, and logic.

The splendid and gigantic edifice of Sassanian Iran, which had functioned with such magnificence and precision, crumbled to pieces in the space of a few years. But the Arabs did not owe their success to their political superiority or to the genius of their military leaders. It was the ancient world, the world of Asia, Europe, and Africa, that gave them their victory, a world exhausted by war, undermined by social and religious strife and powerless to resist a united, inspired, fanatical, and resolute enemy.

Conclusion

MORE than three thousand years elapsed between the moment when prehistoric man left his caves to settle in the plains and valleys and the arrival of the Iranians on the Plateau. During this long span of time man acquired and improved his knowledge of agriculture, learnt to domesticate animals, and made his first essays in metallurgy. The art of painting pottery, almost certainly invented on the Plateau, made rapid progress, and spread far afield. Life was never isolated. Village communities sprang up, and contacts with other human groups were established and gradually expanded.

From time immemorial foreign peoples have passed across or settled on the Iranian Plateau, but in the present state of our knowledge there is little direct evidence of population movements during the prehistoric period. At the beginning of the Iron Age, however, the arrival of the Iranians from the steppes led to great changes in Iran. The westward advance of these new-comers who settled in the hills, was halted on the Plateau which forms a bridge between the Eurasian steppe zone and the great western deserts that stretch as far as Africa; there, in the fertile oases of Mesopotamia and the Nile valley, advanced urban civilizations had already developed. The geographical position of the Iranians profoundly affected their history and civilization. They never lost their connexion with their native steppes, and on several occasions in their history they succeeded in dominating the nomadic peoples who lay beyond the natural eastern frontiers of Iran. But once their society became organized and a regular government was established they turned towards the Mesopotamian world and controlled this prosperous area for over twelve hundred years. They thus developed a culture that drew simultaneously on the rich inheritance of two very different worlds. With the East, their original homeland, they remained closely linked by atavism, and its influence is evident in their style of animal portraiture, in metal-work, such as the rich and varied horse-trappings and distinctively decorated vases, and in jewellery. From the West they learnt the principles of urban life, architecture, applied art, and science.

It was a hybrid civilization that owed its character on the one hand to its geographical position between two worlds, and on the other to the gifted and vigorous character of the Iranians themselves; its highest achievements won universal admiration.

The Iranians were checked by the barrier of Asiatic Powers, but they profited from their enforced halt of four centuries to acquire the culture of the ancient urban civilizations on whose borders they stood. Eventually they in their turn embarked on a successful conquest of the Asiatic world. In Asia Minor and on the shores of the Aegean they came face to face with Greek civilization, with its concept of the liberty of the citizen and his city state. The oligarchic Achaemenian monarchy engaged in a struggle with the democratic empire of Greece; the acropolis of Persepolis stood opposed to that of Athens. Two pictures, but how different one from the other; here, the people, magistrates, priests, and young men worshipped their gods; there, marshalled by the royal bodyguard, the conquered peoples brought tribute to their sovereign. No gods were visible, the king alone was the focal point of the Empire, and towards him millions of human beings directed their efforts. Art reflects two widely different concepts, for whereas the one people revered the gods, the other glorified a single man, the emanation of god on earth.

There is a tendency to criticize Achaemenian civilization for depending too much on the achievements of others, particularly in the sphere of art. But even if a study of the surviving monuments lends support to this view, it only illustrates the old truth that peoples living in close relationship inevitably exert a reciprocal influence. Greece for all her genius drew on the artistic and spiritual riches of the Orient; and Rome, after she had harvested the riches of her immediate neighbours, the Etruscans and Campanians, peoples of greater refinement and with more aesthetic taste than her own, inherited the riches of Greece.

The ancients thought of the world as divided between two civilized countries, Persia and Greece, possessing different types of political and economic organization but nevertheless complementary. Each was the product of a long evolution due

to man's creative activity, but each sought to impose its own
way of life on the rest of the ancient world. The Iranians
created a world empire, and they inspired it with a new spirit
of tolerance and justice. They advanced the frontiers of the
civilized world far to the east, to the line of the Jaxartes. For
over two centuries political life was focused on the Great King.
The glorious role of defender of the treasures of ancient
oriental civilization devolved on Iran, which transmitted them
to more backward regions; the writing of the Persian chancellery gave rise to the oldest script of India; the art of the
Maurya dynasty imitated that of the Great King; the sea routes
between the Far East and the Mediterranean were explored;
the principles of urban life and irrigation were introduced to
the countries lying between the Oxus and Jaxartes. But the attempt to break the resistance of the Greeks failed, more as the
result of Persian mistakes than of Greek strength. Failure to
achieve the political and economic unity of the Empire, the
decay of the Achaemenian dynasty, the delegation of military
responsibility to Greek mercenaries, on the one hand, and on
the other, the awakening of Hellenistic sentiments under the
aegis of Macedonia, delivered Iran into the hands of Alexander
the Great. His conquest inaugurated a new era. It was the '*conscience Européenne*' of the fourth century B.C. that led to the
campaign of Alexander, carried Hellenism throughout Western Asia, and advanced the frontiers of Europe to the Indus
and Central Asia. It was an economic and social rather than a
political revolution. Iran was drawn into the orbit of world
trade; it became a consumer of foreign products as well as an
exporting and transit country. It raised its social standards to
the level of the more advanced western States. Under Alexander, monarchy by divine right became an institution of Hellenism, and seated on the throne of Darius, the Conqueror planned
to re-establish the empire of the Achaemenians and to realize
his dream of fusing the two great peoples and civilizations.

The Greek domination lasted for nearly two centuries and
permanently influenced Iran. It is hard to assess the extent of
Greek penetration, and equally difficult to determine how
rapidly and how completely the Greeks of Iran fell under Iran-

ian influence. The impressionable nature of the Iranian and his readiness to collaborate with the foreign element were certainly the chief factors in a delicate relationship. As regards the outward and material aspects of civilization, Hellenism undoubtedly made far-reaching and relatively rapid progress, but it had far less influence on the spiritual and religious life of the people. A comparison with modern times is instructive, for it shows that the external and material features of a foreign culture are adopted far more quickly than the spiritual, and that there is moreover a marked contrast in the reaction of town and country. In general Hellenism may be said to have suffered a defeat in Iran; its leaders could never escape from a political, social, and economic antinomy. There was constant conflict between the Eastern and Western way of life, between the city state and the oriental monarchy, and between an economic system based on liberty and private enterprise and a controlled oriental economy. Hellenism was unable to solve 'the eternal problem of human society', the conflict between ruler and subject, the propertied classes and the disinherited, the *bourgeoisie* and the proletariat.

A reaction set in against the penetration of Hellenism and its imposition on a foreign substratum; in the East there sprang up the Parthians and Kushans, and in the West, Carthage and Rome. All these peoples were on the fringes of the Hellenistic world, and were to a greater or lesser extent affected by Hellenism, but they had nevertheless preserved their individual and national characters. The last century of the pre-Christian and the first centuries of the Christian era witnessed the greatest expansion of the Iranian world. Under the Parthians Iran advanced to the frontiers of Egypt; the Kushan Empire occupied most of India, Russian Turkestan, and part of Chinese Turkestan; the Sarmatians, who swarmed over the Eurasian steppes, became masters of a great part of the northern shore of the Black Sea, reached the borders of the Danubian world, and spread into Central Asia. The Iranian world took its revenge on that of Greece by attacking its two eastern outposts. The Greco-Bactrian kingdom disappeared under the onslaught of the Yüeh-chih, the later Kushans, and the Greek settlements of the Black Sea coast were overrun by the Sarmatians. Iran maintained its pressure against the Romans when they appeared in Asia and the wars of Mithridates of Pontus represent the resistance of the Asiatics under Iranian leadership. From this titanic duel Iran emerged victorious over the dying Seleucid Empire.

A certain parallel may be observed in the history of the Parthians and the Kushans, for both took over a Hellenistic inheritance and subsequently experienced a national revival. But the formidable task of defending the old oriental civilization on two fronts fell to the Parthians. They were involved in continuous fighting and had to withdraw in order the better to ward off attack, but by their stubborn resistance they prepared the ground for the Sassanian conquests. There seems to have been no nationalistic feeling under the Arsacids, and their kings adopted a tolerant attitude to foreign peoples. Their long reign prevented the reaction against foreign influence from being too violent, and was a transition period which enabled the Iranian nation to add to what remained of its patrimony and to assimilate its Hellenistic inheritance. Politically the Parthians prepared the ground for the Sassanians. They maintained the Mazdian faith, which enjoyed a brilliant period under the later dynasty, and they preserved the traditions of the national art which, reinforced by contact with the peoples of outer Iran, experienced a revival.

Five and a half centuries separated the end of the Achaemenian Empire from the beginning of the Sassanian dynasty. Throughout this long stretch of years Iran suffered from the onslaught of the two worlds between whom it acted as liaison. The Greek advance from the West was matched by that of the Parthians coming from the eastern steppes. During these centuries opposed elements and contrasting principles were fused together as it were in a gigantic crucible. Western influence left a permanent impression on the Iranian spirit and gave rise to Irano-oriental forms that have come to the fore during the present century.

The Sassanian dynasty, which was rooted in the old Irano-oriental culture, came to the throne at a propitious moment for the flowering of Iranian civilization. After its military and political successes against the Romans in the West and the Kushans in the East, Sassanian Persia once again opened its doors to foreign influences and the culture of the Roman eastern provinces was grafted on to that of the regenerated Iranian element. The Sassanian age can only be understood in the light of this new fusion.

While thus remaining receptive to foreign cultures, Iranian civilization had a wider influence during this period than ever before. Its art radiated as far west as the Atlantic and in the form of the new Irano-Buddhist movement spread to China; religions that had sprung up on its soil, but had met with resistance in Europe and Africa, penetrated to the deserts of Central Asia; the organization of its army foreshadowed medieval chivalry, and its administrative system influenced the Court of Charlemagne.

Sassanian Iran stood like a great shield in defence of the culture of Western Asia, halting the onrush of nomads that beat against its northern frontiers. But the effort required for the defence of oriental civilization and the struggle with Rome for mastery of the land and sea routes and for markets and sources of raw materials exhausted the nation. Iran and the India of the Gupta had derived much mutual benefit from their friendship and peaceful intercourse. If only such relations could have been extended to the West, contact might have been established through the medium of Iran between the Greco-Roman world and India and China and 'the future of Eurasia might have been changed for the better'.

Society, economic organization, and religion were becoming much more uniform throughout the civilized world and there was far greater interdependence among the nations. From the Indus to Egypt, from Constantinople to Italy, Spain, and Gaul, fortified palaces were springing up, the strongholds of a brilliant and cultured aristocracy. Both in Rome and Iran the State fought against the power of these nobles, but in vain, and the two empires foundered in the new age of feudalism. The aristocracy saved itself and became guardian of the old traditions, but at what a cost! Millions of human beings bound to the soil, to a garden, work-bench, or trade without hope of escape from their fate. No trace remained of the dawning liberty that had briefly appeared in the Hellenistic world. The popularity enjoyed by the great monotheistic religions in the first centuries of the Christian era sprang from the oppression of the masses in the Roman and Sassanian Empires. Labour voluntarily undertaken and fairly rewarded, as known in Hellenistic society, was replaced by a harsh servitude that killed all desire to work. The accumulation of wealth no longer offered an incentive, men sought escape from labour in prayer and meditation. The world had nothing to offer, but the misery endured in this life ensured peace for the soul in the next. It was this oppressed and suffering world, plunged in misery and despair, that encouraged the spread of Christianity. The Western world was ripe to receive it. Three centuries later, the East was ready to accept Islam in place of the Zoroastrian faith, which, hide-bound by rigid formulas, stood remote from human suffering.

The condition of the agricultural element in the population was not, however, entirely negative. The new peoples, the Germans, Slavs, Turks, and Arabs, found a state of affairs in existence that in the course of the following centuries they transformed into an urban economy. The machinery of State, and the administration of the churches and great estates, passed into their hands, and on these foundations arose the cultures of Christendom and Islam. Thus, despite its decadence, the ancient culture suffered no break in continuity; on the contrary, its future was assured.

The resounding and repeated defeats which the two great empires turn and turn about inflicted on each other exhausted them both and placed them at the mercy of the Arabs. East and West suffered a common disaster in the triumph of a new power that destroyed the foundations of their existence. The East fell under the influence of Islam, the West under that of Christianity – the inevitable consequence of the analogous circumstances prevailing in the two areas. The similarities, both spiritual and political, that can be observed between all the civilized peoples of the Middle Ages, lying west of India and

China, may be ascribed to an identical cause – the tragic but victorious struggle waged by the dying ancient world in defence of its patrimony.

The later history of Iran is beyond the scope of this book. The Sassanian Empire was the finest period in the history of Iran, and might be taken to illustrate the saying that every 'renaissance prepares the way for a new civilization'. Despite the moral and political deterioration of the Iranians, which was aggravated by the democratization introduced by Islam, the old traditions survived and continued at the Court of the Caliphs. After the decline of these rulers, there was a fresh renaissance of the Iranian spirit under the Samanids.

In the course of their long history the Iranian people have given proof of an astonishing vitality. They were able to adapt and assimilate the great urban civilization of the land of the two rivers; after the Macedonian conquest, they experienced the impact of a powerful Western influence, but although drawing largely on this foreign civilization they remained Iranian; in the face of later invasions, Arab, Turk, and Mongol, they had the strength not only to survive but also to absorb the foreign elements. The revival of Iran during the last twenty-five years has taken the form of a national renaissance which seems likely to restore the nation to its ancient place among the peoples of Western Asia. Modern Iran has once again adopted the outward forms of Western civilization, but in spirit remains faithful to its native traditions. Its geographical position, rich natural resources, and industrious population, steeped in the tradition of one of the oldest cultures of the world, ensure that, in the future, it will occupy in the concert of Asiatic peoples a place worthy of its past.

Selected Bibliography

The following works may be of interest to general readers who wish to pursue some of the topics mentioned in this book and to see how problems which are often controversial have been approached by other authorities. The works cited have extensive bibliographies which make it unnecessary to prolong this short list given below.

ARCHAEOLOGY

E. Herzfeld, *Archaeological History of Iran*, the Schweich Lectures of the British Academy 1934, published by Oxford University Press (1935).

E. Herzfeld, *Iran in the Ancient East*, Oxford University Press (1941).

PREHISTORY

V. Gordon Childe, *New Light on the Most Ancient East* (rewritten 1952), Routledge and Kegan Paul Ltd. Discusses the prehistoric and proto-historic evidence of Iranian archaeology in relation to its Western Asiatic background.

HISTORY

A. T. Olmstead, *History of the Persian Empire* (Achaemenid Period), University of Chicago Press.

George G. Cameron, *Histoire de l'Iran antique*, Paris (Payot), (1937). (Translated from the English version which is now out of print.)

P. Sykes, *Persia*, Oxford University Press (1922).

Cambridge Ancient History, Vols I–XII (1928 ff.).

Cambridge Medieval History, Vol. I (1911).

N. C. Debevoise, *A Political History of Parthia* (1938).

RELIGION

Jacques Duchesne-Guillemin, *Zoroastre*, Paris (Maisonneuve), (1948). Contains references to the principal authorities on what is still a highly controversial subject.

H. S. Nyberg, *Die Religionen des alten Iran* (1938). Translated into German from the Swedish.

G. Widengren, *Hochgottglaube im Alten Iran*, Uppsala (1938).

LANGUAGE

R. G. Kent, *Old Persian Grammar, Texts, Lexicon*. American Oriental Society, New Haven, Connecticut (1950). Discusses the linguistic setting of Old Persia and the Script, and contains authoritative translations of the Achaemenian texts, with notes.

George G. Cameron, *Persepolis Treasury Tablets*, University of Chicago Press (1948); the introduction deals with a number of interesting problems on Economic History, Religion, History, Archaeology, and Language.

SPECIAL SUBJECTS

Arthur Christensen, *L'Iran sous les Sassanides*, published by Ejnar Munksgaard, Copenhagen (1944). Contains also interesting discussion of the later religious movements within Iran.

T. Mommsen, *The Provinces of the Roman Empire from Caesar to Diocletian* (in 2 volumes), translated from the German, Macmillan (1909). Chapter I, Vol. 2, discusses in detail the Euphrates Frontier and the Parthians.

M. Rostovtzeff, *The Social and Economic History of the Hellenistic World* (3 volumes). Oxford, Clarendon Press (1941). Lavishly illustrated, contains extensive references to archaeological material and to excavations.

Susa. The excavations conducted by successive French archaeological expeditions have been continually published in the *Mémoires de la délégation en Perse* and have reached Vol. XXXII. M. V. Rutten, *Les Documents épigraphiques de Tchogha Zembil* (1953). R. Ghirshman is the present Field Director of the expeditions to Susa.

Erich F. Schmidt, *Persepolis I*, University of Chicago Oriental Institute Publications, Vol. LXVIII (1951). Sumptuous publication of the excavations at this site, magnificently illustrated.

ART

Arthur Upham Pope (edited), *A Survey of Persian Art*, in 6 volumes (three of text and three of plates). Oxford University Press (1938). This sumptuous work, one of the finest productions of the twentieth century, is magnificently illustrated, and displays a rare choice of Architecture, Pottery, Painting, Textiles, Carpets, Metalwork, Minor Arts. This should be consulted by all phil-Iranians.

Index

Abbasid caliphs, 155, 357
Achaemenes, 139, 164, 189, 190
Achaemenians, 25, 49, 52, 86, 104, 110, 118 ff., 120, 123, 124, 127 ff., 155, 156, 160, 161, 175, 176, 181, 185, 206 ff., 216, 218, 220, 221, 229, 231, 232, 236, 239, 244, 246, 252, 264, 268, 269, 270, 273, 274, 276, 278, 287, 289, 291, 306, 308, 321, 330, 351, 352, 354
Adad Nirari I, 66
Agade, 56, 57
Agesilaus, 198, 206
Agriculture, 28, 29, 71, 86, 87, 91, 93, 182, 183, 184, 203, 208, 239, 241, 285, 341, 343
Ahriman, 161, 162
Ahuramazda, 104, 120, 139, 140, 153, 154, 155, 160, 161, 162, 165, 269, 314, 317, 329
Akkad, Akkadians, 53, 56, 63, 64
Albanians, 254, 258, 313
Alexander the Great, 17, 130, 133, 147, 152, 156, 175, 181, 189, 206–219, 229, 237, 241, 258, 262, 264, 271, 282, 352
Alexandria, 211, 306
Anahita, 103, 156, 160, 204, 228, 246, 268, 269, 270, 282, 290, 314, 315, 318, 333
Animal portraiture, 68, 100, 101, 102, 104, 108, 109, 111, 168, 176, 281, 325, 334, 350
Animals, 31, 238, 239, 265, 266, 284, 313
Annubanini, King, 55, 56
Anshan, 119, 120, 125, 134
Antioch, 220, 223, 244, 292, 299, 304, 306, 326
Antiochus I, 221, 227
Antiochus II, 221, 227
Antiochus III, 223–4, 227–8, 236, 237, 245, 246, 263
Antiochus IV, 224, 228, 236, 246, 252, 269, 278
Antiochus VII (Sidates), 248, 249, 263

Arabia, Arabs, 218, 223, 252, 264, 290, 299, 303, 308, 309, 312, 313, 317, 342, 345, 346, 347, 349, 356
Arachosia, 74, 220, 249, 261
Aramaic language, 163, 204, 229
  writing, 164
Arameans, 94, 118, 119, 163
Arboriculture, 182
Architecture, 35–6, 92, 93, 123, 134, 135, 164, 166, 167, 168, 170, 172, 181, 204, 232, 235, 273, 274, 276, 320, 321, 322–6, 330, 350
Ardashir I, 270, 273, 290, 291, 298, 314, 315, 320, 324, 328, 329, 336
Ariarmenes, 120, 121, 124, 125, 129, 140, 163
Armenia, Armenians, 58, 140, 173, 175, 198, 223, 240, 250, 251, 254, 255, 256, 257, 258, 259, 263, 269, 270, 289, 291, 292, 296, 297, 298, 299, 300, 305, 306, 307, 313, 348
Arsace III, 223
Arsaces, 243, 287
Arsacids, 256, 258, 259, 260, 261 ff., 270–3, 280, 283, 286–7, 289, 291, 306, 310, 312, 346, 354
Arsames, 125, 129, 140
Art, 36, 37, 38, 62, 80, 105, 107, 110, 111, 112, 116, 135, 136, 164 ff., 175, 176, 181, 196, 232 ff., 276–7, 278, 286, 296, 299, 318, 332, 347, 348, 350, 351, 352, 354, 355.
Artabanus I, 245
Artabanus II, 249, 259
Artabanus III, 256, 263, 271
Artabanus V, 259, 270, 273, 280, 290, 328
Artaxerxes I, 172, 173, 174, 181, 194 ff.
Artaxerxes II, 155, 160, 197 ff., 201, 204, 269
Artaxerxes III, 174, 189, 201 ff.
Aryans, 17, 28, 74, 75
Asia Minor, 24, 57, 61, 68, 71, 73, 74, 93, 95, 97, 99, 102, 105, 106, 109, 127, 129, 130, 131, 141, 149,

150, 178, 181, 182, 183, 197, 198, 204, 207, 210, 220, 223, 224, 225, 250, 253, 257, 259, 306, 307, 348, 351

Assur, 66, 112, 273

Assurbanipal, 97, 99, 120, 121, 165

Assurnasirpal, 89

Assyria, Assyrians, 26, 50, 61, 65, 66, 67, 70, 75, 77, 84, 87, 88, 89, 90, 91, 92, 93, 94, 95, 96, 97, 98, 99, 101, 104, 105, 106, 107, 110–16, 118, 119, 121, 122, 129, 163, 165, 178, 181, 212, 245, 252, 273, 274

Astyages, 113, 125, 126, 134

Athens, Athenians, 149, 150, 151, 191, 192, 194, 195, 196, 197, 198, 199, 201, 202, 209, 210, 213, 351

Atropates, 216

Avesta, 318, 340

Avroman, parchment of, 230, 271

Azerbaijan (Atropatene), 22, 23, 98, 216, 230, 307

Babylon, Babylonia, Babylonians, 22, 50, 52–4, 56–8, 61–7, 69–72, 92, 94–6, 112–13, 119–21, 125, 126, 128–9, 131, 132, 134, 136, 140, 145, 153–4, 160, 163–6, 185, 186, 188, 190, 191, 194, 195–7, 203, 204, 212, 216, 220, 224–6, 245, 249, 258, 259, 267, 272, 274, 284, 306, 314–17, 322, 341, 343

Bactria, 44, 63, 74, 204, 214, 215, 221, 222, 223, 225, 230, 237, 240, 243, 244, 246, 260, 267, 292

Bakhtiari mts., district, 27, 91, 119, 122, 123, 236

Banks, Banking, 186, 187, 284, 341, 342, 343

Bardiya, 136, 138, 139, 140

Bas-reliefs, 54, 55, 56, 101, 105, 116, 139, 160, 163, 172, 176, 230, 233, 274, 279, 280, 294, 321, 327, 328, 329, 330, 332

Bishapur, 315, 320, 321, 322, 323, 324, 326, 329, 332

Black Sea, district, 61, 88, 97, 148, 183, 203, 218, 238, 257, 260, 342, 353, 354

Bosphorus, district, 61, 73, 257, 306

Bronze, use of, 58, 60, 68, 71, 72, 78, 79, 80, 81, 87, 88, 99 ff., 100, 102, 107, 111, 150, 156, 175, 236, 278, 281

Buddhism, 162, 314, 315, 316, 317, 318, 348

Building materials, 29, 32, 35, 52, 57, 58, 84, 123, 166, 170, 183, 239, 273, 274, 321, 322, 324

Burial customs, 30, 33, 36, 48, 77, 104, 156, 162, 270, 271, 332

Byzantium, 148, 150, 297, 299, 300, 304, 305, 306, 307, 339, 340

Cambyses I, 125, 133, 136–9, 140

Cambyses II, 140, 141, 142, 144

Canals, 25, 93, 146, 182, 203, 218, 219, 238, 304, 245–6

Cappadocia, 46, 129, 223, 270, 294, 299, 306

Caravans, caravan routes, 54, 56, 62, 145, 261, 283, 284

Carrhae, battle of, 251, 252, 265, 266, 291

Carthage, Carthaginians, 129, 137, 216, 353

Caspian Gates, 65, 90, 261

Caspian Sea, district, 17, 21, 22, 23, 24, 61, 65, 128, 218, 222, 238, 240, 243, 244, 260, 304

Caucasus, Caucasians, 23, 61, 74, 94, 96, 97, 106, 183, 240, 254, 257, 291, 299, 301, 307

Cemeteries, 77, 84, 87, 88, 104, 105

Central Asia, 21, 23, 24, 46, 52, 182, 222, 249, 271, 317, 339, 352, 353, 355

Characene, 245, 249, 263

Charioteers, Chariotry, 89, 99, 212

China, 35, 105, 222, 238, 260, 261, 281, 283, 284, 285, 286, 296, 336, 342, 348, 355, 357

Chinese Turkestan, 248, 261, 284, 296, 353

Chosroes I, 291, 303, 304, 305, 308, 310, 313, 314, 340, 344, 346

Chosroes II, 306, 307, 308

Christianity, 17, 204, 297, 298, 299, 300, 303, 305, 306, 307, 311, 315, 316, 317, 318, 340, 356

Cilicia, 97, 129, 200, 204, 207, 210

Cimmerians, 62, 96 ff., 106, 116
Climate, 25, 91, 114, 166
Coinage, 176, 178, 181, 185, 186, 200, 218, 246, 254, 256, 260, 263, 266, 269, 341
Colonists, 115, 225, 226, 239, 266, 314, 342
Commerce, 71, 72, 86, 88, 113, 130, 131, 146, 148, 163, 181, 184, 185, 199, 209, 219, 222, 229, 237, 238, 240, 241, 245, 250, 257, 261, 284, 312, 341, 342, 343
Communist movement, 289, 302, 346
Constantine the Great, 297, 317
Crassus, proconsul, 251, 252, 283, 287
Croesus, king of Lydia, 87, 129, 130, 181
Ctesiphon, 245, 258, 259, 272, 273, 290, 297, 304, 307, 308, 322, 326, 340
Cyaxares, 106, 112, 113, 125, 140
Cylinder seals, 80, 81, 176
Cyprus, 149, 183, 200, 202, 203, 207, 246, 258
Cyrus the Great, 83, 125, 126, 127, 128 ff., 137, 141, 142, 144, 146, 156, 160, 181, 189
Cyrus the Younger, 190, 197, 213, 227
Cyrus I, 120, 122, 140
Cyrus II, 113, 140

Daiakku (Deioces), 95, 96, 114
Damascus, 99, 204, 210, 284, 306
Damghan (Hecatompylos), 25, 42, 46, 214
Darabgerd, 272, 273, 290
Darius, 96, 112, 124, 125, 127, 128, 132, 135, 139 ff., 152, 153-4, 163, 164, 176, 178, 181, 182, 185, 189, 199, 227, 273
Darius II, 196, 197 ff.
Darius III, 17, 206, 209, 210, 211, 212, 214, 296
Deification, 217, 227
Deities, 64, 65, 67, 282
Delian League, 192, 194, 195
Demavend, Mt (Bikni), 22, 89, 94, 98
Demetrius II, 246, 248, 263, 279

Diocletian, 317, 346
Divans (ministries), 311
Divinities, 62, 162, 236, 237. See also Gods
Diyala river, district, 56, 66, 94, 112
Dura-Europos, 270, 272, 273, 284, 327

Ecbatana (Hamadan), 25, 112, 115, 125, 126, 129, 134, 140, 141, 146, 160, 178, 204, 212, 216, 223, 226, 228, 245, 248, 249, 251, 261, 269, 279
Economics, 18 ff., 219, 237, 238, 282 ff., 301, 341
Egypt, Egyptians, 35, 44, 61, 65, 71, 73, 86, 96, 99, 106, 114, 127, 129, 130, 132, 137, 138, 141, 142, 145, 146, 147, 151, 152, 161, 163, 166, 182, 183, 190, 194, 196, 197, 198, 200, 201, 202, 203, 206, 211, 217, 219, 220, 224, 238, 251, 258, 259, 261, 306, 311, 317, 339, 348, 353, 355
Elam, Elamites, 42, 44, 49, 50, 52, 53, 56, 57, 58, 63, 64, 65, 66, 67, 71, 75, 90, 95, 96, 103, 113, 118 ff., 129, 140, 163, 164, 166, 183, 225, 236
Elburz, mts, 22, 23, 25, 70
Elymais, 245, 246, 254, 263, 269, 278, 279
Embassies, 283, 285
Ephthalites, 289, 297, 298, 299, 300, 301, 302, 305, 307, 313
Ethiopia, 137, 138, 166, 201, 306
Eunuchs, 150, 206
Euphrates, river, valley, 22, 56, 61, 75, 91, 94, 183, 200, 211, 212, 218, 223, 237, 245, 248, 250, 252, 255, 258, 259, 261, 263, 272, 287, 291, 299, 318
Eurasia, 61, 76, 110, 280, 350, 353, 355
Exports, specialized, 342-3

Fars (Parsa), 92, 120, 124, 125, 163, 167, 184, 289, 290, 314, 317, 328
Figurines, 39, 40, 44, 102, 103, 105, 282

Firuzabad, 320, 321, 323, 324, 328
Fiscal system, 85, 210, 228, 240, 303, 304, 345, 346
Forestry, forests, 21, 24, 25, 91, 183, 239
Furnishings, of houses, 47–8
  funerary, 48, 71, 77, 159, 270, 282

Gaumata, the Magian, 138, 139
Gaza, 211, 306
Gimirrai see Cimmerians
Giyan, 42, 46, 58, 67, 68, 69, 70, 80, 88, 94
Glyptics, 49, 105
Gods, 55, 56, 63, 64, 65, 66, 102, 103, 104, 120, 130–3, 137–40, 191, 204, 211, 228, 246, 268, 270, 272, 284, 317, 318, 329, 332–3, 337, 348, 351. See also Divinities
Gold, 58, 60, 107, 108, 109, 110, 111, 147, 175
Gondophares, 249–50, 260
Gor-Firuzabad, 272, 273
Gotarzes II, 279, 285
Granicus, the, 209–10
Greco-Bactria, 243, 249, 260, 353
Greece, Greeks, 127, 129, 130, 131, 132, 133, 137, 138, 146, 147, 148, 149, 150, 151, 173, 175, 182, 186, 189, 191, 192, 193, 196, 198, 199, 202, 203, 206–14, 216–18, 220–9, 230, 231, 232, 239, 240, 241, 242, 246, 249, 250, 259, 264, 266 ff., 272, 286, 294, 306, 314, 340, 351, 352, 353, 354
Guilds, 343
Gundeshapur, 320, 342
Gupta state, 348, 355
Guti, 44, 50, 53, 56, 57, 58, 70

Hadrian, 258
Halys, river, valley, 97, 113, 130, 206, 211
Hamadan (Ecbatana), 25, 42, 53, 64, 65, 90, 94, 96, 98, 112, 113, 116, 120, 125, 139, 145, 225, 279, 309
Hammurabi, 64, 153
Haoma, 159, 162, 188
Harran, 112, 113, 126, 130, 145

Hatra, 258, 259, 272, 273, 274, 276, 321
Hecatompylos (Damghan), 25, 244–245, 249, 261
Heraclius, Emperor, 307, 344
Herat, 25, 90, 245, 249, 261, 291
Herod, 253, 254
Herodotus, 26, 95, 96, 97, 98, 106, 113, 116, 119, 125, 128, 130, 148, 151, 154, 156, 268
Hieroglyphics, 109
Hindu Kush, 63, 74, 215, 223, 260, 261, 284, 292, 299
Hissar, 44, 46, 50, 63, 67, 70
Hittites, 73, 109
Hormizd I, 294
Hormizd II, 296
Hormizd IV, 305–6
Horse, 34, 62, 65, 74, 80, 88, 91, 94, 98, 106, 130, 144, 145, 178, 182, 236
Housing, 29, 32, 36, 46, 47, 284
Huns, 299, 301, 303, 305, 306
Hurrians, 61, 62, 69, 91, 105
Hyrcania, 221, 222, 244, 246, 256, 260, 263
Hystaspes, 125, 139, 141, 161

India, Indians, 26, 35, 62, 72, 74, 127, 146, 162, 163, 183, 185, 204, 215, 216, 220, 222, 223, 238, 240, 249–50, 260, 261, 284, 299, 323, 340, 342, 348, 349, 352, 353, 355, 356
Indo-Europeans, 60, 61, 62, 63, 64, 65, 68, 73, 74, 76, 80, 83, 97
Indo-Iranians, 61, 62, 74
Indus, river, valley, 44, 145, 146, 215, 217, 218, 250, 260, 261, 292, 352, 355
Industry, 184, 186, 238, 241, 285, 336, 342, 343
Ionia, 97, 148, 149, 150, 166, 175, 192, 193, 194, 198, 199, 253
Ipsus, battle of, 219
Iron, Iron Age, 26, 71, 78, 81, 86, 87, 88, 99, 100, 350
Irrigation, 24–5, 34, 93, 114, 182, 203, 239, 352
Isfahan, 25, 57, 90, 245, 278, 290
Islam, 264, 337, 339, 341, 356, 357

Istakhr, 25, 231, 233, 270, 316
Italy, 283

Jaxartes, river, district, 46, 52, 129,
  131, 142, 147, 215, 238, 352
Jerusalem, 253, 272, 306
Jewellery, 30, 32, 34, 41, 48, 58, 70,
  71, 78, 84, 87, 107, 159, 175, 176,
  184, 281, 347, 350
Jews, 115, 131, 132, 133, 138, 141,
  153, 195, 196, 197, 204, 252, 258,
  272, 298, 300, 341, 342
Judaea, 96, 141, 196
Judaism, 272, 316, 317
Justice, 154, 229, 267, 311. *See also*
  Law

Kabul river, 63, 145, 146, 260, 284
Kangavar, 226, 228, 231, 233-4
Kanishka, King, 261, 262, 292, 317,
  346
Karnak, 211
Kartir, 316, 317
Kasham (Siyalk), 25, 29, 77
Kassites, 22, 50, 62, 63, 64 ff., 74
Kavad, 300, 301, 302, 303
Kazbek treasure, 110
Kazvin, 25, 65
Kengavar, 269
Kermanshah, 53, 99, 139, 225, 236
Khabur valley, 56, 68, 69
Khorasan, 23, 90, 183
Khshathrita (Phraortes), 96, 97, 98,
  106, 119
Khuzistan, 24, 151, 294, 336, 346
Kujala Kadphises, King, 260, 261
Kurash, 122. *See* Cyrus I
Kurdistan, Kurds, 23, 44, 91, 107,
  118, 230
Kushans, 260, 261, 267, 271, 281,
  284, 289, 291, 292, 294, 296, 299,
  309, 313, 317, 323, 346, 353, 354,
  355
Kutir-Nahunte, 64, 66

Labour, labour exchanges, 34, 188,
  343, 356
Lake Urmia, 90, 93, 97, 98, 106,
  107, 123

Lake Van, 75, 91, 94, 306
Languages, 163, 204, 229
Laodicea (Nihawand), 226, 227
Law, 152, 153, 154, 302, 304, 311
Literature, 340-1
Lucullus, 251, 263
Lullubi, 50, 53, 55, 58
Luristan, 22, 24, 64, 68, 70, 80,
  99 ff., 104, 105, 106, 111, 146, 278
Lydia, 97, 113, 129, 130, 181, 197,
  200, 270

Macedonia, Macedonians, 148, 189,
  202, 206, 207, 208, 209, 210, 211,
  213, 217, 219, 220, 224, 225, 227,
  229, 232, 282, 352, 357
Magi (*mobads*), 104, 156, 159, 160,
  188, 195, 264, 270, 271, 315, 316,
  317, 318
Mani, prophet, 315, 316
Manicheans, Manicheanism, 315,
  316, 317, 318, 348
Mannai, Mannians, 91, 93, 95, 96,
  98, 106, 107, 108, 112, 113
Marathon, battle of, 151
Marduk, 66, 67, 133
Matriarchies, 28, 44
Mazdakite movement, 302, 303, 346
Medes (Madai), 65, 73, 90, 91, 94,
  97, 98, 99, 104, 106, 111, 112,
  113, 115, 116, 119, 120, 125, 126,
  129, 140, 151, 156, 166, 178, 254
Media, Medians, 58, 95, 96, 106,
  112 ff., 125, 129, 135, 140, 197,
  223, 225, 231, 245, 246, 254, 256,
  263, 270, 271
Memphis, 137, 138
Merchants, 57, 72, 86, 219, 303, 342
Merv, 44, 249, 252, 260, 261, 284,
  291, 309
Mesopotamia, 22, 24, 26, 38, 42, 45,
  46, 47, 48, 49, 50, 56, 57, 58, 61,
  64, 71, 75, 86, 91, 92, 105, 114,
  127, 176, 178, 182, 186, 211, 224,
  248, 258, 259, 272, 273, 284, 292,
  296, 301, 303, 308, 317, 350
Metals, metalwork, 26, 30, 34, 35,
  40, 52, 58, 60, 65, 66, 72, 86, 87,
  88, 166, 183, 184, 238, 239, 240,
  284, 350
Midas, King, 97

Miletus, 130
Military reforms, 304, 313
Minerals, 25, 26, 57, 58, 86, 91, 151
Mining, 86, 88
Mitanni, rulers of, 61, 62, 63, 65, 68, 69, 72, 74, 86
Mithra, 62, 155, 156, 204–5, 269, 270, 318, 332, 348
Mithridates I, 245, 246, 248, 250, 255, 266, 269, 278–9
Mithridates II, 249, 250, 279
Mithridates III, 251
Mithridates Eupator of Pontus, 250, 251, 354
Mixed marriages, 229, 230
Mongols, 23
Monuments, 54, 55, 56, 84, 107, 109, 116, 131, 160, 163, 191, 233, 278, 279, 280, 281, 321, 326, 328

Nabatians, 44, 252, 253
Nabonidus, 113, 126, 130, 131, 132, 140
Nanaia (Anahita), 103, 228, 269
Naqsh-i-Rustam, 152, 153, 156, 157, 160, 231, 232–3, 269, 271, 292
Naram-Sin, 52, 53, 55, 56
Narsah, 296, 297, 317
Nationalism, 154, 155, 287, 318, 347, 354
Nebuchadrezzar I, 67, 112, 113
Nebuchadrezzar III, 140
Neo-Hittites, 73, 105
Nero, 260, 268
Nestorians, 300, 303, 348
Nihawand (Laodicea), 42, 228, 231, 236, 309
Nineveh, 98, 112, 115, 121, 125
Nomads, 24, 52, 74, 120, 131, 133, 147, 161, 221, 222, 225, 243, 244, 245, 248, 249, 257, 258, 262, 263, 264, 265, 266, 267, 271, 280, 281, 287, 289, 290, 292, 297, 299, 301, 304, 350, 355
Nysa, 226, 236, 270

Oases, 24, 25, 26, 42, 90, 137, 303
Oil, 26, 123
Orodes II, 251, 252, 253, 254
Osroes, King, 258

Oxus, river, district, 46, 63, 129, 131, 221, 249, 260, 261, 292, 305, 352

Pacorus, 253, 259, 272, 287
Pahlavi-Arsacid alphabet, 256
Palace of Darius, 164, 165, 166, 170, 172
Palestine (Edom), 61, 68, 73, 97, 99, 113, 132, 138, 147, 183, 218, 219, 220, 252, 253, 258, 271, 284
Palmyra, 255, 284, 294
Papak, 290
Parsa (Fars), 120, 125
Parsua, 93, 94, 95
Parsumash (Parsuash), 91, 98, 119, 120, 122, 123, 125
Partatua (Protothyes), 98, 106, 107
Parthava see Parthians
Parthia, Parthians, 90, 103, 104, 131, 139, 141, 220, 221, 222, 223, 224, 226, 227, 229, 230, 232, 233, 236, 237, 241, 242, 243 ff., 255, 257, 258, 259, 260 ff., 270 ff., 290–2, 309, 310, 313, 318, 320, 321, 328, 330, 347, 353, 354
Particularism, 114
Pasargadae, 25, 92, 123, 124, 125, 133, 134, 135, 156, 160, 167, 197, 215, 232, 269
Peloponnesian War, 196, 197
Peroz, 300, 301
Persepolis, 17, 25, 42, 44, 92, 111, 124, 125, 136, 142, 145, 152, 160, 161, 164, 167, 168, 172, 173, 174, 175, 176, 178, 187, 188, 193, 204, 213, 214, 231, 233, 235, 279, 324, 330, 351
Persia, Persians, 44, 90, 91, 92, 93, 98, 112, 113, 118 ff., 128 ff., 263, 289, 299, 351, 352
Persian Gulf, 21, 26, 32, 45, 52, 66, 183, 223, 238, 258, 278
Persis (Bushire), 125, 140, 141, 223, 225, 231, 245, 246, 263, 269, 290
Philip of Macedon, 202, 206, 208, 212
Philip the Arab, 292
Phoenicia, Phoenicians, 99, 132, 137, 147, 191, 192, 200, 210, 211, 224

Phraates II, 246, 248, 249, 251
Phraates IV, 254, 255, 279, 286
Phraates V, 255, 286
Phrygia, Phrygians, 73, 97, 197
Piracy, 282
Plague, 259
Planticulture, 239
Plastics, 239
Police system, 284
Polycrates, 137, 146-7
Pompey, 251, 263, 270, 282
Pontus, 251, 270
Pottery, 28, 29, 33, 34, 36, 42, 44, 45, 46, 49, 50, 58, 60, 67, 68, 69, 70, 72, 80, 82, 83, 104, 184, 239, 278, 281, 282, 350
Proto-Elamite script, 66
Psammatichus III, 137

Qumm, 25, 42
Quteiba, 303

Rainfall, 24, 25, 27, 114
Religion, 17, 18, 25, 44, 62, 93, 132, 133, 135, 138, 139, 175, 193, 204, 227, 230, 231, 240, 242, 256, 268-72, 276, 280, 289, 294, 297, 298, 300, 302, 311, 314 ff., 323-4, 340, 341, 348, 349, 355, 356
Rhages (Raga), 115, 140, 226
Roads, 145, 146, 186, 187, 219, 241, 284, 304
Rock tombs, 116, 117, 118, 124, 156, 157
Rome, Romans, 220, 221, 223, 224, 237, 238, 245, 250-61, 263-8, 270, 272, 273, 282, 283, 284 ff., 298, 299, 301, 302, 303, 305, 307, 311, 314, 317, 318, 320, 322, 329, 330, 336, 344, 346, 347, 348, 351, 353-6
Rusas I, 94, 95, 97
Russia, 23, 26, 61, 110, 147, 178, 222, 238, 243, 280, 282

Sakiz, 106 ff.
Salamis, 192
Samaria, 95
Sarcophagi, 270, 271, 282

Sardis, 130, 137, 145, 149, 196, 204
Sarduris II, 94
Sargon of Agade, 52, 53, 57, 58
Sargon II, 87, 95, 96, 97
Sarmatians, 353, 354
Sassan, 290, 315
Sassanians, 17, 18, 23, 166-7, 230, 233, 241, 242, 257, 260, 262, 264, 268, 270, 273, 274, 277, 278, 286, 288, 289-349, 354-5, 356, 357
Satraps, satrapies, 143, 144, 149, 150, 178, 181, 195, 196-201, 209, 210, 212, 213, 214, 215, 216, 219, 220, 221, 223, 224, 227, 243, 244, 264, 267, 280, 308, 311, 312
Science, 203, 318
Scylax of Caryanda, 146, 185, 218
Scythians, 62, 96 ff., 105, 106, 107, 111, 112, 116, 120, 147, 148, 176, 178, 203, 243, 244, 248, 249, 260-261, 291
Seals, 41-2, 46, 48, 49, 176
Seistan, 44, 80, 245, 249, 250, 261, 274, 291, 294, 309, 313, 346
Seleucia, 220, 221, 223, 225, 226, 245, 246, 256, 264, 267, 268, 273, 298
Seleucids, 145, 219 ff., 229, 232, 236, 237-8, 239, 241, 243, 244, 245, 246, 248, 251, 263, 272, 282, 287, 354
Seleucus I, 150, 219, 220, 237
Seleucus II, 221, 223, 244
Semites, 52, 53, 75, 252, 258, 267
Sennacherib, 96, 119
Serfs, 183, 184, 228, 239, 264, 265, 266, 310, 344-5, 347
Shalmaneser III, 90
Shalmaneser IV, 93
Shami statue, 278, 279
Shamsi-Adad V, 90
Shapur I, 262, 271, 290, 291, 292, 294, 296, 315, 316, 317, 320, 321, 324, 329, 340, 346
Shapur II, 296, 297, 298-9, 309, 317, 320
Shapur III, 298, 299
Shilhak-Inshushinak, 66, 67
Shiraz, 25
Shirkari (Shilka(ki)), 94
Shiz, 270, 271, 315
Shustar, 27, 91, 119, 122, 342

Shutruk-Nahunte, 66
Simash, 57, 58
Sin, temple of, 113, 131
Sinope, 97, 207
Siyalk, 17, 29, 32 ff., 42, 44, 46, 47,
 48, 49, 50, 58, 67, 70, 71, 77, 80, 82,
 83, 84, 87, 88, 94, 104, 105, 278
Slavery, slaves, 151, 184, 209, 228,
 238, 286, 302, 346
Social structure, 84, 85, 86, 229,
 240, 242, 285, 298, 299, 302, 304,
 308, 309 ff., 341, 347, 355
Sparta, Spartans, 130, 149, 151, 191,
 194, 196, 197, 198, 199, 200, 210
Sport, 347
Stakhr, 308, 314, 322
State monopolies, 240, 342, 343
Stock-breeding, 29, 31, 85, 86, 285
Stone-age man, settlement, 25, 28,
 29, 34, 40
Sulla, 250
Sumerians, 25, 52, 115
Surena, 251, 252, 265
Susa, 17, 24, 42, 44, 45, 46, 47, 48,
 50, 52, 53, 57, 58, 63, 66, 67, 102,
 121, 125, 134, 137, 142, 145, 146,
 150, 151, 152, 153, 160, 163, 164,
 165, 167, 168, 172, 174, 175, 178,
 190, 193, 199, 202, 204, 206, 209,
 212, 213, 214, 215, 216, 220, 223,
 236, 264, 267, 269, 270, 271, 279,
 280, 282, 320, 335, 342
Susiana, 24, 42, 52, 75, 125, 140, 290
Syria, 61, 68, 73, 95, 97, 99, 105,
 109, 113, 126, 127, 132, 147, 182,
 195, 200, 218, 219, 220, 223, 224,
 225, 244, 248, 251, 252, 253, 256,
 258, 259, 262, 271, 282, 284, 287,
 292, 294, 299, 304, 306, 317, 342,
 348

Taxation, 85, 144, 151, 181, 184,
 187, 195, 199, 200, 227, 231, 240,
 266, 284, 300, 304, 307, 308, 310,
 311, 312, 342, 343, 344, 345
Teheran, 25, 29, 53, 65, 70, 80, 89,
 115, 140
Teispes, 119, 120, 122, 123, 140,
 163
Terraces, 123, 124, 168, 233, 235,
 279

Textiles, 336, 342
Thebes, 199, 209, 210
Thermopylae, 191
Thrace, Thracians, 73, 97, 148,
 348
Tiglath-pileser III, 94
Tigranes, 250, 251
Tigris, river, valley, 22, 66, 75, 93,
 119, 129, 140, 145, 150, 183, 211,
 220, 223, 225, 237, 245, 246, 256,
 258, 259, 264, 273, 296, 307
Tiridates, 243, 244, 256, 263, 268,
 269, 287
Tokhari (Yueh-chi), 249
Tombs, 58, 70, 74, 83, 84, 87, 99,
 106, 110, 116, 117, 118, 133, 152,
 156, 164, 178, 213, 231, 270, 271,
 337
Toruetic, 333, 339
Trade, trade routes, 25, 26, 31, 32,
 35, 49, 54, 56, 87, 129, 145, 185,
 186, 219, 223, 224, 237–8, 245,
 260, 261, 262, 266, 272, 278, 283,
 284, 292, 336, 342, 343, 348, 352,
 355
Trajan, 257, 258, 259, 329
Troy, 209
Turcomans, 23
Turco-Tartars, 23
Turkestan, 342, 348
Turks, 305, 306, 307
Tyre, 211

Untash-Gal (Untash-Huban), 66,
 122
Ur, 57, 58, 48
Urartu, 75, 88, 90, 91, 92, 93, 94,
 95, 96, 97, 98, 113, 114, 123, 129,
 178
Urban development, 225, 226, 227,
 228, 229, 241, 272, 285, 286, 346,
 350, 352, 356, 357
Uruk, 45, 64, 267

Vahram I, 294, 329
Vahram II, 294, 296, 297, 316, 329
Vahram III, 296
Vahram IV, 298
Vahram V, 299
Valerian, Emperor, 292, 325, 329

Vannic inscriptions, 91
Vardanes, 285
Vedic tribes, 74
Vologases I, 256, 268, 271
Vologases II, 258
Vologases III, 259, 262, 280
Vologases IV, 262
Vologases V, 259
Vologasia, 257
Vonones I, 255, 256

Wages, 181, 182, 187, 188, 237, 342, 344
Warrior-horsemen, 97, 98, 105, 243, 265
Weights and Measures, 181
Western Asia, 21, 57, 60, 62, 71, 73, 105, 113, 185, 259, 262, 273, 287, 355, 357
Woman, rôle in society, 28, 44, 302, 347
Writing, 38, 39, 45, 46, 48–9, 53, 66, 120, 121, 163 ff., 267, 318, 352

Xerxes, 172, 174, 175, 181, 182, 189, 190 ff., 199, 209, 212, 213, 223

Yazdgard I, 298
Yazdgard II, 300
Yazdgard III, 308, 309
Yueh-chi (Tokhari), 249, 260, 353

Zab, 52, 56, 93
Zagros, mts, district, 21, 22, 24, 25, 26, 42, 52, 57, 61, 62, 64, 66, 68, 69, 70, 72, 75, 88, 89, 90, 91, 94, 95, 99, 106, 112, 118
Zeno, Emperor, 300
Zeus-Ammon, 217
Zikirtu, 90
Zoroastrianism, 17, 161, 162, 163, 205, 268, 269, 270, 298, 300, 303, 306, 311, 314, 315, 316, 317, 318, 340, 341, 347, 356